Habits:
The Mother's
Secret of Success

Charlotte Mason

ISBN: 978-1508401650
ISBN-13: 1508401659

DEDICATION

To devoted parents and teachers everywhere.

CONTENTS

FOREWORD

I've been a long-time fan of Charlotte Mason's educational ideas, but probably my all-time favorite idea of hers doesn't even apply strictly to education. It's the concept of developing habits into the life of a child as they grow. Mason had much to say on establishing good habits in children. Habits (good or bad) are like the ruts in a path from a wheelbarrow going down the same trail again and again. As time goes on, it becomes increasingly difficult to run the wheelbarrow outside the rut, but the wheel will always run smoothly down the well-worn rut in the path.

By training children in good habits, the school day (and home life in general) goes more smoothly. Focus on one habit at a time for 4-6 weeks rather than attempting to implement a long list of new habits all at once. The habit formation pages of my copy of Mason's book, *Home Education*, are nearly dog-eared from consistently referring back to them for inspiration and reference, so I decided to put together a small volume with the pertinent information all in one place. I hope the volume you hold in your hand inspires you to read more of Charlotte Mason's work and discover the wealth of ideas her writing continues to impart to modern day parents, educators and homeschoolers throughout the world. Not only is habit building a great tool for child-training, it's also an excellent way to implement new growth into your own life, as well.

Deborah Taylor-Hough
Seattle 2015

1

HABIT MAY SUPPLANT 'NATURE'

'Habit is ten natures.' If that be true, strong as nature is, habit is not only as strong, but tenfold as strong. Here, then, have we a stronger than he, able to overcome this strong man armed.

Habit Runs on the Lines of Nature

But habit runs on the lines of nature: the cowardly child habitually lies that he may escape blame; the loving child has a hundred endearing habits; the good-natured child has a habit of giving; the selfish child, a habit of keeping. Habit, working thus according to nature, is simply nature in action, growing strong by exercise.

Habit May be a Lever

But habit, to be the lever to lift the child, must work contrary to nature, or at any rate, independently of her. Directly we begin to look out for the working of habit on these lines, examples crowd upon us: there are the children trained in careful habits, who never soil their clothes; those trained in reticent habits, who never speak of what is done at home, and answer indiscreet questions with 'I don't know'; there are the children brought up in courteous habits, who make way for their elders with gentle grace, and more readily for the poor woman with the basket than for the well-dressed lady; and there are children trained in grudging habits, who never offer to yield, or go, or do.

A Mother Forms Her Children's Habits Involuntarily

Such habits as these, good, bad, or indifferent, are they natural to the children? No, but they are what their mothers have brought them up to; and as a matter of fact, there is nothing which a mother cannot bring her child up to, and there is hardly a mother anywhere who has not some two or three—crotchets sometimes, principles sometimes—which her children never violate. So that it comes to this—given, a mother with liberal views on the subject of education, and she simply cannot help working her own views into her children's habits; given, on the other hand, a mother whose final question is, 'What will people say? What will people think? How will it look?' and the children grow up with habits of seeming, and not of being; they are content to appear well-dressed, well-mannered, and well intentioned to outsiders, with very little effort after beauty, order, and goodness at home, and in each other's eyes.

Habit Forces Nature into New Channels

The extraordinary power of habit in forcing nature into new channels hardly requires illustration; we have only to see a small boy at a circus riding two barebacked ponies with a foot on the back of each, or a pantomime fairy dancing on air, or a clown behaving like an India rubber ball, or any of the thousand feats of skill and dexterity which we pay our shillings to see—mental feats as well as bodily, though, happily, these are the rarer—to be convinced that exactly anything may be accomplished by training, that is, the cultivation of persistent habits. And the power of habit is not seen in human beings alone. The cat goes in search of her dinner always at the same time and to the same place—that is, if it is usual to feed her in one spot. Indeed, the habit of place is so much to the cat, that she will often rather die of famine than forsake the house to which she is accustomed. As for the dog, he is still more a 'bundle of habits' than his master. Scatter the crumbs for the sparrows at nine o'clock every morning, and at nine o'clock they will come for their breakfast, crumbs or no crumbs. Darwin inclines to think that the terror and avoidance shown towards man by the wild birds and lesser animals is simply a matter of transmitted habit; he tells us how he landed upon certain of the Pacific islands where the birds had never seen man before, and they lighted upon him and flew about him with utter fearlessness. To come nearer home, what evidence of the mastery of habit is more sad and more overwhelming than the habits of the drunkard, for instance, persisted in, in spite of reason, conscience, purpose, religion, every motive which should influence a thinking being?

Parents and Teachers Must Lay Down Lines of Habit

All this is nothing new; we have always known that 'use is second nature,' and that 'man is a bundle of habits.' It was not the fact, but the application of the fact, and the physiology of habit, that were new and exceedingly valuable ideas to me, and I hope they may be of some use to the reader. It was new to me, for instance, to perceive that it rests with parents and teachers to lay down lines of habit on which the life of the child may run henceforth with little jolting or miscarriage, and may advance in the right direction with the minimum of effort.

The Laying Down of Lines of Habit

'Begin it, and the thing will be completed!' is infallibly true of every mental and moral habitude: completed, not on the lines you foresee and intend, but on the lines appropriate and necessary to that particular habitude. In the phrase 'unconscious cerebration' we are brought face to face with the fact that, whatever seed of thought or feeling you implant in a child whether through inheritance or by early training—grows, completes itself, and begets after its kind, even as does a corporeal organism. It is a marvelous and beautiful thing to perceive an idea when the idea itself is a fine one—developing within you of its own accord, to find your pen writing down sentences whose logical sequence delights you, and yet in the conception of which you have had no conscious part. When the experienced writer 'reels off' in this fashion, he knows that so far as the run of the words, the ordering of the ideas, go, his work will need no revision. So fine a thing is this, that the lingering fallacy of the infallible reason established itself thereupon. The philosopher, who takes pleasure in observing the ways of his own mind, is a thinker of high thoughts, and he is apt to forget that the thought which defiles a man behaves in precisely the same way as that which purifies: the one, as the other, develops, matures, and increases after its kind.

We Think as We are Accustomed to Think

How does this bear on the practical work of bringing up children? In this way. We think, as we are accustomed to think; ideas come and go and carry on a ceaseless traffic in the rut— let us call it—you have made for them in the very nerve substance of the brain. You do not deliberately intend to think these thoughts; you may, indeed, object strongly to the line they are taking (two 'trains' of thought going on at one and the same time!), and objecting, you may be able to barricade the way, to put up 'No Road' in big letters, and to compel the busy populace of the brain-world to take another route.

But who is able for these things? Not the child, immature of will, feeble in moral power, unused to the weapons of the spiritual warfare. He depends upon his parents; it rests with them to initiate the thoughts he shall think, the desires he shall cherish, the feelings he shall allow. Only to initiate; no more is permitted to them; but from this initiation will result the habits of thought and feeling which govern the man—his character, that is to say. But is not this assuming too much, seeing that, to sum up roughly all we understand by heredity, a child is born with his future in his hands? The child is born, doubtless, with the tendencies which should shape his future; but every tendency has its branch roads, its good or evil outcome; and to put the child on the right track for the fulfilment of the possibilities inherent in him, is the vocation of the parent.

Direction of Lines of Habit

This relation of habit to human life—as the rails on which it runs to a locomotive—is perhaps the most suggestive and helpful to the educator; for just as it is on the whole easier for the locomotive to pursue its way on the rails than to take a disastrous run off them, so it is easier for the child to follow lines of habit carefully laid down than to run off these lines at his peril. It follows that this business of laying down lines towards the unexplored country of the child's future is a very serious and responsible one for the parent. It rests with him to consider well the tracks over which the child should travel with profit and pleasure; and, along these tracks, to lay down lines so invitingly smooth and easy that the little traveler is going upon them at full speed without stopping to consider whether or no he chooses to go that way.

Habit and Free Will

But,—supposing that the doing of a certain action a score or two of times in unbroken sequence forms a habit which it is as easy to follow as not; that, persist still further in the habit without lapses, and it becomes second nature, quite difficult to shake off; continue it further, through a course of years, and the habit has the strength of ten natures, you cannot break through it without doing real violence to yourself,—grant all this, and also that it is possible to form in the child the habit of doing and saying, even of thinking and feeling, all that it is desirable he should do or say, think or feel,—and do you not take away the child's free-will, make a mere automaton of him by this excessive culture?

Habit Rules 99 in 100 of Our Thoughts and Acts

In the first place, whether you choose or no to take any trouble about the formation of his habits, it is habit, all the same, which will govern ninety-nine one-hundredths of the child's life: he is the mere automaton you describe. As for the child's becoming the creature of habit, that is not left with the parent to determine. We are all mere creatures of habit. We think our accustomed thoughts, make our usual small talk, go through the trivial round, the common task, without any self-determining effort of will at all. If it were not so—if we had to think, to deliberate, about each operation of the bath or the table—life would not be worth having; the perpetually repeated effort of decision would wear us out. But, let us be thankful, life is not thus laborious. For a hundred times we act or think, it is not necessary to choose, to will, say, more than once. And the little emergencies, which compel an act of will, will fall in the children's lives just about as frequently as in our own. These we cannot save them from, nor is it desirable that we should. What we can do for them is to secure that they have habits which shall lead them in ways of order, propriety, and virtue, instead of leaving their wheel of life to make ugly ruts in miry places.

Habit Powerful Even Where the Will Decides

And then, even in emergencies, in every sudden difficulty and temptation that requires an act of will, why, conduct is still apt to run on the lines of the familiar habit. The boy who has been accustomed to find both profit and pleasure in his books does not fall easily into idle ways because he is attracted by an idle schoolfellow. The girl who has been carefully trained to speak the exact truth simply does not think of a lie as a ready means of getting out of a scrape, coward as she may be. But this doctrine of habit, is it, after all, any more than an empirical treatment of the child's symptoms? Why should the doing of an act or the thinking of a thought, say, a score of times in unbroken succession, have any tendency to make the doing of that act or the thinking of that thought a part of the child's nature? We may accept the doctrine as an act of faith resting on experience; but if we could discover the raison d'être of this enormous force of habit it would be possible to go to work on the laying down of habits with real purpose and method.

2

THE PHYSIOLOGY OF HABIT

A work of Dr. Carpenter's was perhaps the first which gave me the clue I was in search of. In his Mental Physiology—a most interesting book, by the way—he works out the analogy between mental and physical activity, and shows that the correspondence in effect is due to a correspondence in cause.

Growing Tissues Form Themselves to Modes of Action

To state roughly the doctrine of the school Dr. Carpenter represents—the tissues, as muscular tissue, for instance, undergo constant waste and as constant reparation. Even those modes of muscular action which we regard as natural to us, as walking and standing erect, are in reality the results of a laborious education; quite as much so as many modes of action which we consciously acquire, as writing or dancing; but the acquired modes become perfectly easy and natural. Why? Because it is the law of the constantly growing tissues that they should form themselves according to the modes of action required of them.

In a case where the brain is repeatedly sending down to the muscles, under nervous control as they are, the message to have a certain action done, that action becomes automatic in the lower centre, and the faintest suggestion from outside comes to produce it without the intervention of the brain. Thus, the joints and muscles of the child's hand very soon accommodate themselves to the mode of action required of them in holding and guiding the pen.

Observe, it is not that the child learns with his mind how to use his pen, in spite of his muscles; but that the newly growing muscles themselves take form according to the action required of them. And here is the explanation of all the mountebank feats which appear simply impossible to the untrained looker-on. They are impossible to him, because his joints and muscles have not the same powers which have been produced in the mountebank by a process of early training.

Children Should Learn Dancing, Swimming, etc., at an Early Age

So much for mere bodily activities. And here we have the reason why children should learn dancing, riding, swimming, calisthenics, every form of activity which requires a training of the muscles, at an early age: the fact being, that muscles and joints have not merely to conform themselves to new uses, but to grow to a modified pattern; and this growth and adaptation take place with the greatest facility in early youth.

Of course, the man whose muscles have kept the habit of adaptation picks up new games, new muscular exercises, without very great labour. But teach a ploughman to write, and you see the enormous physical difficulty which unaccustomed muscles have in growing to any new sort of effort. Here we see how important it is to keep watch over the habits of enunciation, carriage of the head, and so on, which the child is forming hour by hour. The poke, the stoop, the indistinct utterance, is not a mere trick to be left off at pleasure 'when he is older and knows better,' but is all the time growing into him becoming a part of himself, because it is registered in the very substance of his spinal cord. The part of his nervous system where consciousness resides (the brain) has long ago given a standing order, and such are the complications of the administration, that to recall the order would mean the absolute re-making of the parts concerned. And to correct bad habits of speaking, for instance, it will not be enough for the child to intend to speak plainly and to try to speak plainly; he will not be able, to do so habitually until some degree of new growth has taken place in the organs of voice whilst he is making efforts to form the new habit.

Moral and Mental Habits Make Their Mark Upon Physical Tissues

But, practically, everybody knows that the body, and every part of the body, accommodates itself very readily to the uses it is put to: we know that if a child accustom herself to stand on one foot, thus pushing up one shoulder, the habit will probably end in curvature of the spine; that to permit drooping shoulders, and, consequently, contracted chest, is to prepare the way for lung disease. The physical consequences of bad habits of this sort are so evident, that we cannot blind ourselves to the relation of cause and effect.

What we are less prepared to admit is, that habits which do not appear to be in any sense physical—a flippant habit, a truthful habit, an orderly habit—should also make their mark upon a physical tissue, and that it is to this physical effect the enormous strength of habit is probably due. Yet when we consider that the brain, the physical brain, is the exceedingly delicate organ by means of which we think and feel and desire, love and hate and worship, it is not surprising that that organ should be modified by the work it has to do; to put the matter picturesquely, it is as if every familiar train of thought made a rut in the nervous substance of the brain into which the thoughts run lightly of their own accord, and out of which they can only be got by an effort of will.

Persistent Trains of Thought

Thus, the mistress of the house knows that when her thoughts are free to take their own course, they run to cares of the house or the larder, to tomorrow's dinner or the winter's clothing; that is, thought runs into the rut which has been, so to speak, worn for it by constant repetition. The mother's thoughts run on her children, the painter's on pictures, the poet's on poems; those of the anxious head of the house on money cares, it may be, until in times of unusual pressure the thoughts beat, beat, beat in that well-worn rut of ways and means, and decline to run in any other channel, till the poor man loses his reason, simply because he cannot get his thoughts out of that one channel made in the substance of his brain. And, indeed, "that way madness lies" for every one of us, in the persistent preying of any one train of thought upon the brain tissue. Pride, resentment, jealousy, an invention that a man has laboured over, an opinion he has conceived, any line of thought which he has no longer the power to divert, will endanger a man's sanity.

Incessant Regeneration of Brain Tissue

If we love, hate, think, feel, worship, at the expense of actual physical effort on the part of the brain, and consequent waste of tissue, how enormous must be the labour of that organ with which we, in fact, do everything, even many of those acts whose final execution falls to the hands or feet! It is true: and to repair this excessive waste, the brain consumes the lion's share of the nourishment provided for the body.

As we have already seen, fully a sixth or a fifth of all the blood in the body goes to repair the waste in the king's house; in other words, new brain tissue is being constantly formed at a startlingly rapid rate: one wonders at what age the child has no longer any part left of that brain with which he was born. The new tissue repeats the old, but not quite exactly, just as a new muscular growth adapts itself to any now exercise required of it, so the new brain tissue is supposed to 'grow to' any habit of thought in force during the time of growth—'thought' here including, of course, every exercise of mind and soul. "The cerebrum of man grows to the modes of thought in which it is habitually exercised," says an able physiologist; or, in the words of Dr. Carpenter, "Any sequence of mental action which has been frequently repeated, tends to perpetuate itself; so that we find ourselves automatically prompted to think, feel, or do what we have been before accustomed to think, feel, or do, under like circumstances, without any consciously formed purpose or anticipation of results.

"For there is no reason to regard the cerebrum as an exception to the general principle, that whilst each part of the organism tends to form itself in accordance with the mode in which it is habitually exercised, this tendency will be specially strong in the nervous apparatus, in virtue of that incessant regeneration which is the very condition of its functional activity.

"It scarcely, indeed, admits of a doubt, that every state of ideational consciousness which is either very strong or is habitually repeated, leaves an organic impression on the cerebrum, in virtue of which the same state may be reproduced at any future time in correspondence to a suggestion fitted to excite it."

Artificial Reflex Actions May be Acquired

Or, to take Huxley's way of putting the case: "By the help of the brain we may acquire an infinity of artificial reflex actions; that is to say, an action may require all our attention and all our volition for its first, second, or third performance, but by frequent repetition it becomes, in a manner, part of our organisation, and is performed without volition or even consciousness.

"As everyone knows, it takes a soldier a long time to learn his drill—for instance, to put himself into the attitude of 'attention' at the instant the word of command is heard. But after a time the sound of the word gives rise to the act, whether the soldier be thinking of it or not. There is a story, which is credible enough, though it may not be true, of a practical joker who, seeing a discharged veteran carrying home his dinner, suddenly called out 'Attention!' whereupon the man instantly brought his hands down, and lost his mutton and potatoes in the gutter. The drill had been thorough, and its effects had become embodied in the man's nervous structure.

"The possibility of all education (of which military drill is only one particular form) is based upon the existence of this power which the nervous system possesses, of organising conscious actions into more or less unconscious, or reflex, operations. It may be down laid as a rule, that if any two mental states be called up together, or in succession, with due frequency and vividness, the subsequent production of the one of them will suffice to call up the other, and that whether we desire it or not.

Intellectual and Moral Education

"The object of intellectual education is to create such indissoluble associations of our ideas of things, in the order and relation in which they occur in nature; that of a moral education is to unite as fixedly, the ideas of evil deeds with those of pain and degradation, and of good actions with those of pleasure and nobleness."

But it is the intimate interlocking of mind and matter which is more directly important to the educator—the idea which we have put broadly under the (by no means scientifically accurate) figure of a rut. Given, that the constant direction of the thoughts produces a certain set in the tissues of the brain, this set is the first trace of the rut or path, a line of least resistance, along which the same impression, made another time, will find it easier to travel than to take another path. So arises a right-of way for any given habit of action or thought.

Character Affected by Acquired Modification of Brain Tissue

What follows? Why, that the actual conformation of the child's brain depends upon the habits which the parents permit or encourage; and that the habits of the child produce the character of the man, because certain mental habitudes once set up, their nature is to go on forever unless they should be displaced by other habits. Here is an end to the easy philosophy of, 'It doesn't matter,' 'Oh, he'll grow out of it,' 'He'll know better by-and-by,' 'He's so young, what can we expect?' and so on. Every day, every hour, the parents are either passively or actively forming those habits in their children upon which, more than upon anything else, future character and conduct depend.

Outside Influence

And here comes in the consideration of outside influence. Nine times out of ten we begin to do a thing because we see someone else do it; we go on doing it, and—there is the habit! If it is so easy for ourselves to take up a new habit, it is tenfold as easy for the children; and this is the real difficulty in the matter of the education of habit. It is necessary that the mother be always on the alert to nip in the bud the bad habit her children may be in the act of picking up from servants or from other children.

3

THE FORMATION OF HABIT

The Forming of a Habit—'Shut the Door After You'
Do Ye Next Thinge

"Lose this day loitering,and 'twill be the same story To-morrow;
and the next, more dilatory: The indecision brings its own delays,
And days are lost, lamenting o'er lost days," ... says Marlowe, who,
like many of us, knew the misery of the intellectual indolence
which cannot brace itself to "Do ye next thinge." No question
concerning the bringing up of children can, conceivably, be trivial,
but this, of dilatoriness, is very important.

The effort of decision, we have seen, is the greatest effort of
life; not the doing of the thing, but the making up of one's mind as
to which thing to do first. It is commonly this sort of mental
indolence, born of indecision, which leads to dawdling habits. How
is the dilatory child to be cured? Time? She will know better as she
grows older? Not a bit of it: "And the next, more dilatory" will be
the story of her days, except for occasional spurts. Punishments?
No; your dilatory person is a fatalist. 'What can't be cured must be
endured,' he says, but he will endure without any effort to cure.
Rewards? No; to him a reward is a punishment presented under
another aspect: the possible reward he realises as actual; there it is,

within his grasp, so to say; in foregoing the reward he is punished; and he bears the punishment.

What remains to be tried when neither time, reward, nor punishment is effectual? That panacea of the educationist: 'One custom overcometh another.' This inveterate dawdling is a habit to be supplanted only by the contrary habit, and the mother must devote herself for a few weeks to this cure as steadily and untiringly as she would to the nursing of her child through measles.

Having in a few—the fewer the better—earnest words pointed out the miseries that must arise from this fault, and the duty of overcoming it, and having so got the (sadly feeble) will of the child on the side of right-doing, she simply sees that for weeks together the fault does not recur.

The child goes to dress for a walk; she dreams over the lacing of her boots—the tag in her fingers poised in midair—but her conscience is awake; she is constrained to look up, and her mother's eye is upon her, hopeful and expectant. She answers to the rein and goes on; midway, in the lacing of the second boot, there is another pause, shorter this time; again she looks up, and again she goes on. The pauses become fewer day by day, the efforts steadier, the immature young will is being strengthened, the habit of prompt action acquired.

After that first talk, the mother would do well to refrain from one more word on the subject; the eye (expectant, not reproachful), and, where the child is far gone in a dream, the lightest possible touch, are the only effectual instruments. By-and-by, 'Do you think you can get ready in five minutes to-day without me?' 'Oh yes, mother.' 'Do not say "yes" unless you are quite sure.' 'I will try.' And she tries, and succeeds.

Now, the mother will be tempted to relax her efforts—to overlook a little dawdling because the dear child has been trying so hard. This is absolutely fatal. The fact is, that the dawdling habit has made an appreciable record in the very substance of the child's brain. During the weeks of cure new growth has been obliterating the old track, and the track of a new habit is being formed. To permit any reversion to the old bad habit is to let go all this gain.

To form a good habit is the work of a few weeks; to guard it is a work of incessant, but by no means anxious, care. One word more,—prompt action on the child's part should have the reward of absolute leisure, time in which to do exactly as she pleases, not granted as a favour, but accruing (without any words) as a right.

Habit a Delight in Itself

Except for this one drawback, the forming of habits in the children is no laborious task, for the reward goes hand in hand with the labour; so much so, that it is like the laying out of a penny with the certainty of the immediate return of a pound. For a habit is a delight in itself; poor human nature is conscious of the ease that it is to repeat the doing of anything without effort; and, therefore, the formation of a habit, the gradually lessening sense of effort in a given act, is pleasurable.

This is one of the rocks that mothers sometimes split upon: they lose sight of the fact that a habit, even a good habit, becomes a real pleasure; and when the child has really formed the habit of doing a certain thing, his mother imagines that the effort is as great to him as at first, that it is virtue in him to go on making this effort, and that he deserves, by way of reward, a little relaxation—she will let him break through the new habit a few times, and then go on again. But it is not going on; it is beginning again, and beginning in the face of obstacles. The 'little relaxation' she allowed her child meant the forming of another contrary habit, which must be overcome before the child gets back to where he was before. As a matter of fact, this misguided sympathy on the part of mothers is the one thing that makes it a laborious undertaking to train a child in good habits; for it is the nature of the child to take to habits as kindly as the infant takes to his mother's milk.

Tact, Watchfulness, and Persistence

For example, and to choose a habit of no great consequence except as a matter of consideration for others: the mother wishes her child to acquire the habit of shutting the door after him when he enters or leaves a room. Tact, watchfulness, and persistence are the qualities she must cultivate in herself; and, with these, she will be astonished at the readiness with which the child picks up the new habit.

Stages in the Formation of a Habit

'Johnny,' she says, in a bright, friendly voice, 'I want you to remember something with all your might: never go into or out of a room in which anybody is sitting without shutting the door.' 'But if I forget, mother?' 'I will try to remind you.' 'But perhaps I shall be in a great hurry.' 'You must always make time to do that.' 'But why, mother?' 'Because it is not polite to the people in the room to make them uncomfortable.' 'But if I am going out again that very minute?' 'Still, shut the door, when you come in; you can open it again to go out. Do you think you can remember?' 'I'll try, mother.' 'Very well; I shall watch to see how few "forgets" you make.'

For two or three times Johnny remembers; and then, he is off like a shot and halfway downstairs before his mother has time to call him back. She does not cry out, 'Johnny, come back and shut the door!' because she knows that a summons of that kind is exasperating to big or little. She goes to the door, and calls pleasantly, 'Johnny!' Johnny has forgotten all about the door; he wonders what his mother wants, and, stirred by curiosity, comes back, to find her seated and employed as before. She looks up, glances at the door, and says, 'I said I should try to remind you.' 'Oh, I forgot,' says Johnny, put upon his honour; and he shuts the door that time, and the next, and the next. But the little fellow has really not much power to recollect, and the mother will have to adopt various little devices to remind him; but of two things she will be careful—that he never slips off without shutting the door, and that she never lets the matter be a cause of friction between herself and the child, taking the line of his friendly ally to help him against that bad memory of his.

By and by, after, say, twenty shuttings of the door with never an omission, the habit begins to be formed; Johnny shuts the door as a matter of course, and his mother watches him with delight come into a room, shut the door, take something off the table, and go out, again shutting the door.

The Dangerous Stage

Now that Johnny always shuts the door, his mother's joy and triumph begin to be mixed with unreasonable pity. Poor child,' she says to herself, 'it is very good of him to take so much pains about a little thing, just because he is bid!' She thinks that, all the time, the child is making an effort for her sake; losing sight of the fact that the habit has become easy and natural, that, in fact, Johnny shuts the door without knowing that he does so. Now comes the critical moment.

Some day Johnny is so taken up with a new delight that the habit, not yet fully formed, loses its hold, and he is half-way downstairs before he thinks of the door. Then he does think of it, with a little prick of conscience, strong enough, not to send him back, but to make him pause a moment to see if his mother will call him back. She has noticed the omission, and is saying to herself, 'Poor little fellow, he has been very good about it this long time; I'll let him off this once.' He, outside, fails to hear his mother's call, says, to himself—fatal sentence!—'Oh, it doesn't matter,' and trots off. Next time he leaves the door open, but it is not a 'forget.' His mother calls him back in a rather feeble way. His quick ear catches the weakness of her tone, and, without coming back, he cries, 'Oh, mother, I'm in such a hurry,' and she says no more, but lets him off. Again he rushes in, leaving the door wide open. 'Johnny!'—in a warning voice. 'I'm going out again just in a minute, Mother,' and after ten minutes' rummaging he does go out, and forgets to shut the door. The mother's mis-timed easiness has lost for her every foot of the ground she had gained.

4

INFANT HABITS

The whole group of habitudes, half physical and half moral, on which the propriety and comfort of everyday life depend, are received passively by the child; that is, he does very little to form these habits himself, but his brain receives impressions from what he sees about him; and these impressions take form as his own very strongest and most lasting habits.

Some Branches of Infant Education

Cleanliness, order, neatness, regularity, punctuality, are all 'branches' of infant education. They should be about the child like the air he breathes, and he will take them in as unconsciously. It is hardly necessary to say a word about the necessity for delicate cleanliness in the nursery. The babies get their share of tubbing, and unlimited washing is done on their behalf; but, indeed, scrupulous as mothers of the cultured class are, a great deal rests with the nurses, and it needs much watchfulness to secure that there shall not be the faintest odour about the infant or anything belonging to him, and that the nurseries be kept sweet and thoroughly aired. One great difficulty is, that there are still some nurses who belong to a class to which an open window is an abomination; and another is, they do not all know the meaning of odours: they cannot see 'a smell,' and, therefore, it is not easy to persuade them that a smell is matter, microscopic particles which the child takes into him with every breath he draws.

A Sensitive Nose

By the way, a very important bit of physical education for a child is to train in him a sensitive nose—nostrils which sniff out the least 'stuffiness' in a room, or the faintest odour attached to clothes or furniture. The sense of smell appears to have been given us not only as an avenue of pleasure, but as a sort of danger-signal to warn us of the presence of noxious matters: yet many people appear to go through the world without a nose at all; and the fact tends to show that a quick sense of smell is a matter of education and habit. The habit is easily formed. Encourage the children to notice whether the room they enter 'smells' quite fresh when they come in out of the open air, to observe the difference between the air of the town and the fresher air beyond; and train them to perceive the faintest trace of pleasant or harmless odours.

The Baby is Ubiquitous

To return to the nursery. It would be a great thing if the nurse could be impressed with the notion that the baby is ubiquitous, and that he not only sees and knows everything, but will keep, for all his life, the mark of all he sees:—" If there's a hole in a' your coats, I pray ye, tent it; A chiel's amang ye takin' notes, And, faith, he'll prent it":—…'prent it' on his own active brain, as a type for his future habits. Such a notion on the nurse's part might do something to secure cleanliness that goes beyond that of clean aprons. One or two little bits of tidiness that nurses affect are not to be commended on the score of cleanliness—the making up of the nursery beds early in the morning, and the folding up of the children's garments when they take them off at night. It is well to stretch a line across the day nursery at night, and hang the little garments out for an airing, to get rid of the insensible perspiration with which they have been laden during the day. For the same reason, the beds and bedclothes should be turned down to air for a couple of hours before they are made up.

Personal Cleanliness as an Early Habit

The nursery table, if there be one, should be kept as scrupulously nice as that of the dining-room. The child who sits down to a crumpled or spotted tablecloth, or uses a discoloured metal spoon, is degraded—by so much. The children, too, should be encouraged to nice cleanliness in their own persons. We have all seen the dainty baby-hand stretched out to be washed; it has got a smudge, and the child does not like it. May they be as particular when they are big enough to wash their own hands! Not that they should be always clean and presentable; children love to 'mess about' and should have big pinafores for the purpose. They are all like that little French prince who scorned his birthday gifts, and entreated to be allowed to make dear little mud-pies with the boy in the gutter. Let them make their mud pies freely; but that over, they should be impatient to remove every trace of soil, and should do it themselves.

Young children may be taught to take care of their fingernails, and to cleanse the corners of eyes and ears. As for sitting down to table with unwashed hands and unbrushed hair, that, of course, no decent child is allowed to do. Children should be early provided with their own washing materials, and accustomed to find real pleasure in the bath, and in attending to themselves.

There is no reason why a child of five or six should not make himself thoroughly clean without all that torture of soap in the eyes and general pulling about and poking which children hate, and no wonder. Besides, the child is not getting the habit of the daily bath until he can take it for himself, and it is important that this habit should be formed before the reckless era of school-life begins.

Modesty and Purity

The operations of the bath afford the mother many opportunities to give necessary teaching and training in habits of decency, and a sense of modesty. To let her young child live and grow in Eden-like simplicity is, perhaps, the most tempting and natural course to the mother. But alas! we do not live in the Garden, and it may be well that the child should be trained from the first to the conditions under which he is to live.

To the youngest child, as to our first parents, there is that which is forbidden. In the age of unquestioning obedience, let him know that not all of his body does Almighty God allow him to speak of, think of, display, handle, except for purposes of cleanliness. This will be the easier to the mother if she speak of heart, lungs, etc., which, also, we are not allowed to look at or handle, but which have been so enclosed in walls of flesh and bone that we cannot get at them. That which is left open to us is so left, like that tree in the Garden of Eden, as a test of obedience; and in the one case, as in the other, disobedience is attended with certain loss and ruin.

The Habit of Obedience and the Sense of Honour

The sense of prohibition, of sin in disobedience, will be a wonderful safeguard against knowledge of evil to the child brought up inhabits of obedience; and still more effective will be the sense of honour, of a charge to keep—the motive of the apostolic injunctions on this subject. Let the mother renew this charge with earnestness on the eve, say, of each birthday, giving the child to feel that by obedience in this matter he may glorify God with his body; let her keep watch against every approach of evil; and let her pray daily that each one of her children may be kept in purity for that day. To ignore the possibilities of evil in this kind is to expose the child to frightful risks. At the same time, be it remembered that words which were meant to hinder may themselves be the cause of evil, and that a life full of healthy interests and activities is amongst the surest preventives of secret vice.

Order Essential

What has been said about cleanliness applies as much to order—order in the nursery, and orderly habits in the nurse. One thing under this head: the nursery should not be made the hospital for the disabled or worn-out furniture of the house; cracked cups, chipped plates, jugs and teapots with fractured spouts, should be banished. The children should be brought up to think that when once an article is made unsightly by soil or fracture it is spoiled, and must be replaced; and this rule will prove really economical, for when children and servants find that things no longer 'do,' after some careless injury, they learn to be careful. But, in any case, it is a real detriment to the children to grow up using imperfect and unsightly makeshifts.

The pleasure grown-up people take in waiting on children is really a fruitful source of mischief;—for instance, in this matter of orderly habits. Who does not know the litter the children leave to be cleared up after them a dozen times a day, in the nursery, garden, drawing-room, wherever their restless little feet carry them? We are a bit sentimental about scattered toys and faded nosegays, and all the tokens of the children's presence; but the fact is, that the lawless habit of scattering should not be allowed to grow upon children. Everybody condemns the mother of a family whose drawers are chaotic, whose possessions are flung about heedlessly; but at least some of the blame should be carried back to her mother. It is not as a woman that she has picked up a miserable habit which destroys the comfort, if not the happiness, of her home; the habit of disorder was allowed to grow upon her as a child, and her share of the blame is, that she has failed to cure herself.

The Child of Two Should Put Away His Playthings

The child of two should be taught to get and to replace his

playthings. Begin early. Let it be a pleasure to him, part of his play, to open his cupboard, and put back the doll or the horse each in its own place. Let him always put away his things as a matter of course, and it is surprising how soon a habit of order is formed, which will make it pleasant to the child to put away his toys, and irritating to him to see things in the wrong place. If parents would only see the morality of order, that order in the nursery becomes scrupulousness in after life, and that the training necessary to form the habit is no more, comparatively, than the occasional winding of a clock, which ticks away then of its own accord and without trouble to itself, more pains would be taken to cultivate this important habit.

Neatness Akin to Order

Neatness is akin to order, but is not quite the same thing: it implies not only 'a place for everything, and everything in its place,' but everything in a suitable place, so as to produce a good effect; in fact, taste comes into play. The little girl must not only put her flowers in water but arrange them prettily, and must not be put off with some rude kitchen mug or jug for them, or some hideous pink vase, but must have jar or vase graceful in form and harmonious in hue, though it be but a cheap trifle.

In the same way, everything in the nursery should be 'neat'—that is, pleasing and suitable; and children should be encouraged to make neat and effective arrangements of their own little properties. Nothing vulgar in the way of print, picture-book, or toy should be admitted—nothing to vitiate a child's taste or introduce a strain of commonness into his nature. On the other hand, it would be hard to estimate the refining, elevating influence of one or two well-chosen works of art, in however cheap a reproduction.

Regularity

The importance of regularity in infant education is

beginning to be pretty generally acknowledged. The young mother knows that she must put her baby to bed at a proper time, regardless of his cries, even if she leave him to cry two or three times, in order that, for the rest of his baby life, he may put himself sweetly to sleep in the dark without protest. But a good deal of nonsense is talked about the reason of the child's cries—he is supposed to want his mother, or his nurse, or his bottle, or the light, and to be 'a knowing little fellow,' according to his nurse, quite up to the fact that if he cries for these things he will get them.

Habits of Time and Place

The fact is, the child has already formed a habit of wakefulness or of feeding at improper times, and he is as uneasy at his habits being broken in upon as the cat is at a change of habitation; when he submits happily to the new regulation, it is because the new habit is formed, and is, in its turn, the source of satisfaction.

According to Dr Carpenter, "Regularity should begin even with infant life, as to times of feeding, repose, etc. The bodily habit thus formed greatly helps to shape the mental habit at a later period. On the other hand, nothing tends more to generate a habit of self-indulgence than to feed a child, or to allow it to remain out of bed, at unseasonable times, merely because it cries. It is wonderful how soon the actions of a young infant (like those of a young dog or horse) come into harmony with systematic 'training' judiciously exercised."

The habit of regularity is as attractive to older children as to the infant. The days when the usual programme falls through are, we know, the days when the children are apt to be naughty.

5

CHILDHOOD & NURSERY HABITS

Physical Exercises

Give the child pleasure in light and easy motion—the sort of delight in the management of his own body that a good rider finds in managing his horse—dancing, drill, calisthenics, some sort of judicious physical exercise, should make part of every day's routine. Swedish drill is especially valuable, and many of the exercises are quite suitable for the nursery. Certain moral qualities come into play in alert movements, eye-to-eye attention, prompt and intelligent replies; but it often happens that good children fail in these points for want of physical training.

Drill of Good Manners

Just let them go through the drill of good manners: let them rehearse little scenes in play,—Mary, the lady asking the way to the market; Harry, the boy who directs her, and so on. Let them go through a position drill—eyes right, hands still, heads up. They will invent a hundred situations, and the behaviour proper to each, and will treasure hints thrown in for their guidance; but this sort of drill should be attempted while children are young, before the tyranny of *mauvaise honte* sets in. Encourage them to admire and take pride in light springing movements, and to eschew a heavy gait and clownish action of the limbs.

Training of the Ear and Voice

The training of the ear and voice is an exceedingly important part of physical culture. Drill the children in pure vowel sounds, in the enunciation of final consonants; do not let them speak of 'walkin and 'talkin',' of a 'fi-ine da-ay,' 'ni-ice boy-oys.' Drill them in pronouncing difficult words—'imperturbability,' 'ipecacuanha,' 'Antananarivo,'—with sharp precision after a single hearing; in producing the several sounds of each vowel and the sounds of the consonants without attendant vowels. French, taught orally, is exceedingly valuable as affording training for both ear and voice.

The Habit of Music

As for a musical training, it would be hard to say how much that passes for inherited musical taste and ability is the result of the constant hearing and producing of musical sounds, the habit of music, that the child of musical people grows up with. Mr. Hullah maintained that the art of singing is entirely a trained habit—that every child may be, and should be, trained to sing. Of course, transmitted habit must be taken into account. It is a pity that the musical training most children get is of a random character; that they are not trained, for instance, by carefully graduated ear and voice exercises, to produce and distinguish musical tones and intervals.

Let Children Alone

In conclusion, let me say that the education of habit is successful in so far as it enables the mother to let her children alone, not teasing them with perpetual commands and directions— a running fire of Do and Don't; but letting them go their own way and grow, having first secured that they will go the right way, and grow to fruitful purpose. The gardener, it is true, 'digs about and dungs,' prunes and trains, his peach tree; but that occupies a small fraction of the tree's life: all the rest of the time the sweet airs and sunshine, the rains and dews, play about it and breathe upon it, get into its substance, and the result is—peaches. But let the gardener neglect his part, and the peaches will be no better than sloes.

6

HABITS OF MIND & MORALS

Allow me to say once more, that I venture to write upon subjects bearing on home education with the greatest deference to mothers; believing, that in virtue of their peculiar insight into the dispositions of their own children, they are blest with both knowledge and power in the management of them which lookers on can only admire from afar.

At the same time, there is such a thing as a science of education, that does not come by intuition, in the knowledge of which it is possible to bring up a child entirely according to natural law, which is also Divine law, in the keeping of which there is great reward.

Education in Habit Favours an Easy Life

We have seen why Habit, for instance, is such a marvelous force in human life. I find this view of habit very encouraging, as giving a scientific reasonableness to the conclusions already reached by common experience. It is pleasant to know that, even in mature life, it is possible by a little persistent effort to acquire a desirable habit. It is good, if not pleasant, to know, also, with what fatal ease we can slip into bad habits. But the most comfortable thing in this view of habit is, that it falls in with our natural love of an easy life. We are not unwilling to make efforts in the beginning with the assurance that by-and-by things will go smoothly; and this is just what habit is, in an extraordinary degree, pledged to effect.

The mother who takes pains to endow her children with good habits secures for herself smooth and easy days; while she who lets their habits take care of themselves has a weary life of endless friction with the children. All day she is crying out, 'Do this!' and they do it not; 'Do that!' and they do the other. 'But,' you say, 'if habit is so powerful, whether to hinder or to help the child, it is fatiguing to think of all the habits the poor mother must attend to. Is she never to be at ease with her children?'

Training in Habit Becomes a Habit

Here, again, is an illustration of that fable of the anxious pendulum, overwhelmed with the thought of the number of ticks it must tick. But the ticks are to be delivered tick by tick, and there will always be a second of time to tick in. The mother devotes herself to the formation of one habit at a time, doing no more than keep watch over those already formed. If she be appalled by the thought of overmuch labour, let her limit the number of good habits she will lay herself out to form. The child who starts life with, say, twenty good habits, begins with a certain capital which he will lay out to endless profit as the years go on.

The mother who is distrustful of her own power of steady effort may well take comfort in two facts. In the first place, she herself acquires the habit of training her children in a given habit, so that by-and-by it becomes, not only no trouble, but a pleasure to her. In the second place, the child's most fixed and dominant habits are those which the mother takes no pains about, but which the child picks up for himself through his close observation of all that is said and done, felt and thought, in his home.

Habits Inspired in the Home Atmosphere

We have already considered a group of half physical habits—order, regularity, neatness—which the child imbibes, so to speak, in a way. But this is not all: habits of gentleness, courtesy, kindness, candour, respect for other people, or—habits quite other than these, are inspired by the child as the very atmosphere of his home, the air he lives in and must grow by.

7

THE HABIT OF ATTENTION

Let us pass on, now, to the consideration of a group of mental habits which are affected by direct training rather than by example. First, we put the habit of attention, because the highest intellectual gifts depend for their value upon the measure in which their owner has cultivated the habit of attention.

To explain why this habit is of such supreme importance, we must consider the operation of one or two of the laws of thought. But just recall, in the meantime, the fixity of attention with which the trained professional man—the lawyer, the doctor, the man of letters—listens to a roundabout story, throws out the padding, seizes the facts, sees the bearing of every circumstance, and puts the case with new clearness and method; and contrast this with the wandering eye and random replies of the uneducated;—and you see that to differentiate people according to their power of attention is to employ a legitimate test.

A Mind at the Mercy of Associations

We will consider, then, the nature and the functions of attention. The mind—with the possible exception of the state of coma—is never idle; ideas are forever passing through the brain, by day and by night, sleeping or walking, mad or sane. We take a great deal too much upon ourselves when we suppose that we are the authors and intenders of the thoughts we think. The most we can do is to give direction to these trains of thought in the comparatively few moments when we are regulating the thoughts of our hearts. We see in dreams—the rapid dance of ideas through the brain during lighter sleep how ideas follow one another in a general way. In the wanderings of delirium, in the fancies of the mad, the inconsequent prattle of the child, and the babble of the old man, we see the same thing, i.e.—the law according to which ideas course through the mind when they are left to themselves.

You talk to a child about glass—you wish to provoke a proper curiosity as to how glass is made, and what are its uses. Not a bit of it; he wanders off to Cinderella's glass slipper; then he tells you about his godmother who gave him a boat; then about the ship in which Uncle Harry went to America; then he wonders why you do not wear spectacles, leaving you to guess that Uncle Harry does so.

But the child's ramblings are not whimsical; they follow a law, the law of association of ideas, by which any idea presented to the mind recalls some other idea which has been at any time associated with it—as glass and Cinderella's slipper; and that, again some idea associated with it. Now this law of association of ideas is a good servant and a bad master. To have this aid in recalling the events of the past, the engagements of the present, is an infinite boon; but to be at the mercy of associations, to have no power to think what we choose when we choose, but only as something 'puts it into our head,' is to be no better than an imbecile.

Wandering Attention

A vigorous effort of will should enable us at any time to fix our thoughts. Yes; but a vigorous self-compelling will is the flower of a developed character; and while the child has no character to speak of, but only natural disposition, who is to keep humming-tops out of a geography lesson, or a doll's sofa out of a French verb?

Here is the secret of the weariness of the home school

room—the children are thinking all the time about something else than their lessons; or rather, they are at the mercy of the thousand fancies that flit through their brains, each in the train of the last. "Oh, Miss Smith," said a little girl to her governess, "there are so many things more interesting than lessons to think about!" Where is the harm? In this: not merely that the children are wasting time, though that is a pity; but that they are forming a desultory habit of mind, and reducing their own capacity for mental effort.

The Habit of Attention to be Cultivated in the Infant

The help, then, is not the will of the child but in the habit of attention, a habit to be cultivated even in the infant. A baby, notwithstanding his wonderful powers of observation, has no power of attention; in a minute, the covered plaything drops from listless little fingers, and the wandering glance lights upon some new joy. But even at this stage the habit of attention may be trained: the discarded plaything is picked up, and, with 'Pretty!' and dumb show, the mother keeps the infant's eyes fixed for fully a couple of minutes—and this is her first lesson in attention. Later, as we have seen, the child is eager to see and handle every object that comes in his way. But watch him at his investigations: he flits from thing to thing with less purpose than a butterfly amongst the flowers, staying at nothing long enough to get the good out of it.

It is the mother's part to supplement the child's quick observing faculty with the habit of attention. She must see to it that he does not flit from this to that, but looks long enough at one thing to get a real acquaintance with it. Is little Margaret fixing round eyes on a daisy she has plucked? In a second, the daisy will be thrown away, and a pebble or buttercup will charm the little maid. But the mother seizes the happy moment. She makes Margaret see that the daisy is a bright yellow eye with white eyelashes round it; that all the day long it lies there in the grass and looks up at the great sun, never blinking as Margaret would do, but keeping its eyes wide open. And that is why it is called daisy, 'day's eye,' because its eye is always looking at the sun which makes the day. And what does Margaret think it does at night, when there is no sun? It does what little boys and girls do; it just shuts up its eye with its white lashes tipped with pink, and goes to sleep till the sun comes again in the morning.

By this time the daisy has become interesting to Margaret; she looks at it with big eyes after her mother has finished speaking, and then, very likely, cuddles it up to her breast or gives it a soft little kiss. Thus the mother will contrive ways to invest every object in the child's world with interest and delight.

Attention to 'Things'; Words a Weariness

But the tug of war begins with the lessons of the schoolroom. Even the child who has gained the habit of attention to things, finds words a weariness. This is a turning point in the child's life, and the moment for mother's tact and vigilance. In the first place, never let the child dawdle over copybook or sum, sit dreaming with his book before him.

When a child grows stupid over a lesson, it is time to put it away. Let him do another lesson as unlike the last as possible, and then go back with freshened wits to his unfinished task. If mother or governess have been unwary enough to let the child 'moon' over a lesson, she must just exert her wits to pull him through; the lesson must be done, of course, but must be made bright and pleasant to the child.

Lessons Attractive

The teacher should have some knowledge of the principles of education; should know what subjects are best fitted for the child considering his age, and how to make these subjects attractive; should know, too, how to vary the lessons, so that each power of the child's mind should rest after effort, and some other power be called into play. She should know how to incite the child to effort through his desire of approbation, of excelling, of advancing, his desire of knowledge, his love of his parents, his sense of duty, in such a way that no one set of motives be called unduly into play to the injury of the child's character. But the danger she must be especially alive to, is the substitution of any other natural desire for that of knowledge, which is equally natural, and is adequate for all the purposes of education.

Time-Table; Definite Work in a Given Time

I shall have opportunities to enter into some of these points later; meantime, let us look in at a home schoolroom managed on sound principles. In the first place, there is a timetable, written out fairly, so that the child knows what he has to do and how long each lesson is to last. This idea of definite work to be finished in a given time is valuable to the child, not only as training him in habits of order, but in diligence; he learns that one time is not 'as good as another'; that there is no right time left for what is not done in its own time; and this knowledge alone does a great deal to secure the child's attention to his work. Again, the lessons are short, seldom more than twenty minutes in length for children under eight; and this, for two or three reasons.

The sense that there is not much time for his sums or his reading, keeps the child's wits on the alert and helps to fix his attention; he has time to learn just so much of any one object as it is good for him to take in at once: and if the lessons be judiciously alternated—sums first, say, while the brain is quite fresh; then writing, or reading—some more or less mechanical exercise, by way of a rest; and so on, the program varying a little from day to day, but the same principle throughout—a 'thinking' lesson first, and a 'painstaking' lesson to follow,—the child gets through his morning lessons without any sign of weariness.

Even with regular lessons and short lessons, a further stimulus may be occasionally necessary to secure the attention of the child. His desire of approbation may ask the stimulus, not only of a word of praise, but of something in the shape of a reward to secure his utmost efforts. Now, rewards should be dealt out to the child upon principle: they should be the natural consequences of his good conduct.

A Natural Reward

What is the natural consequence of work well and quickly done? Is it not the enjoyment of ampler leisure? The boy is expected to do two right sums in twenty minutes: he does them in ten minutes; the remaining ten minutes are his own, fairly earned, in which he should be free for a scamper in the garden, or any delight he chooses. His writing task is to produce six perfect m's: he writes six lines with only one good m in each line, the time for the writing lesson is over and he has none for himself; or, he is able to point out six good m's in his first line, and he has the rest of the time to draw steamboats and railway trains.

This possibility of letting the children occupy themselves variously in the few minutes they may gain at the end of each lesson, is compensation which the home school room offers for the zest which the sympathy of numbers, and emulation, are supposed to give to schoolwork.

Emulation

As for emulation, a very potent means of exciting and holding the attention of children, it is often objected that a desire to excel, to do better than others, implies an unloving temper, which the educator should rather repress than cultivate. Good marks of some kind are usually the rewards of those who do best, and it is urged that these good marks are often the cause of ungenerous rivalry.

Now, the fact is, the children are being trained to live in the world, and in the world we all do get good marks of one kind or another, prize, or praise, or both, according as we excel others, whether in football or tennis, or in picture painting or poem-making. There are envyings and heart burnings amongst those who come in second best; so it has been from the beginning, and doubtless will be to the end. If the child is go out into an emulous world, why, it may be possibly be well that he should brought up in an emulous school.

But here is where the mother's work comes in. She can teach her child to be first without vanity, and to be last without bitterness; that is, she can bring him up in such a hearty outgoing of love and sympathy that joy in his brother's success takes the sting out of his own failure, and regret for his brother's failure leaves no room for self-glorification.

Again, if a system of marks be used as a stimulus to attention and effort, the good marks should be given for conduct rather than for cleverness—that is, they should be within everybody's reach: every child may get his mark for punctuality, order, attention, diligence, obedience, gentleness; and therefore, marks of this kind may be given without danger of leaving a rankling sense of injustice in the breast of the child who fails.

Emulation becomes suicidal when it is used as the incentive to intellectual effort, because the desire for knowledge subsides in proportion as the desire to excel becomes active. As a matter of fact, marks of any sort, even for conduct, distract the attention of children from their proper work, which is in itself interesting enough to secure good behaviour as well as attention.

Affection as a Motive

`That he ought to work hard to please his parents who do so much for him, is a proper motive to bring before the child from time to time, but not too often: if the mother trade on her child's feelings, if, 'Do this or that to please mother,' 'Do not grieve poor mother,' etc., be brought too frequently before the child as the reason for right doing, a sentimental relation is set up which both parent and child will find embarrassing, the true motives of action will be obscured, and the child unwilling to appear unloving, will end in being untrue.

Attractiveness of Knowledge

Of course, the most obvious means of quickening and holding the attention of children lies in the attractiveness of knowledge itself, and in the real appetite for knowledge with which they are endowed. But how successful faulty teachers are in curing children of any desire to know, is to be seen in many a school room. I shall later, however, have an opportunity for a few words on this subject.

What is Attention?

It is evident that attention is no 'faculty' of the mind; indeed, it is very doubtful how far the various operations of the mind should be described as 'faculties' at all. Attention is hardly even an operation of the mind, but is simply the act by which the whole mental force is applied to the subject in hand. This act, of bringing the whole mind to bear, may be trained into a habit at the will of the parent or teacher, who attracts and holds the child's attention by means of a sufficient motive.

Self-Compelled

As the child gets older, he is taught to bring his own will to bear; to make himself attend in spite of the most inviting suggestions from without. He should be taught to feel a certain triumph in compelling himself to fix his thoughts. Let him know what the real difficulty is, how it is the nature of his mind to be incessantly thinking, but how the thoughts, if left to themselves, will always run off from one thing to another, and that the struggle and the victory required of him is to fix his thoughts upon the task in hand. 'You have done your duty,' with a look of sympathy from his mother, is a reward for the child who has made this effort in the strength of his growing will. But it cannot be too much borne in mind that attention is, to a great extent, the product of the educated mind; that is, one can only attend in proportion as one has the intellectual power of developing the topic.

It is impossible to overstate the importance of this habit of attention. It is, to quote words of weight, "within the reach of everyone, and should be made the primary object of all mental discipline"; for whatever the natural gifts of the child, it is only so far as the habit of attention is cultivated in him that he is able to make use of them.

The Secret of Overpressure

If it were only as it saves wear and tear, a perpetual tussle between duty and inclination, it is worthwhile for the mother to lay herself out to secure that her child never does a lesson into which he does not put his heart. And that is no difficult undertaking; the thing is, to be on the watch from the beginning against the formation of the contrary habit of inattention.

A great deal has been said lately about overpressure, and we have glanced at one or two of the causes whose effects go by this name. But truly, one of the most fertile causes of an overdone brain is a failure in the habit of attention. I suppose we are all ready to admit that it is not the things we do, but the things we fail to do, which fatigue us, with the sense of omission, with the worry of hurry in overtaking our tasks. And this is almost the only cause of failure in the work in the case of the healthy schoolboy or schoolgirl: wandering wits hinder a lesson from being fully taken in at the right moment; that lesson becomes a bugbear, continually wanted henceforth and never there; and the sense of loss tries the young scholar more than would the attentive reception of a dozen such lessons.

The Schoolboy's Homework

In the matter of homework, the parents may still be of great use to their boys and girls after they begin to go to day school; not in helping them, that should not be necessary; but let us suppose a case: 'Poor Annie does not her finish her lessons till half past nine, she really has so much to do'; 'Poor Tom is at his books till ten o'clock; we never see anything of the children in the evening,' say the distressed parents; and they let their children go on in a course which is absolutely ruinous both to bodily health and brain power.

Wholesome Home Treatment for Mooning

Now, the fault is very seldom in the lessons, but in the children; they moon over their books, and a little wholesome home treatment should cure them of that ailment. Allow them, at the utmost, an hour and a half for their home-work; treat them tacitly as defaulters if they do not appear at the end of that time; do not be betrayed into word or look of sympathy; and the moment the time for lessons is over, let some delightful game or storybook be begun in the drawing room.

By-and-by they will find that it is possible to finish lessons in time to secure a pleasant evening afterwards, and the lessons will be much better done for the fact that concentrated attention has been bestowed upon them. At the same time the custom of giving home-work, at any rate to children under fourteen, is greatly to be deprecated. The gain of a combination of home and school life is lost to the children; and a very full scheme of school work may be carried through in the morning hours.

Rewards and Punishments Should be Relative
Consequences of Conduct

In considering the means of securing attention, it has been necessary to refer to discipline—the dealing out of rewards and punishments,—a subject which every tyro of a nursery maid or nursery governess feels herself very competent to handle. But this, too, has its scientific aspect: there is a law by which all rewards and punishments should be regulated: they should be natural, or, at any rate, the relative consequences of conduct; should imitate, as nearly as may be without injury to the child, the treatment which such and such conduct deserves and receives in after life. Miss Edgeworth, in her story of Rosamond and the Purple Jar, hits the right principle, though the incident is rather extravagant. Little girls do not often pine for purple jars in chemists' windows; but that we should suffer for our willfulness in getting what is unnecessary by going without what is necessary, is precisely one of the lessons of life we all have to learn, and therefore is the right sort of lesson to teach a child.

Natural and Elective Consequences

It is evident that to administer rewards and punishments on this principle requires patient consideration and steady determination on the mother's part. She must consider with herself what fault of disposition the child's misbehaviour springs from; she must aim her punishment at that fault, and must brace herself to see her child suffer present loss for his lasting gain. Indeed, exceedingly little actual punishment is necessary where children are brought up with care.

But this happens continually—the child who has done well gains some natural reward (like that ten minutes in the garden), which the child forfeits who has done less well; and the mother must brace herself and her child to bear this loss; if she equalise the two children she commits a serious wrong, not against the child who has done well, but against the defaulter, whom she deliberately encourages to repeat his shortcoming.

In placing her child under the discipline of consequences, the mother must use much tact and discretion. In many cases, the natural consequence of the child's fault is precisely that which it is her business to avert, while, at the same time, she looks about for some consequence related to the fault which shall have an educative bearing on the child: for instance, if a boy neglects his studies, the natural consequences is that he remains ignorant; but to allow him to do so would be criminal neglect on the part of the parent.

8

THE HABIT OF THINKING

The habits of mental activity and of application are trained by the very means employed to cultivate that of attention. The child may plod diligently through his work who might be trained to rapid mental effort. The teacher herself must be alert, must expect instant answers, quick thought, rapid work. The tortoise will lag behind the hare, but the tortoise must be trained to move, every day, a trifle quicker. Aim steadily at securing quickness of apprehension and execution, and that goes far towards getting it.

Zeal Must be Stimulated

So of application. The child must not be allowed to get into the mood in which he says, 'Oh, I am so tired of sums,' or 'of history.' His zeal must be stimulated; and there must be always a pleasing vista before him; and the steady, untiring application to work should be held up as honourable, while fitful, flagging attention and effort are scouted.

A Lion' Operations Included in Thinking

The actual labour of the brain is known to psychologists under various names, and divided into various operations: let us call it thinking, which, for educational purposes, is sufficiently exact; but, by 'thinking,' let us mean a real conscious effort of mind, and not the fancies that flit without effort through the brain. This sort of thing, for instance, an example quoted by Archbishop Thompson in his Laws of Thought [This example, offered by so able a psychologist, is so admirable that I venture to quote it more than once]:—

"[W]hen Captain Head was travelling across the pampas of South America, his guide one day suddenly stopped him, and pointing high into the air, cried out 'A lion!' Surprised at such an exclamation, accompanied with such an act, he turned up his eyes, and with difficulty perceived, at an immeasurable height, a flight of condors, soaring in circles in a particular spot. Beneath this spot, far out of sight of himself of himself or guide, lay the carcass of a horse, and over that carcass stood, as the guide well knew, a lion, whom the condors were eyeing with envy from their airy height. The signal of the birds was to him what the sight of the lion alone would have been to the traveler—a full assurance of its existence.

"Here was an act of thought which cost the thinker no trouble, which was easy to him as to cast his eyes upward, yet which from us, unaccustomed to the subject, would require many steps and some labour.

"The sight of the condors convinced him that there was some carcass or other; but as they kept wheeling far above it, instead of swooping down to their feast, he guessed that some beast had anticipated them. Was it a dog, or a jackal? No; the condors would not fear to drive away, or share with, either: it must be some large beast, and as there were lions in the neighbourhood, he concluded that one was here."

And all these steps of thought are summed in the words 'A lion.' This is the sort of thing that the children should go through, more or less, in every lesson—a tracing of effect from cause, or of cause from effect; a comparing of things to find out wherein they are alike, and wherein they differ; a conclusion as to causes or consequences from certain premises.

9

THE HABIT OF IMAGINING

The Sense of Incongruous

All their lessons will afford some scope for some slight exercise of the children's thinking power, some more and some less, and the lessons must be judiciously alternated, so that the more mechanical efforts succeed the more strictly intellectual, and that the pleasing exercise of the imagination, again, succeed efforts of reason.

By the way, it is a pity when the sense of the ludicrous is cultivated in children's books at the expense of better things. *Alice in Wonderland* is a delicious feast of absurdities, which none of us, old or young, could afford to spare; but it is doubtful whether the child who reads it has the delightful imaginings, the realising of the unknown, with which he reads *The Swiss Family Robinson*. This point is worth considering in connection with Christmas books for the little people. Books of 'comicalities' cultivate no power but the sense of the incongruous; and though life is the more amusing for the possession of such a sense, when cultivated to excess it is apt to show itself a flippant habit. *Diogenes and the Naughty Boys of Troy* is irresistible, but it is not the sort of thing the children will live over and over, and 'play at' by the hour, as we have all played at Robinson Crusoe finding the footprints. They must have 'funny books,' but do not give the children too much nonsense reading.

Commonplace Tales: Tales of Imagination

Stories, again, of the Christmas holidays, of George and Lucy, of the amusements, foibles, and virtues of children in their own condition of life, leave nothing to the imagination. The children know all about everything so well that it never occurs to them to play at the situations in any one of these tales, or even to read it twice over. But let them have tales of the imagination, scenes laid in other lands and other times, heroic adventures, hairbreadth escapes, delicious fairy tales in which they are never roughly pulled up by the impossible—even where all is impossible, and they know it, and yet believe.

Imagination and Great Conceptions

And this, not for the children's amusement merely: it is not impossible that posterity may write us down a generation blest with little imagination, and, by so far, the less capable of great conceptions and heroic efforts, for it is only as we have it in us to let a person or a cause fill the whole stage of the mind, to the exclusion of self-occupation, that we are capable of large hearted action on behalf of that person or cause. Our novelists say there is nothing left to imagine; and that, therefore, a realistic description of things as they are is all that is open to them. But imagination is nothing if not creative, unless it see, not only what is apparent, but what is conceivable, and what is poetically fit in given circumstances.

Imagination Grows

Now imagination does not descend, full grown, to take possession of an empty house; like every other power of the mind, it is the merest germ of a power to begin with, and grows by what it gets; and childhood, the age of faith, is the time for its nourishing. The children should have the joy of living in far lands, in other persons, in other times—a delightful double existence; and this joy they will find, for the most part, in their story books.

Their lessons, too, history and geography, should cultivate their conceptive powers. If the child does not live in the times of his history lesson, be not at home in the climes of his geography book describes, why, these lessons will fail of their purpose. But let lessons do their best, and the picture gallery of the imagination is poorly hung if the child have not found his way into the realms of fancy.

Thinking Comes By Practice

How the children's various lessons should be handled so as to induce habits of thinking, we shall consider later; but this for the present: thinking, like writing or skating, comes by practice. The child who has never thought, never does think, and probably never will think; for are there not people enough who go through the world without any deliberate exercise of their own wits? The child must think, get at the reason why of things for himself, every day of his life, and more each day than the day before.

Children and parents both are given to invert this educational process. The child asks 'Why?' and the parent answers, rather proud of this evidence of thought in his child. There is some slight show of speculation even in wondering 'Why?' but it is the slightest and most superficial effort the thinking brain produces. Let the parent ask 'Why?' and the child produce the answer, if he can. After he has turned the matter over and over in his mind, there is no harm in telling him—and he will remember it—the reason why. Every walk should offer some knotty problem for the children to think out—"Why does that leaf float on the water, and this pebble sink?" and so on.

10

THE HABIT OF REMEMBERING

Memory is the storehouse of whatever knowledge we possess; and it is upon the fact of the stores lodged in the memory that we take rank as intelligent beings. The children learn in order that they may remember. Much of what we have learned and experienced in childhood, and later, we cannot reproduce, and yet it has formed the groundwork of after knowledge; later notions and opinions have grown out of what we once learned and knew. That is our sunk capital, of which we enjoy the interest though we are unable to realise. Again, much that we have learned and experienced is not only retained in the storehouse of memory, but is our available capital, we can reproduce, recollect upon demand. This memory which may be drawn upon by the act of recollection is our most valuable endowment.

A 'Spurious' Memory

There is a third kind of (spurious) memory—facts and ideas floating in the brain which yet make no part of it, and are exuded at a single effort; as when a barrister produces all his knowledge of a case in his brief, and then forgets to tell about it; or when the schoolboy 'crams' for an examination, writes down what he has thus learned, and behold, it is gone from his gaze forever: as Ruskin puts it, "They cram to pass, and not to know, they do pass, and they don't know." That this barrister, the physician, should be able thus to dismiss the case on which he has ceased to be occupied, the publisher the book he has rejected, is well for him, and this art of forgetting is not without its uses: but what of the schoolboy who has little left after a year's work but his place in a class list?

Memory a Record in the Brain Substance

To say anything adequate on the subject of memory is impossible here; but let us try to answer two or three queries which present themselves on the surface. How do we come to 'remember' at all? How do we gain the power to utilize remembered facts— that is, to recollect? And under what conditions is knowledge acquired that neither goes to the growth of brain and mind, nor is available on demand, but is lightly lodged in the brain for some short period, and is then evacuated at a single throw?

We are interested in a wonderful invention—an instrument which records spoken words, and will deliver, say a century hence, speech or lecture on the very words and in the very tones of the speaker. Such an instrument is that function of the brain called memory, whereby the impressions received by the brain are recorded mechanically—at least, such is the theory pretty generally received now by physiologists. That is, the mind takes cognisance of certain facts, and the nerve substance of the brain records that cognisance.

Made Under What Conditions

Now, the questions arise, under what conditions is such an imprint of fact or event made upon the substance of the brain? Is the record permanent? And is the brain capable of receiving an indefinite number of such impressions? It appears, both from common experience and from an infinite number of examples quoted by psychologists, that any object or idea which is regarded with attention makes the sort of impression on the brain which is said to fix it in the memory.

In other words, give an instant's undivided attention to anything whatsoever, and that thing will be remembered. In describing this effect, the common expression is accurate beyond its intention. We say, "Such and such a sight or sound, or sensation, made a strong impression on me." And that is precisely what has happened: arrest the attention upon any fact or incident, that fact or incident is remembered; it is impressed, imprinted upon the brain substance. The inference is plain. You want a child to remember? Then secure his whole attention, the fixed gaze of his mind, as it were, upon the fact to be remembered; then he will have it: by a sort of photographic (!) process, that fact or idea is 'taken' by his brain, and when he is an old man, perhaps, the memory of it will flash across him.

Recollection and the Law of Association

But it is not enough to have a recollection flash across one incidentally; we want to have the power of recalling at will: and for this, something more is necessary than an occasional act of attention producing a solitary impression.

Supposing, for instance, that by good teaching you secure the child's attention to the verb *avoir*, he will remember it; that is to say, some infinitely slight growth of brain tissue will record and retain that one French verb. But one verb is nothing; you want the child to learn French, and for this you must not only fix his attention upon each new lesson, but each must be so linked into the last that it is impossible for him to recall one without the other following in its train.

The physical effect of such a method appears to be that

each new growth of the brain tissue is, so to speak, laid upon the last; that is, to put it figuratively, a certain tract of the brain may be conceived of as being overlaid with French. This is to make a practical use of that law of association of ideas of which one would not willingly become the sport; and it is the neglect of this law which invalidates much good teaching. The teacher is content to produce a solitary impression which is only recalled as it is acted upon by a chance suggestion; whereas he should forge the links of a chain to draw his bucket out of the well. Probably the reader may have heard, or heard of, a Dr Pick, who grounded a really philosophical system of mnemonics on these two principles of attention and association. Whatever we may think of his application of it, the principle he asserted is the right one.

Every Lesson Must Recall the Last

Let every lesson gain the child's entire attention, and let each new lesson be so interlaced with the last that the one must recall the other; that again, recalls the one before it, and so on to the beginning.

No Limit to the Recording Power of the Brain

But the 'lightly come, lightly go' of a mere verbal memory follows no such rules. The child gets his exercise 'by heart,' says it off like a parrot, and behold, it is gone; there is no record of it upon the brain at all. To secure such a record, there must be time; time for that full gaze of the mind we call attention, and for the growth of the brain tissue to the new idea. Given these conditions, there appears to be no limit of quantity to the recording power of the brain.

Except in this way: a girl learns French, and speaks it fairly well; by the time she is a grandmother she has forgotten it entirely, has not a word left. When this is the case, her French has been disused; she has not been in the habit of reading, hearing, or speaking French from youth to age. Whereby it is evident that, to secure right-of-way to that record of French imprinted on her brain, the path should have been kept open by frequent goings and comings.

But Links of Association a Condition of Recollection

To acquire any knowledge or power whatsoever, and then to leave it to grow rusty in a neglected corner of the brain, is practically useless. Where there is no chain of association to draw the bucket out of the well, it is all the same as if there were no water there. As to how to form these links, every subject will suggest a suitable method. The child has a lesson about Switzerland today, and one about Holland tomorrow, and the one is linked to the other by the very fact that the two countries have hardly anything in common; what the one has, the other has not. Again, the association will be of similarity, and not of contrast. In our own experience we find that colours, places, sounds, odors recall persons or events; but links of this sensuous order can hardly be employed in education. The link between any two things must be found in the nature of the things associated.

11

THE HABIT OF PERFECT EXECUTION

The Habit of Turning Out Imperfect Work

'Throw perfection into all you do' is a counsel upon which a family may be brought up with great advantage. We English, as a nation, think too much of persons, and too little of things, work, execution. Our children are allowed to make their figures or their letters, their stitches, their dolls' clothes, their small carpentry, anyhow, with the notion that they will do better by-and-by. Other nations—the Germans and the French, for instance—look at the question philosophically, and know that if children get the habit of turning out imperfect work, the men and women will undoubtedly keep that habit up.

I remember being delighted with the work of a class of about forty children, of six and seven, in an elementary school at Heidelberg. They were doing a writing lesson, accompanied by a good deal of oral teaching from a master, who wrote each word on the blackboard. By-and-by the slates were shown, and I did not observe one faulty or irregular letter on the whole forty slates. The same principle of 'perfection' was to be discerned in a recent exhibition of schoolwork held throughout France. No faulty work was shown, to be excused on the plea that it was the work of children.

A Child Should Execute Perfectly

No work should be given to a child that he cannot execute perfectly, and then perfection should be required from him as a matter of course. For instance, he is set to do a copy of strokes, and is allowed to show a slateful at all sorts of slopes and all sorts of intervals; his moral sense is vitiated, his eye is injured. Set him six strokes to copy; let him, not bring a slateful, but six perfect strokes, at regular distances and at regular slopes. If he produces a faulty pair, get him to point out the fault, and persevere until he has produced his task; if he does not do it today, let him go on tomorrow and the next day, and when the six perfect strokes appear, let it be an occasion of triumph.

So with the little tasks of painting, drawing, or construction he sets himself—let everything he does be well done. An unsteady house of cards is a thing to be ashamed of. Closely connected with this habit of 'perfect work' is that of finishing whatever is taken in hand. The child should rarely be allowed to set his hand to a new undertaking until the last is finished.

12

THE HABIT OF OBEDIENCE

It is disappointing that, in order to cover the ground at all, we must treat those moral habits, which the mother owes it to her children to cultivate in them, in a slight and inadequate way; but the point to be borne in mind is, that all has been already said about the cultivation of habit applies with the greatest possible force to each of these habits.

The Whole Duty of a Child

First and infinitely the most important, is the habit of obedience. Indeed, obedience is the whole duty of the child, and for this reason—every other duty of the child is fulfilled as a matter of obedience to his parents. Not only so: obedience is the whole duty of man; obedience to conscience, to law, to Divine direction.

It has been well observed that each of the three recorded temptations of our Lord in the wilderness is a suggestion, not of an act of overt sin, but of an act of willfulness, that state directly opposed to obedience, and out of which springs all that foolishness which is bound up in the heart of a child.

Obedience No Accidental Duty

Now, if the parent realise that obedience is no mere

accidental duty, the fulfilling of which is a matter that lies between himself and the child, but that he is the appointed agent to train the child up to the intelligent obedience of the self-compelling, law-abiding human being, he will see that he has no right to forego the obedience of his child, and that every act of disobedience in the child is a direct condemnation of the parent. Also, he will see that the motive of the child's obedience is not the arbitrary one of, 'Do this, or that, because I have said so,' but the motive of the apostolic injunction, "Children, obey your parents in the Lord, for this is right."

Children Must Have the Desire to Obey

It is only in proportion as the will of the child is in the act of obedience, and he obeys because his sense of right makes him desire to obey in spite of temptations to disobedience—not of constraint, but willingly—that the habit has been formed which will, hereafter, enable the child to use the strength of his will against his inclinations when these prompt him to lawless courses.

It is said that the children of parents who are most strict in exacting obedience often turn out ill; and that orphans and other poor waifs brought up under strict discipline only wait their opportunity to break into license. Exactly so; because, in these cases, there is no gradual training of the child in the habit of obedience; no gradual enlisting of his will on the side of sweet service and a free will offering of submission to the highest law: the poor children are simply bullied into submission to the will, that is, the willfulness, of another; not at all, 'for it is right'; only because it is convenient.

Expect Obedience

The mother has no more sacred duty than that of training her infant to instant obedience. To do so is no difficult task; the child is still "trailing clouds of glory ... from God, who is his home"; the principle of obedience is within him, waiting to be

65

called into exercise. There is no need to rate the child, or threaten him, or use any manner of violence, because the parent is invested with authority which the child intuitively recognises. It is enough to say, 'Do this,' in a quiet, authoritative tone, and expect it to be done.

The mother often loses her hold over children because they detect in the tone of her voice that she does not expect them obey her behests; she does not think enough of her position; has not sufficient confidence in her own authority. The mother's great stronghold is in the habit of obedience. If she begin by requiring that her children always obey her, why, they will always do so as a matter of course; but let them once get the thin end of the wedge in, let them discover that they can do otherwise than obey, and a woeful struggle begins, which commonly ends in the children doing that which is right in their own eyes.

This is the sort of thing which is fatal: The children are in the drawing room, and a caller is announced. 'You must go upstairs now.' 'Oh, mother dear, do let us stay in the window-corner; we will be as quiet as mice!' The mother is rather proud of her children's pretty manners, and they stay. They are not quiet, of course; but that is the least of the evils; they have succeeded in doing as they chose and not as they were bid, and they will not put their necks under the yoke again without a struggle.

It is in little matters that the mother is worsted. 'Bedtime, Willie!' 'Oh, mamma, just let me finish this'; and the mother yields, forgetting that the case in point is of no consequence; the thing that matters is that the child should be daily confirming a habit of obedience by the unbroken repetition of acts of obedience.

It is astonishing how clever the child is in finding ways of evading the spirit while he observes the letter. 'Mary, come in.' 'Yes, mother'; but her mother calls four times before Mary comes. 'Put away your bricks'; and the bricks are put away with slow reluctant fingers. 'You must always wash your hands when you hear the first bell.' The child obeys for that once, and no more.

To avoid these displays of willfulness, the mother will

insist from the first on an obedience which is prompt, cheerful, and lasting—save for lapses of memory on the child's part. Tardy, unwilling, occasional obedience is hardly worth the having; and it is greatly easier to give the child the habit of perfect obedience by never allowing him in anything else, than it is to obtain this mere formal obedience by a constant exercise of authority.

By-and-by, when he is old enough, take the child into confidence; let him know what a noble thing it is to be able to make himself do, in a minute, and brightly, the very thing he would rather not do. To secure this habit of obedience, the mother must exercise great self-restraint; she must never give a command which she does not intend to see carried out to the full. And she must not lay upon her children burdens, grievous to be borne, of command heaped upon command.

Law Ensures Liberty

The children who are trained to perfect obedience may be trusted with a good deal of liberty: they receive a few directions which they know they must not disobey; and for the rest, they are left to learn how to direct their own actions, even at the cost of some small mishaps; and are not pestered with a perpetual fire of 'Do this' and 'Don't do that!'

13

HABITS OF TRUTH & TEMPER

It is unnecessary to say a word of the duty of Truthfulness; but the training of the child in the habit of strict veracity is another matter, and one which requires delicate care and scrupulosity on the part of the mother.

Three Causes of Lying—All Vicious

The vice of lying causes: carelessness in ascertaining the truth, carelessness in stating the truth, and a deliberate intention to deceive. That all three are vicious, is evident from the fact that a man's character may be ruined by what is no more than a careless mis-statement on the part of another; the speaker repeats a damaging remark without taking the trouble to sift it; or he repeats what he has heard or seen with so little care to deliver the truth that his statement becomes no better than a lie.

Only One Kind Visited on Children

Now, of the three kinds of lying, it is only, as a matter of fact, the third which is severely visited upon the child; the first and the second he is allowed in. He tells you he has seen 'lots' of spotted dogs in the town—he has really seen two; that 'all the boys' are collecting crests—he knows of three who are doing so; that 'everybody' says Jones is a 'sneak'—the fact is he has heard Brown say so. These departures from strict veracity are on matters of such slight importance that the mother is apt to let them pass as the 'children's chatter'; but, indeed, ever such lapse is damaging to the child's sense of truth—a blade which easily loses its keenness of edge.

Accuracy of Statement

The mother who trains her child to strict accuracy of statement about things small and great fortifies him against temptations to the grosser forms of lying; he will not readily colour a tale to his own advantage, suppress facts, equivocate, when the statement of the simple fact has become a binding habit, and when he has not been allowed to form the contrary vicious habit of playing fast and loose with words.

Exaggeration and Ludicrous Embellishments

Two forms of prevarication, very tempting to the child, will require great vigilance on the mother's part—that of exaggeration and that of clothing a story with ludicrous embellishments. However funny a circumstance may be as described by the child, the ruthless mother must strip the tale of everything over and above the naked truth: for, indeed, a reputation for facetiousness is dearly purchased by the loss of that dignity of character, in child or man, which accompanies the habit of strict veracity; it is possible, happily, to be humorous, without any sacrifice of truth.

Reverence

As for reverence, consideration for others, respect for persons and property, I can only urge the importance of a sedulous cultivation of these moral qualities—the distinguishing marks of a refined nature—until they become the daily habits of the child's life; and the more, because a self-assertive, aggressive, self-seeking temper is but too characteristic of the times we live in.

Temper—Born in a Child

I am anxious, however, to a say a few words on the habit of sweet temper. It is very customary to regard temper as constitutional, that which is born in you and is neither to be helped nor hindered. 'Oh, she is a good tempered little soul; nothing puts her out!' 'Oh, he has his father's temper; the least thing that goes contrary makes him fly into a passion,' are the sorts of remarks we hear constantly.

Not Temper, But Tendency

It is no doubt true that children inherit a certain tendency to irascibility or to amiability, to fretfulness, discontentment, peevishness, sullenness, murmuring, and impatience; or to cheerfulness, trustfulness, good-humour, patience, and humility. It is also true that upon the preponderance of any of these qualities— upon temper, that is—the happiness or wretchedness of child and man depends, as well as the comfort or misery of the people who live with him.

We all know people possessed of integrity and of many excellent virtues who make themselves intolerable to their belongings. The root of evil is, not that these people were born sullen, or peevish, or envious that might have been mended; but that they were permitted to grow up in these dispositions. Here, if anywhere, the power of habit is invaluable: it rests with the parents to correct the original twist, all the more so if it is from them the child gets it, and to send their child into the world best with an even, happy temper, inclined to make the best of things, to look on the bright side, to impute the best and kindest motives to others, and to make no extravagant claims on his own account—fertile source of ugly tempers. And this, because the child is born with no more than certain tendencies.

Parents Must Correct Tendency by New Habit of Temper

It is by force of habit that a tendency becomes a temper; and it rests with the mother to hinder the formation of ill tempers, to force that of good tempers. Nor is it difficult to do this while the child's countenance is as an open book to his mother, and she reads the thoughts of his heart before he is aware of them himself.

Remembering that every envious, murmuring, discontented thought leaves a track in the very substance of the child's brain for such thoughts to run in again and again—that this track, this rut, so to speak, is ever widening and deepening with the traffic in ugly thoughts—the mother's care is to hinder at the outset the formation of any such track. She sees into her child's soul— sees the evil temper in the act of rising: now is her opportunity.

Change the Child's Thoughts

Let her change the child's thoughts before ever the bad temper has had time to develop into conscious feeling, much less act: take him out of doors, send him to fetch or carry, tell him or show him something of interest,—in a word, give him something else to think about; but all in a natural way, and without letting the child perceive that he is being treated. As every fit of sullenness leaves place in the child's mind for another fit of sullenness to succeed it, so every such fit averted by the mother's tact tends to obliterate the evil traces of former sullen tempers. At the same time, the mother is careful to lay down a highway for the free course of all sweet and genial thoughts and feelings.

I have been offering suggestions, not for a course of intellectual and moral training, but only for the formation of certain habits which should be, as it were, the outworks of character. Even with this limited programme, I have left unnoticed many matters fully as important as those touched upon. In the presence of an embarrassment of riches, it has been necessary to adopt some principle of selection; and I have thought it well to dwell upon considerations which do not appear to me to have their full weight with educated parents, rather than upon those of which every thoughtful person recognises the force.

14

CHARLOTTE MASON'S LIST OF HABITS

The following list of habits to instill in children was gleaned from the preceding writings by Charlotte Mason on the subject of habit formation. This definitely isn't an exhaustive list of habits we can work on with our families, but it gives a good sense of the types of things Charlotte Mason thought could be formed in people simply through the power of habit. Some people may be surprised to see things like attitudes and temperaments covered as things that can be formed through habitual training.

-Deborah Taylor-Hough, 2015

- Courage
- Loving
- Good-nature
- Giving
- Unselfishness
- Carefulness
- Clean clothes
- Reticence
- Descretion
- Courteousness
- Making way for elders

- Not holding a grudge
- Ability to yield
- Temperance
- Pure thoughts
- Willpower
- Moral power
- Spiritual weapons
- Thankfulness
- Order
- Propriety
- Virtue
- Pleasure and profit from reading books
- Speaking the exact truth
- Decisiveness
- Tact
- Watchfulness
- Persistence
- Cleanliness
- Neatness
- Regularity
- Punctuality
- A sensitive nose
- Care of fingernails
- Clean eyes and ears
- Washed hands
- Brushed hair
- Modesty
- Purity
- Obedience
- Sense of humor
- Caring for possessions

- Putting away toys
- Appreciation of beauty
- Regularity of schedule
- Sleeping at bedtime
- Dancing
- Calisthenics
- Eye contact with others
- Prompt and intelligent replies
- Good manners
- Light, springy movements
- Training of ear and voice
- Pure vowel sounds
- Pronunciation of difficult words
- Musical training
- Singing
- Gentleness
- Courtesy
- Kindness
- Candor
- Respect for others
- Attention
- Self-compelling will
- Sense of duty
- Desire to excel
- Be first without vanity
- Be last without bitterness
- Sportsmanship
- Joy in others' success
- Appetite for knowledge
- Zeal for work
- Imagination

- Thinking of the "why" of things
- Undivided attention
- Perfect execution
- Handwriting
- Finishing work that's been started
- Obedience to conscience
- Obedience to the law
- Obedience to Divine direction
- Promptness
- Cheerfulness
- Self-restraint
- Truthfulness
- Carefulness
- Attention to detail
- Factualness
- Accuracy
- Reverence for others
- Respect for persons and property
- Sweet temper
- Trustfulness
- Good humor
- Patience
- Humility
- Contentment
- Amiability
- An even temper
- Inclined to make the best of things
- To look on the bright side
- To impute the best and kindest motives to others
- To make no extravagant claims

ABOUT THE EDITOR

Deborah Taylor-Hough, long-time homeschooling mother of three, is the author of a number of popular books including *Frugal Living For Dummies*® and the bestselling *Frozen Assets* cookbook series. Debi also worked as Outreach Director and Youth Director at her church, and regularly teaches classes, workshops and seminars throughout the USA and Canada to women's groups, conferences, churches, and community education programs.

Her workshop topics include:

- living within your means
- simple living
- cooking for the freezer
- general homemaking
- writing, publishing and publicity
- identifying personal priorities
- simplifying the holidays
- easy educational ideas for children
- Charlotte Mason home education
- ... and more!

Visit Deborah online:

TheSimpleMom.com
CharlotteMasonHome.com

Also available from Deborah Taylor-Hough:

Frozen Assets: Cook for a Day, Eat for a Month
ISBN: 9781402218590 (Sourcebooks)
This breakthrough cookbook delivers a program for readers to cook a week or month's worth of meals in just one day by using easy and affordable recipes to create a customized meal plan. The author, who saved $24,000 on her family's total grocery bill during a five-year period, offers up kid-tested and family approved recipes in Frozen Assets, plus bulk-cooking tips for singles, shopping lists, recipes for two-week and 30-day meal plans, and a ten-day plan to eliminate cooking over the holidays. Cooking for the freezer allows you to plan ahead, purchase items in bulk, cut down on waste, and stop those all-too-frequent trips to the drive-thru.

Frozen Assets Lite and Easy
ISBN: 9781402218606 (Sourcebooks)
Taylor-Hough is back with a book of low-fat, lower-calorie meal plans that use the same time-saving and cost-effective methods. *Frozen Assets Lite and Easy* shows readers how to eat healthy food while still saving time and money, with shopping lists, recipes, and detailed instruction on how to make freezer cooking work for you.

Frugal Living For Dummies®
ISBN: 9780764554032 (Wiley)
Need help keeping that New Year's resolution to eliminate credit card debt and live within your means? Packed with tips on cutting costs on everything from groceries to gifts for all occasions, this practical guide shows you how to spend less on the things you need and save more for those fun things you want.

Made in the USA
Las Vegas, NV
15 July 2022

51632069R00046

THE CAPTIVATOR

THE CAPTIVATOR

ANDREW YORK

PUBLISHED FOR THE CRIME CLUB BY
DOUBLEDAY & COMPANY, INC.
GARDEN CITY, NEW YORK
1974

The characters and events in this novel are invented; any resemblance to real characters or events is coincidental and unintended.

ISBN: 0-385-08432-3
Library of Congress Catalog Card Number 73–82251
Printed in the United States of America
First edition in the United States of America

CONTENTS

Man is only great when he acts from the passions.

Benjamin Disraeli

PART ONE

THE IDEALIST

CHAPTER 1

During the night a sea mist had gathered over the southern North Sea. Now, as dawn approached, the gentle southwesterly breeze blew it towards the low-lying shore, sent it swirling across the Flemish banks to leave the whistle buoys mournfully proclaiming their presence to anxious navigators, shrouded the high buildings of Ostend, accumulated densely over the great mole at Zeehrugge. On it whispered, now tinged pink in the east, round the lonely tip of Walcheren, rendering the grey warships in the Helder ever more sinister, reaching for the Frisians with their romantic names, Terschelling, Ameland, Schiermonnikoog in the Netherlands, and across the Ems to Borkum, Juist, Nordeney, Langeoog, Spiekeroog, and Wangerooge in Germany, at last gaining the Elbe itself, turning the constant stream of ships moving up river with the tide for Hamburg and the Kiel Canal into a ghost armada, following their sirens into the gathering gloom.

The yacht had left Nordeney at half tide, as soon as the incoming water had raised her from her mud bed. In the five o'clock half light the mooring warps had been brought in, and with purring diesel she had swept around the curving harbour, pausing at the mouth to set main and genoa, before disappearing into the mist. She was a beautiful ship, built for speed, her bows sheering from twelve metres over-all to nine on the waterline, her hull gleaming white. She had come into the harbour the previous afternoon, found a berth in the marina, and spent a quiet night. Her crew consisted of four young people, two men and two girls, but apart from a walk ashore they had spent the evening on board their vessel. Her name was *Fair Winds*.

Now she was leaving as quietly as she had come. Her de-

parture interested no one, not even the fishermen on the pierheads. There was mist every morning in the Frisians, especially
in late spring, and in any event, the watt channels through the
sandbanks were well marked. Nor would she be going far, as
she turned towards the east. Perhaps to Norddeich on the mainland, more likely to Langeoog, to reach the huge sheltered harbour at high water, and allow her crew ashore for a ride in the
multi-coloured train, for a day of utter relaxation. She flew the
German ensign.

Weber leaned on the tiller, sitting on the transom with his
feet against the lee gunwale, although the ship heeled only
slightly in this gentle breeze. Early as it was, he smoked a pipe,
which left his mouth only when he sucked a gulp of steaming
coffee from the mug in his left hand. He was in his middle thirties, his beard a matching yellow to the near whiteness of his
sun-bleached hair, to the paleness of his blue eyes. He wore sea
boots, jeans, and a heavy sweater. Seemingly relaxed, he gazed
into the mist with a frown of concentration, glanced at the chart
resting on the seat beside him, as each buoy loomed out of the
grey cloud. And he listened. With a strong tide and a light
breeze, and surrounded by invisible sandbanks, he needed every
inch of space available in the narrow watt, and had no wish
suddenly to encounter a swift-moving barge while on the wrong
side of the channel.

Parks sat in the hatchway, carefully folding the next large-
scale chart for use when his skipper had exhausted the current
one. Unlike Weber, he was of dark complexion with a ruddy
face and lank black hair. He wore a polo-necked sweater over
his jeans, deck shoes but no socks. "Bit of a sharp left-hand bend
coming up," he said in English. "And the watt dries."

"But the tide has already risen five feet, so we are all right."
Weber's English was tinged with accent. "You are still afraid
of alarming your Michelle? I think she is proving an excellent
sailor, and a most charming companion. You know, I was worried about this trip. It's not what I usually do."

"You'll probably get a medal," Parks said. "What's that
noise?"

The German cocked his head. "An engine. Two engines, I think. A motor cruiser. I hope they have more sense than to be travelling at speed in this fog."

The Englishman stood up, braced against the hatch coaming, binoculars in his hands, and swept the horizon ahead and astern. "Not a thing."

The noise grew louder.

"Coming up astern," Weber decided. "I think we should give them a hoot, Olly."

"Aye, aye, Skipper." Oliver Parks reached into the hatchway and produced a compressed-air foghorn, which he proceeded to squeeze twice. The noise blared around the ship, struck the fog wall, and seemed to rebound. "I must say, I was once out in the North Sea in a howling gale, and I didn't like it much. But this is a hell of a lot worse."

Weber smiled. "That was with Jonas Wilde, from Dunkirk to Dover."

"Now, how the hell . . . don't tell me you know that bastard?"

"We have worked together. In fact, I think I may claim to be his friend. And he doesn't have that many."

"You can say that again. So he told you about that little adventure."

"Some of it. He found it amusing. In retrospect."

"Not at the time. He even dented my skull for me because he wasn't sure that *I* was going to be his friend."

"Well, as I remember his story, you were trying to arrest him. Good morning, Ilse. I apologise for the noise, but there is another ship too close."

"You disturbed Michelle." Ilse Weenink was Dutch, as blond as the captain, but half his size, a short, solid young woman with broad features, handsome rather than pretty, with very straight pale yellow hair. She still wore her dressing gown. "Where is this other ship?" Like Weber's, her English was accented.

"That's our trouble, doll," Parks pointed out. "We can hear

the blighter, but we can't see him. How about a spot of breakfast? It's pushing six."

"Ugh. I will see if Michelle is ready to get up." She began to lower herself down the companion ladder, and checked. "There is your mystery ship."

Weber turned his head. Astern of them, coming slowly out of the mist, was a large twin-screw motor yacht, roughly their own length but with a shallow draft which made her far more at home in these restricted waters than the deep-keel sloop. "So, what were we worrying about, Olly?" He pointed. In front of the flying bridge a small radar scanner slowly revolved. "She has been watching us all the time."

Parks levelled the binoculars. "One chap on the bridge, and that appears to be it."

Weber sucked on his pipe. "Well, now she can see us with the naked eye and can see we're under sail, it's her business to keep out of our way." He put down the coffee cup and altered course, trimming the mainsheet as he did so away from the sandbank which had appeared on their starboard bow. "Providing we don't crowd her."

Parks continued to stare through the binoculars. "No ensign."

"Thus, presumably, she is a German vessel in her home waters," Weber pointed out. "You are nervous, Olly. Now that surprises me. Perhaps it *is* the fog."

Parks grunted, and lowered the glasses. "Can't be too careful, old man. I'm sure your friend Wilde will have told you that often enough."

"Oh, indeed. But for him it is a matter of life and death. We are merely protectors, and besides, no one even knows who we are. You are supposed to be on holiday, Olly. You want to relax. And for God's sake stop standing around Michelle like a, how do you say it? A cat on hot bricks? She is only flesh and blood, you know. And her blood is not really blue."

"There's a world of difference between the German attitude to royalty and the British," Parks said.

"We have had far too much of it, if that is what you mean. What is the news about breakfast?"

Ilse had reappeared in the saloon, changed into jeans and a sweater. "Any moment now. Michelle is hungry." She gazed through the hatchway. "Mmmm. Now *there* is a boat. I bet *they* cook with electricity. And have television on board. Why Michelle chose to go to sea in this tub I shall never know."

"She comes from a sailing family," Parks said. "I say, old man, isn't she coming a bit *too* close?"

Weber glanced over his shoulder once again. The motor yacht had inched up astern and now lay within fifty feet of the sloop, engines gently purring; she was obviously travelling well below her cruising speed, which made sense in thick visibility. Her name was clearly discernible, *Nemo,* painted in black letters on each white bow.

"Yeah," Weber agreed, and waved his hand. The man on the bridge waved back.

"Silly lout," Parks said.

"What is the matter, Oliver?"

Both men turned as the tall girl came into the cockpit. Like them, she wore jeans and a seaman's sweater and deck shoes. Yet on her the clothes looked different. Because she moved differently, sat differently, regarded the approaching yacht differently. The world, to her, was a different place. She spoke with the faintest of foreign accents.

"Sorry to wake you up this early, Michelle," Parks said. "It's a lousy German showing his lack of seamanship."

Weber grinned. "Perhaps he is lost," he said good-naturedly. "And wishes to follow us to Langeoog."

Michelle turned round to look forward. "It is a bit thick, isn't it? Oliver, your chauvinism is showing. Is that coffee I smell?"

She ducked her head and went down the companion ladder. Weber continued to grin at Parks. "You know, you are sweating? You British really make me smile."

"Even friend Jonas?"

"Even he, from time to time, with his absurd ideas on personal confrontation. Although less so than the rest of you. Wave good-bye to your friend."

The motor yacht had apparently decided it had waited long enough. Now the helm went to port, and the engine increased power. The boat surged forward, moving up alongside the yacht, and the young man on the flying bridge grinned and waved again.

"Clear off, you great ugly monster," Parks growled. "There's going to be a wash," he called down the hatchway.

The motorboat swung away from the sloop, holding the centre of the channel until it was half a length in front, and then suddenly slewed across in front of the sailing ship.

"Christalmighty," Parks bellowed.

Weber said nothing, but his instinctive reaction was to put the helm up. The sloop came round into the wind and the sails flapped. The motorboat turned off again, at the same time reducing speed to remain directly in front of the sailing yacht, which had meanwhile lost way so as to be entirely at the mercy of the current.

While Parks remained frozen in the hatchway, now joined by the two girls crowding up to see what had happened, Weber desperately put the helm down again, trying to gybe the yacht and get way on once more. But it was too late. *Fair Winds* had turned broadside to the channel and was swept forward and to one side; a moment later her keel grated on the first of the sand.

"Quickly," Weber shouted. "Into the lee scuppers."

Parks scrambled out of the hatch, followed by Ilse and more slowly by the girl called Michelle. They slid across the cabin roof and landed on the lee rail, forcing the yacht right over on to her beam ends. The keel lifted as Weber had intended, but then the topsides themselves grated on the bottom, and the yacht came to rest, the deck almost perpendicular, the boom free and dipping into the water, which coursed along the scuppers and threatened to lap into the cockpit itself, the sails drooping towards the sea.

"Christalmighty," Parks said again.

Weber had released the tiller and crawled forward. "Get

those sails down," he snapped at Parks. "Or we'll lose the mast. Help him, Ilse. I'll anchor. We'll lift off in half an hour."

"Can't I help?" Michelle demanded.

"By staying in the cockpit, if you please." Weber hurried forward, swinging from shroud to shroud, stepping on ventilators and sheet winches.

"Bloody swine." Parks crawled on to the coach roof and released the main halliard. "If you'll excuse my language, Michelle."

"I'm inclined to echo it." Michelle had regained the cockpit and now stood on the lee coaming to look over the weather gunwale at the motorboat, which had come round in a complete circle until it was once again astern of them. "What's the idiot doing now?"

There was a rasp of chain as Weber let the anchor go from the foredeck. He looked over his shoulder. "Go away," he bawled. "You've caused enough trouble."

"Don't you need assistance?" asked the young man on the flying bridge, surprisingly speaking in English. A woman had now joined him, together with two more men, both young, and all wearing sea clothes.

"We can get ourselves off, thank you." Parks tugged and strained at the mainsail, which was now thoroughly wet, and with its weight holding the yacht over on her side, although she was already trying to lift as the tide rose. Ilse worked beside him.

"But we must help you," said the captain of the motorboat, putting his engines astern so as to check his vessel immediately behind the stranded yacht. He gave a command to his two deckhands, who hurried forward to release their anchor. Thus held, but with her much shallower draft still floating, the *Nemo* swung gently round on the tide.

"Not *there*," Weber called, scrambling aft. "She'll swing into us. For heaven's sake. Fend off, ma'am." He landed in the cockpit as Michelle hoisted herself onto the transom, thrusting her feet over the stern in an attempt to check the motorboat from hitting them.

The captain left the bridge, accompanied by the woman. "What's a little paint?" he asked quietly. "Will you please keep very still, Mr. Weber?"

Weber raised his head, gazed into the muzzle of an M-16 rifle.

CHAPTER 2

The house stood by itself; the village was a mile up the road, the nearest building estate three miles over the downs. Alike in its situation, its size, and the acreage with which it was surrounded, not to mention the high wall which enclosed the whole, it was a reminder of a more gracious, less democratic past.

The wall, Wilde remembered, was not electrified. Because of the dogs. Presumably, tonight, the dogs had been chained. Did that mean the electricity had been turned on, for the night?

He brought the hired SL 300 to a gentle halt before the gates, watched them swing open before him. Certainly there was a lot of electricity around.

The car waited, humming gently. A nice car. A luxury for a man who normally only drove when he had to, and then took whatever came to hand. The roof was down, and the slight breeze ruffled his hair. It was thinning hair, with perhaps even a thread of grey here and there amidst the dark brown. He wore it fashionably long at the back, and his sideburns reached to below his earlobes, but even they left his features too exposed, large and gaunt, granite-hard when relaxed, suggestive of a boulder stranded by the falling tide. Only his pale blue eyes were mild and thoughtful. Tonight, decidedly thoughtful.

He wore a white dinner jacket that accentuated the width of his shoulders, just as the black pants made his narrow hips appear more slender than they really were. Evening dress suited him, although he seldom wore it. He was a tall man, a shade over six feet, and the seat was pushed back to allow his long legs room to stretch. Even sitting still, both hands on the wheel, he suggested energy; he breathed slowly and deeply. Now he took one hand off the wheel and looked at it; there was sweat on his palm.

Which was reasonable. He had only visited this house twice before. The first time he had come in Felicity Adams' car, blindfolded in a grotesque caricature of his real business. The second time he had also come secretly, with Catherine Light, his mind a jumbled chaos of fear and anger. Tonight he was driving up to the front door with an invitation in his pocket. This was so unlikely a situation that he could hardly believe it even now. Yet when a summons came from this source, it had to be obeyed.

Apparently no dogs tonight. He pressed the accelerator and the car slipped forward. Now he could see the house itself. There was light at every window, and he calculated there were forty-eight windows facing him. The summons had said black tie. For a quiet supper *à trois?* Sir Gerald Light at one end of the table, Catherine at the other, and in between them, Wilde. Something out of a Vincent Price movie. "You've met Jonas, of course, my dear? But of course, you worked together once. He kills, you know. For me. And when he is not doing that, he makes love to you. Silly fellow. But then, silly you, my darling Kate, for responding. His enemies say that he is the most dangerous man in the world, you know, Kate. But *you* know, and I know, that that is nonsense. Jonas merely does what I tell him to do, which must mean that *I* am the most dangerous man in the world. Of course, I never lose my temper, never even get angry. Or at least, never show it. As for jealousy, that is an unworthy emotion for a man like me. And yet, it *is* pleasant, isn't it, Jonas, isn't it, Kate, to have you both sitting here at dinner with me, drinking my wine, eating my food, wondering what I have in store for you."

It occurred to Wilde that he was becoming quite a pessimist in his old age. But the truly remarkable aspect of the situation was that he was here. The Mercedes glided to a halt outside the front door. Another surprise. One, two, four, eight . . . there were twelve cars parked here, five of them Rollses, and only one a Mini. There was music, issuing from the windows. And there was Rodrigues, waiting to welcome him at the top of the short staircase. Wilde invited to a party? At the Lights'?

The door of the car swung shut behind him, and he went up the steps. His instincts tingled. He lived by them, survived by humouring their every warning. For Wilde the civilised world was a jungle, through which he stalked as a lonely predator, with every man's hand raised against him, save only the man who employed him. Who had always employed him, to this moment.

"Good evening, Mr. Wilde." Rodrigues allowed himself a brief smile. He was a stocky little man; Wilde recalled that he had the physique and the strength of a bull.

"Good evening, Rodrigues. I'm wondering if I got my numbers right."

"Oh, indeed, Mr. Wilde. You are expected. Just walk in; it's an informal party tonight."

"You do surprise me." His heels clicked on the parquet of the hall. The double doors on his left were open, but he hesitated for an instant before entering. There were perhaps twenty men and women in there, all wearing evening dress, all chatting while white-coated waiters passed trays of champagne and cocktail food. There was a three-piece group playing some extraordinarily square music in the background. Sir Gerald and Lady Light, entertaining.

He stepped inside and was accosted by an enormous man six feet seven inches tall with a cavernous, gloomy face. "Jonas. How good to see you."

"Is it, Commander? I suppose I should say it's good to be here. I wish my head would stop swinging."

"It's a changing world, Jonas," Commander Mocka said sententiously. "Even people like you, and myself, of course, are allowed existence nowadays."

"Rodney Mocka. You must introduce me to your friend." She was fortyish, inclined to stoutness, and she gushed.

"Jonas Wilde," Mocka explained. "A chap from the ministry, you know, Cynthia. I must get you both a drink." He sidled into the crowd.

"Spoken like a gentleman," Wilde murmured. "He is, you know. Dartmouth and all that."

"Jonas Wilde. What a *nice* name," Cynthia said. "But you don't *look* like a civil servant, Mr. Wilde."

"Ah well, you see, I never learned to be civil." Wilde also sidled into the crowd.

"Jonas. *Jonas?* Oh, my God." Catherine Light wore an off-the-shoulder sapphire-blue taffeta gown, and the room was suddenly empty. She was tall, for a woman, and had, he remembered, very long and very lovely legs, which made a too-thin figure irrelevant. But her face made the legs themselves irrelevant. It was shrouded in the straight midnight hair which hung to her shoulders, a piece of sculptured beauty in which the too-short, upturned nose was the only flaw; but the nose itself was reassuring in that it proved her mortality. He felt a sense of awe every time he looked at her; on the rare occasions he had been privileged to hold her in his arms he had known a euphoria quite outside his considerable experience. He lived by women, because women were so often men's weaknesses, and he existed by discovering his enemies' weaknesses and using them to his own advantage. Over fifteen years in his most peculiar profession he had come to regard sex in the same sense as he picked up a strange pistol, curling his hand around the butt to feel the balance, wondering just how many live cartridges were still in the magazine, whether there was one in the chamber, whether the moving parts were in good order and well oiled, whether it would be a help or a hindrance.

But not Catherine Light, and she was the woman who loved him. But then, this was the reason. If Wilde used women, there was scarce a woman who, knowing him, had not come to hate him. Except Catherine Light.

"Didn't you know I was coming?" He inclined towards her, and she put up her cheek to be kissed. She wore Adoration with a carelessness which suggested that her choice was made because she liked the scent, and not merely to establish that she was one of the *few*.

Her head shook from side to side slowly; her cheek brushed up and down his mouth and was withdrawn.

"Um," he said, and released her hand. "Then it would appear

that I've walked into something. I suppose we should start holding our breath. Or would you rather just bust our way out of here?"

She gazed at him, and her tongue came out to circle her lips, quickly. It was an idiosyncrasy he adored. She wasn't afraid. Catherine Light scarcely knew the meaning of the word regarding herself. But she was afraid for him. Despite all she knew about him, she also knew he was no match for her husband.

"Your champagne, Jonas." Mocka loomed over them. "Of course, you know Lady Light. I keep forgetting that."

"We shared an adventure once," Wilde said. "When you had been nobbled, as I remember, Rodney. I suppose you wouldn't know what I am doing here?"

"Sir Gerald's idea, my dear fellow. As I said, he feels there has been enough of this cloak-and-dagger stuff, wants us to be more, how shall I put it, armour-clad diplomats in the future. Ah, Sir Gerald, Wilde has arrived."

"Jonas." Gerald Light came through the crowd, hand outstretched. His mouth smiled, but the pleasure did not reach his eyes, which remained a soft brown opaquely empty of any emotion at all. The neutrality of expression covered his face as well; it had always done so, and presumably, Wilde thought, it always would. In the abstract he might almost be considered handsome, through the perfect regularity of his features. Not even the slightest blemish, unlike his wife. Forehead fitted nose and eyes, eyes and nose melded into short upper lip and average-sized flat mouth, which in turn sat well over a squared chin. He walked erect, making the most of his average height, but quite without stiffness. His black tuxedo fitted him like a second skin, and his shirt had an old-fashioned starched front. He affected rubber-heeled shoes even in evening pumps, which might not have been approved by his fellow old Harrovians, but which enabled him to move silently, his only apparent pleasure.

His fingers were limp but dry, as was his palm, and he gave Wilde's face no more than a glance. "So glad you could come, my dear boy. I imagine you were a little surprised by the invitation, eh?"

"Aren't we all?" Wilde asked. "Lady Light nearly had me thrown out."

Sir Gerald turned his smile on his wife. "Do you know, I keep forgetting that she used to work for us and thus knows all about you. To my other friends you are just a chap from the ministry. You do understand that?"

"I got the message, Sir Gerald."

"Good. Good. Now, I tell you what, we don't really want to stand around being bored, do we? I've someone I'm anxious for you to meet. So why don't you have that drink and another, if you wish, and let Catherine introduce you around, and then I'll send Melanie to bring you into the other room. What?"

"That sounds delightful," Wilde murmured and watched his employer's back receding. Mocka had disappeared in the direction of the bar.

"Do you think I could have a cigarette?" Catherine asked.

Wilde took a whaleskin cigarette case from his inside breast pocket. "Turkish on the right. You mean you haven't given them up? Everyone else has."

"Me included." She inhaled, sucking the smoke deep into her system before expelling it into his face. "But there are times . . . you haven't?"

"I figure it's as good a way to die as any, although I must admit I still prefer cigars. His nibs is playing his cards very close to his chest, as usual."

She turned away, smiled at the next couple they encountered. "Lillian, I do want you to meet Jonas Wilde. Mr. Wilde is one of Gerald's bright young men from the ministry, you know. Charles. You haven't met Jonas Wilde, have you?"

"Can't say I have," the baronet admitted. "New, are you, Wilde?"

"Not really, Sir Charles," Wilde said. "Sir Gerald keeps me hidden away, in Records." They passed on, for a moment suspended between groups. "I suppose there is no possibility . . ."

"That he knows about us?" She paused to stub out her cigarette so suddenly that he brushed her arm. She was trembling, and as cold as if she'd been swimming in December. "Oh, he can't. He just can't."

"But you have no idea why I'm here?"

Her smile was back. "Zita, this is Jonas Wilde, one of Gerald's bright young men from the ministry. Peter, do come over here and meet Jonas Wilde, one of Gerald's secretaries."

"Wilde? Wilde? I say, old man, haven't I seen you around the House?"

"Peter is an M.P.," Catherine explained.

"I doubt it," Wilde said. "I've only ever been to the Palace of Westminster once in my life." He was more interested in the woman.

"Zita Richmond," Catherine said a trifle coldly. "We were at school together."

"Katie was my best friend," Zita Richmond confessed. She had black hair, like Catherine, long, but with a peculiarly thin quality; it hung to her thighs and matched the slenderness of her body, leaving the soft roundness of her features, the liquid brown of her eyes somehow exposed in a foreign land. She was above average height, although not so tall as Catherine, and wore a blood-red silk gown, high-necked but shoulderless, to leave her arms bare. It occurred to Wilde that if her body might prove disappointing—and that remained to *be* proved—her eyes had that bottomless quality which indicated a mind well worth possessing. When women interested him, he estimated their potential in terms of colours. Catherine, because of her elusiveness, was mist grey. Zita Richmond could only be thistle.

"Do you think I'll live?" she inquired gently.

"He thinks a great deal, about women," Catherine said.

"I was wondering how any schoolmistress, even at Roedean, had the nerve to take the two of you on at the same time," Wilde admitted. "The name Zita Richmond promises all manner of exotic excitements."

"Zita is a complete mongrel," Catherine said sweetly. "Egyptian mother, French father, eventually English husband, and far too much money all her life. She seems to divide her time between the Seychelles and Long Island. England is slumming. I can't imagine what brought her here this time. She only arrived last night."

"I felt like paying a visit to my oldest friend, darling," Zita reminded her. "I'd have come sooner if I'd known how you'd expanded your circle of friends. I wonder why you've kept Mr. Wilde hidden all these years, Kate."

"You'll have to ask Gerald," Catherine said. "Come along, Jonas. Oh."

She had turned, to find herself facing a very young woman, with dark brown hair and soft eyes, and a pleasantly ugly face. "What is it, Melanie?"

Melanie Bird glanced at Wilde.

"Oh," Catherine said again. "I think she wants you, Jonas."

"How charming," Zita Richmond said. "To be *wanted*, Mr. Wilde."

"I wish I could be sure it was my brain and not my good looks," Wilde said. "I hope we'll meet again, Mrs. Richmond."

"Oh, call me Zita, Mr. Wilde. I'm not really a Mrs. any more; the poor darling went and died. I'm sure we shall. Meet again, I mean."

Catherine took a step beside him. "Jonas . . ."

"Red alert? Darling, not even Gerald would do me dirt with all these people around. I hope." He followed Melanie into the hall, and then towards the back of the house. "Quaint old pile, isn't it, Birdie? Any idea what his nibs has in mind?"

Melanie Bird smiled. When first they had met, only a few months previously, her inability to speak had made him uneasy. She was too symptomatic of Gerald Light's pleasure in surrounding himself with the unusual. He had feared that she might even be something of a freak.

But since then he had learned to respect her intelligence and her unfailing good humour. And, no doubt, her loyalty. To her employer. But then, that had always been Wilde's most attractive quality as well. Loyalty to Gerald Light meant loyalty to Western Civilisation. Sir Gerald said so, often enough, and oddly enough, Wilde believed him. He was *the* representative of that unchanging middle class which had maintained Britain in the forefront of world affairs for some five centuries, more often than not against the wishes of the majority of the population. Wilde even supposed he admired the old bastard. But old bastards should not indulge themselves with pretty young wives. Not pretty young wives like Catherine, anyway.

Melanie led him down three steps, and past a pantry, and then opened a door on the left and stood aside. She still smiled. Wilde stepped into darkness, and a pair of hands closed on his throat.

(ii)

The American, Coolidge Lucinda, one of the only two male friends Wilde possessed in the world, had recently suggested that he was growing old. "Not when on the job, Jonas," he had said. "There's still no one quite like you when you've a target in front of you. But you're given to relaxing too often and too soon. One day the floor is going to get up and hit you."

The words flashed through Wilde's mind as the door slammed shut behind him and the fingers ate into his windpipe, cutting off the flow of oxygen to his brain. They were strong fingers. Dangerous fingers. Instinctively he struck to his right, a scything, right-handed blow, delivered with the edge of his hand, not carrying sufficient weight because of his lack of balance. And he struck a very solid body across the chest. The man was shorter than himself, and therefore reaching upwards.

Now they were close together, and a head was thrust under his chin, supporting the fingers. And now the fingers were all but meeting, and the blackness was serrated by blazing lights flying to and fro in front of his eyes. There were only seconds of consciousness left. But his adversary had made a mistake in coming so close. Wilde brought his hands together, and struck downwards, behind the man, slamming his clenched fists into the small of the back. He did not even raise a murmur. But now he was working up a rhythm, increasing the power with each swing, a rhythm which would increase until he died.

The man grunted, and half turned, as yet another blow

thudded into his kidneys. Another mistake. Wilde brought his hands back in front with tremendous speed, locked his fingers once again, and forced them upwards with all his strength and power. His fists struck the triceps of the arms directed at his throat, and threw them apart as if they were made of straw. The man gasped, and Wilde stepped backwards, sucking air into his lungs, seeking the balance to deliver a killing blow, drawing back his right hand as he did so, and checking as the room suddenly became filled with light.

"Hold that, Wilde." Sir Gerald sat at a desk, on the far side of the room, which was otherwise empty of furniture save for half a dozen straight chairs pushed against the wall. The room was, however, carpeted throughout, which explained the absence of sound. Commander Mocka stood next to Sir Gerald, on the right, and now that the light was on, Melanie reopened the door and came in, closing it behind her.

"Your idea of a joke, Sir Gerald?" Wilde asked coldly.

The man in front of him, only now straightening following the tremendous blows on his back, and still clutching himself there, was perhaps a dozen years younger than himself. A sign of the times; all of Wilde's adversaries nowadays were younger than himself. He was also, as Wilde had deduced, some four inches shorter, with thick shoulders and obviously considerable strength. His features were clipped, in an otherwise broad face; they made Wilde think of Dick Tracy, except for the little black moustache. Altogether, he calculated, and especially remembering the fingers he could still feel at his throat, a dangerous young man. He wore evening dress, like the rest of them, although his shirt front was the worse for wear.

Wilde realised his own tie had come unstuck. He reached up to remove it altogether, and release his top button.

"His name is Paul Fine," Sir Gerald said. "Paul, I want you to meet Jonas Wilde. Code Name Eliminator."

"My pleasure." Paul Fine held out his hand, and after a moment Wilde took it.

"I'm still a little fogged."

"Then sit down," Sir Gerald said. "Melanie, may we have something to drink."

Mocka arranged four of the chairs in front of the desk, and sat down. Wilde and Fine followed his example. Melanie pressed a concealed panel, and part of the right-hand wall slid back to reveal a cocktail bar. She looked over her shoulder at the men.

"Ah, yes," Sir Gerald said. "Wilde has a sweet tooth, and will drink Bacardi and Coca-Cola. I assume you can put rum on top of champagne?"

"They mix very well. But no lemon, if you please, Melanie, and a great deal of ice."

"How ignorant I am," Sir Gerald said sadly. "Fine will drink whisky. Johnny Walker Black, I believe, Paul?"

"When I can get it, Sir Gerald."

"And the commander will join me in a dry sherry. As may you, Melanie. Yes, of course, Wilde, explanations. Well, the fact is, I was interested in seeing how Paul would fare against your, shall we say, greater experience. What did he do wrong?"

"He lacks mental stamina," Wilde said. "When I started to hurt him, he relaxed his grip, whereas, had he put up with the pain for just a few seconds longer, I think I would have blacked out. My head was swinging. Although, of course, perhaps he was not *trying* to kill me."

"Perhaps not." Sir Gerald took the glass from Melanie's tray. "You would say, then, on due reflection, that he would prove a worthy opponent, were he to put his mind to it?"

"I would say that," Wilde agreed. Obviously it was what he was supposed to say.

"That makes me very pleased." Sir Gerald leaned back in his chair. "Gentlemen, our healths." They drank, and Sir Gerald put down his glass. "The fact is, Wilde, we have come to a decision, the P.M. and I, and Hugo Grain, of course, that you have shouldered the burden of being Eliminator by yourself for just too long. How many years is it, now?"

"By myself? Six."

"And before then you still bore the main responsibility. But now that your identity is known to the Russians, not to mention, ah, various other groups, I think we must introduce a certain alternative. Paul, to be precise."

"You chose a peculiar way to go about it."

Sir Gerald smiled. "I am a peculiar man, which is why I am, and always have been, a successful man. Actually, there is method in my madness. Oh, having him assault you was my bit of fun, but, ah, salutary as well, eh, Paul? He is a very dangerous young man, as you have agreed, Jonas. He has been very carefully trained for three years now. And yet, as I warned him, there is someone even more dangerous than himself. Would you now agree with that, Paul?"

"Oh, quite, Sir Gerald," Fine said, unconvincingly.

"Good. Good. It is always essential to recognise the true facts. My reason for having you meet here, of course, Wilde, is that I felt to send Paul to you might be to arouse your suspicions that all was not well. I seem to remember that when the Special Branch, owing to that unfortunate breakdown in liaison between them and myself, sent Inspector Parks along to arrest you, they pretended *he* was your new alter ego."

"And Olly and I nearly killed each other," Wilde agreed. "So he's an inspector now. How nice."

"Oh, indeed. Whereas here, in the presence not only of myself, but of Rodney and Melanie, in fact, of the entire Elimination Section, you can have no doubt that Paul is, ah, the goods. Would you agree?"

Wilde finished his drink, handed the glass to Malanie. As always when in the presence of this man, thought was a waste of time. One listened, absorbed what was said, and left consideration of the situation to a less crowded moment. "Agreed. What exactly do you want me to do, with Fine?"

"Well, of course, our intention is that you should continue to work separately. You have always done very well on your own, and Paul is also, by nature and training, something of a lone wolf. But we naturally desire that you should each be, ah, how shall I put it, barrels of the same gun. So I would esteem it a favour, Wilde, were you to take Paul with you, and for the next couple of months, ah, teach him all you know. You will find that he has a memory almost as good as your own, and a great capacity, as well as desire, for learning. And I am sure you will also find him a congenial companion."

"It'll be a pleasure, Sir Gerald," Wilde said. "Where would you like me to take him?"

Melanie handed him a full glass, sat beside him.

"I think, as we are just entering summer, that you should take him for a voyage in your boat. What is it called? A catamaran? Yes, indeed. You have the perfect cover, there; two yachtsmen enjoying the good weather."

"Suits me," Wilde said. "Know anything about sailing, Fine?"

"Not a thing."

"Well," Sir Gerald said, "you'll have even more to teach him then, won't you. Now tell me, Wilde, where is your, ah, catamaran, at this precise moment?"

"I was actually on my way north when I got your message," Wilde said. "So I've left her in Calais."

"Oh, splendid," Sir Gerald said. "Because I would like you to continue north. At least for a while. I think it would be a splendid idea were you to spend the summer cruising in and around the German Frisians. I understand they are quite delightful at this time of the year."

"I had intended to go up to the Baltic," Wilde pointed out.

"That's even more delightful, at this time of the year. But we shall certainly visit the Frisians, coming and going."

"I should prefer you to stay in that vicinity, Wilde," Sir Gerald said. "Would you excuse me for a moment." He picked up his telephone, on which a red light had started to blink. "Oh, good evening, Hugo. I wondered if you could tell me the latest development in the, ah, Miss Smith situation?"

The Foreign Secretary's voice spoke rapidly at the other end, and Sir Gerald smiled at his assembled staff as he listened.

"Oh, dear," he said at last. "Oh, dear me. Yes. Oh, yes. I don't think we have any alternative. At least, they seem to be reasonable people, don't you know? Oh, yes, my dear fellow. My man Wilde. No, no, no, of course he'll understand that. Yes, yes, yes, he'll be away immediately. Well, Hugo, you see, he's used to this sort of thing. In a slightly different context, of course. Oh, quite, I take full responsibility. Good-bye, Hugo."

He replaced the receiver and gazed at Wilde. "I have a motive for sending you to the Frisians, Wilde. In fact, as you must have surmised, I had a motive in bringing you here at all. I was endeavouring to kill, ah, two birds with one stone, in taking this opportunity to introduce you to Paul. What I really want you to do for me, and I am sure that Paul will be able to give you valuable assistance, is to find me a princess."

(iii)

Wilde discovered that he was in the process of swallowing a piece of ice. He coughed, and Melanie slapped him on the back. He put down his drink and took out his cigar case. "Smoke, Fine? I know this lot don't."

"I'm afraid I don't either," Fine admitted.

"Ah, well, it takes all sorts."

"You mistake me, Wilde," Sir Gerald said. "I seem to remember that your, ah, Jamaican cigars have a rather pleasant taste."

Wilde sighed, handed over his cigar case. Sir Gerald took one, sniffed it, and produced a cutter. Wilde retrieved his case, bit the end off his other cigar, and struck a match. "You're in a devilish humour tonight, Sir Gerald."

Sir Gerald also struck a match, carefully scorched one end of his cigar before allowing the other to touch his lips. "Am I to understand that you do not wish to, ah, rescue this young woman from her predicament?"

"The fact is, my suit of armour needs oiling, and my horse is at the vet. I don't even care much for the little darling."

"Ah. Do you know to whom I am referring?"

"Well, I assumed . . ."

"Don't," Sir Gerald recommended. "It may not have occurred to you, Wilde, but now that we are all, so to speak, one great happy family in Western Europe, we have suddenly accumulated quite a clutch of the, ah, little darlings, as you put it. One or two of them are even crown princesses, which makes matters worse.

Now *you* may suppose you know to whom I am referring, but, if you will excuse my vulgarity, Melanie, I will have the guts of anyone who dares mention her name. For our purpose, she will be called Miss Michelle Smith, a name she selected for herself."

He sipped his sherry. "Miss, ah, Smith, it seems, is fond of sailing. She comes from a sailing family, of course. She is also not fond of publicity, and in the course of her normal duties she has far too much of it. So it was that this summer she elected to take a sailing holiday, ah, incognito. As, in fact, Miss, ah, Smith. As she chose to spend her holiday in the Frisians, having no doubt heard of their remarkable beauty, her holiday was made the concern of three governments. The Germans very kindly supplied the yacht, a twelve-metre sailing vessel with an auxiliary engine, called *Fair Winds*. They also supplied the chief guard, your old friend Carl Weber, Wilde, who was to skipper the vessel. We supplied the second guard, that other old friend of yours, Wilde, Oliver Parks. And the Dutch supplied the third guard, and the necessary female accompaniment to Miss, ah, Smith, in the person of a Miss Ilse Weenink."

"I'm afraid I don't know *her*," Wilde murmured.

"You do surprise me. I understand that she is quite efficient. She is also, by the verdict of a computer, I'm told, the ideal companion for Miss, ah, Smith. They share the same interests, the same tastes in clothing, and, ah, music, and all that sort of thing which seems so important to modern youth. Thus, about ten days ago, the happy ship set off on its idyllic voyage."

Sir Gerald paused to flick ash and have another sip of sherry, and to sigh. Commander Mocka stared at the ceiling. Paul Fine waited expectantly. Wilde finished his second drink and handed the glass to Melanie.

"The, ah, yacht," Sir Gerald continued, "is fitted with a radio telephone, on which Weber was instructed to report every day, to various, ah, stations on the shore, and in addition, Miss Smith was persuaded to give us an itinerary, of her various projected ports of call, so that we could, ah, keep our eyes on the situation. Which is just as well. Four days ago, last Monday to be exact, the, ah, *Fair Winds* left the island of Nordeney, in the

German Frisians, at five o'clock in the morning. An odd hour to start upon a journey, I would have said."

"They may have wanted to catch a tide," Wilde suggested. "Boats have to, from time to time."

"Possibly. They also left in a fog, or at any rate, a thick mist. Does that not seem strange?"

"Not necessarily. There is often a sea mist in the early morning during fine weather, so they'd have expected it to clear as the day went on. And if they were staying inside the islands they'd have had nothing to worry about. The channels are well marked."

"I'm very glad to hear you say so. As it happens, they did intend to stay inside the islands, according to our itinerary, making for the island of Langeoog, which is about ten miles away from Nordeney. Not very far, would you say, Wilde?"

"No," Wilde agreed. "But then, it's impossible to go direct. They would have had to follow the watt channels through the sandbanks, which in some cases might almost carry them back to the mainland. Say fifteen miles, at least."

"Is that so? You do confound me with your expertise. In any event, they never arrived in Langeoog, which was very upsetting for the German agent waiting there. He, fortunately, obeyed his instructions, and contacted his headquarters, which was already alarmed because Weber had failed to report at noon, as he was required to do whenever they were at sea. The situation as it then was caused a, ah, bit of a flap, which naturally was placed in my lap, our continental friends doing us the honour of regarding the British Security Services as the most highly developed of all such organisations. And so, merely as a precaution, I sent for you, Wilde."

"Nursemaiding princesses, oops, young ladies known as Smith, is not really in my line."

"Quite. Although I have no doubt at all that you would prove quite good at it. But you seemed such an obvious choice, as this whole affair would appear to revolve around small boats, and you not only have a small boat yourself, but you have spent most of your life messing about in them. I also had to take into consideration that something more than nursemaiding might be required, and of course, it is absolutely essential that this affair is handled with the strictest secrecy. You are at least used to working in secrecy. And as I said, I could also take the opportunity to introduce you to Paul here. And as it happens, and I may say, as usual, my precautions were very wise. The *Fair Winds* disappeared for a full forty-eight hours. Because of the mist, which, contrary to your supposition, Wilde, persisted all day on Monday, we were unable to send out search aircraft, and I repeat, as it was considered essential to maintain the secrecy we had hitherto observed, a full-scale air and sea search could not be mounted.

"On Tuesday evening, however, the, ah, sloop put into Cuxhaven, which, as you will know, Wilde, is the German seaport at the mouth of the Elbe. It entered the yacht marina there, secured a berth, and requested the harbour master's permission to stay there for a week or two, as the crew, having been delayed by inclement weather, had come to the end of their holiday, and would have to fly home, they having represented themselves as British. They would, they said, make arrangements for the ship to be picked up by a delivery firm. To this, naturally enough, the harbour master agreed. Unfortunately, you see, Cuxhaven was not on Miss Smith's itinerary, as she had not intended going that far north, and so there was no agent on the spot. And again, as there had been no overdue report, the normal authorities were not interested in her at that time. In fact, but for the fact that German agents were by now crawling all over their North Sea coast looking for the vessel, she might have remained there undetected for some time. Luckily, at this stage circumstances did alter slightly in our favour; she was discovered by our Hamburg agent on Wednesday morning."

"Who exactly were the crew, Sir Gerald?" Commander Mocka asked.

"Two young men, who gave their names as Carl Weber and Oliver Parks, and were in possession of passports and papers to prove it."

"Well then, couldn't there be some perfectly reasonable explanation?"

"I'm sure there could, Commander. Only there wasn't. And that was on Wednesday."

"But if they had passports," Fine said.

"Simple," Wilde said. "Yachtsmen often grow beards when at sea, and immigration officials are used to this. The two men would have needed the same general build and colouring as Parks and Weber, but that could have come out of a bottle. The resemblance itself need have been very slight."

"I'm afraid Wilde would appear to be correct, Paul," Sir Gerald said. "And where were the two young ladies? Oh no, it was obvious that some disturbing occurrence had taken place. Unfortunately, once again, the two young men were allowed to depart, and they took a train, ostensibly for Hamburg and the airport. Our agent traced them that far, but there was no record of their ever having caught a plane. But of course, as Wilde has pointed out, no blame could be attached to the harbour officials."

Once again he paused, with the air of a magician whose rabbit had also disappeared. Wilde took his refilled glass from Melanie and squeezed her hand. She smiled at him and sat down. "So you plump for the German Frisians," Wilde said. "I still prefer the Baltic. Supposing they are at sea at all."

"Supposing, Wilde, as you say. But I'm afraid it is most definitely the Frisians. While we were assimilating this information and wondering what to do about it, we received a letter." Sir Gerald opened a drawer of his desk and took out a photostat. "At least, I suppose you could call it a letter. It says, very simply, 'Miss Smith is in good hands. But it will cost you to regain her. Wait for it.' This was received last night. It may be imagined what a disturbance *that* caused in the capitals of Western Europe. Of us all only I, secure in the knowledge that I had already sent for you, Wilde, could remain even reasonably calm." Sir Gerald's mouth widened into what might easily have been mistaken for a smile. "But even I had no alternative other than to, ah, wait for it. Obviously Miss Smith has been kidnapped by some, ah, left-wing group. But which one? Nowadays there are so many."

"And that's the present situation?" Wilde asked. "I assume that the letter was mailed from one of the Frisians, which is why you're assuming they're still there."

"It was mailed from Nordeney, as a matter of fact."

"Which means absolutely nothing. I'd say there is a member of the group in Nordeney, with orders to mail that letter on such and such a date, unless he or she received orders to the contrary. This person would have had no link whatsoever with the actual kidnapping. At least, no link that you'll be able to find. Anyway, you know, Nordeney at the end of June is just about as crowded as Brighton Beach on a bank-holiday afternoon. The Germans like to enjoy their offshore islands."

"But you'd agree that if, as seems certain, Miss Smith was kidnapped between Nordeney and Langeoog, it had to be done by another boat," Mocka objected. "And presumably this boat had to have picked up the *Fair Winds* in Nordeney."

"Then she should be easy enough to trace," Fine said, and looked expectantly at Sir Gerald.

"One would have supposed so, dear boy. Unfortunately, the *Fair Winds* appears to have been the only yacht to leave Nordeney on Monday, at any time during the day. Because of the mist. And the harbour that morning was fairly empty. The previous day having been a Sunday, you see, it had been quite full of boats from the mainland, but most of them had left that afternoon. Quite an armada, I'm told."

"And the boat we want was probably amongst them," Wilde said. "The commander has to be right there. She could have hung around the watts all night, waiting for the *Fair Winds* to come out. It's possible to find very sheltered anchorage in the lee of the sandbanks, and it's quite a common practice, too, so no one would be likely to become suspicious. But whoever was planning that had to have known all about *Fair Winds,* all about her crew, and must have had a copy of her itinerary. That doesn't speak very well for your security blanket."

"My God, yes," Mocka said. "There has to be a leak, somewhere."

"We are working on that, Commander," Sir Gerald said. "But at least we are now agreed as to how, and probably where, the, ah, hijacking of the yacht occurred."

"Irrelevant," Wilde said. "If the hijacking was done early on Monday morning, and the princess was transferred to a high-powered motorboat, which seems the obvious choice for a job like this, that boat could be six hundred miles away, up in Sweden, or well on its way to the south of France by now."

"Oh indeed, Wilde, I'm sure you're right. As it happens, however, the matter has not rested there. We received another communication this morning." Sir Gerald peered at another photostat. "This one is slightly longer. It says, 'Glad you decided to play it softly, folks, we like it that way too. The price for the young lady is five hundred million Deutschmarks, or its equivalent. Cash, please. The money will be placed on board a sailing yacht, which will then cruise inside the German Frisians, from Borkum to Wangerooge and back again, for as long as is necessary until contacted. Her nationality is irrelevant, but she must carry a six man life raft on her foredeck, the case to be painted red.'" Sir Gerald glanced at Wilde. "Is *that* relevant?"

"It'll be conspicuous. Life rafts are usually carried in white, or black, or yellow containers."

"And that is obviously the idea. The message goes on, 'The number and composition of the crew is also irrelevant, but it must be understood that should there be *any* suspicious behaviour, by the crew or by any accompanying vessel or aircraft, Miss Smith will immediately be executed, and her body exposed in a public place. She will not, of course, be on the contacting vessel, so no heroics, please, but we shall be in radio communication with our boat at all times, so this is no idle threat. If it is any comfort to you, the money is not intended for us, but for the starving millions in India. You may mark the notes if you wish, but if you do, Miss Smith will not be released until the money has been changed and has reached its destination. The yacht should be beyond Borkum by Monday morning.'" Sir Gerald restored the photostats to their drawer, and relit his cigar. "They know, of course, that we are completely at their mercy."

"Five hundred million Deutschmarks?" Paul Fine said, in awed tones.

"Something in excess of fifty million pounds," Sir Gerald said. "A considerable sum of money."

"And they don't want any part of it?" Wilde said. "I'd let them get on with it, and the best of luck. It wouldn't do the young lady I'm thinking of any harm to learn something about the true facts of life."

"The young lady you are thinking about does not come into it at all," Sir Gerald said. "I suspect you have always been something of an anarchist at heart, yourself, Wilde. But I may say that if you believe these, ah, people really intend to donate the money to some, ah, charity, you have more faith in human nature than I have. I also find their threat quite horrible, even if they presumably are quite sure that we will never permit such a situation to arise. But quite apart from the rank of Miss Smith, there is the principle involved. Let them get away with this, and heaven knows where they might strike next. The P.M. is even a possibility."

"Or even you, Sir Gerald," Mocka murmured.

"I'm happy to say, Commander, that I have never set foot on any ship smaller than the *Queen Mary,* and now that she is no longer in business I doubt that I shall ever again come within fifty feet of the sea. My stomach does not take to it. Now, Wilde, how long will it take you to sail your boat from Calais to Borkum?"

"Not more than forty-eight hours, if I hurry. The wind is southerly at the moment, which is fine."

"Then I suggest you, ah, hurry. You and Paul will leave now with Commander Mocka and drive into London to collect the, ah, money. We have decided to pay them in English pounds, as this is the easiest to carry. You will then proceed to Ramsgate and take the first hovercraft tomorrow morning to Calais.

Tomorrow being Saturday, that will give you just forty-eight hours to reach Borkum by the stipulated time."

"Provided we can get out of Calais on time," Wilde said. "As I mentioned just now, yachts have to get on with tides. In Calais, for instance, I happen to be in a wet basin which is only opened one hour each side of high water, just to make sure that it stays wet, if you follow me."

Sir Gerald frowned. "So?"

Wilde did a hasty calculation, with the aid of his Yachts-man's Diary. "I think we're all right. High water tomorrow is about ten o'clock, in Calais, and I think the hovercraft starts running about eight in the morning at this time of year. We'll just make it."

"I certainly suggest that you do."

"What exactly are our instructions, Sir Gerald?" Fine asked. "You wish us to find these people and rescue Miss Smith?"

"Certainly *not*, Paul. I'm afraid we must take these people seriously, and *any* sort of, ah, executive action is expressly forbidden. But as I happen to have summoned Wilde already, it occurs to me that I may as well use him. And it will give you a taste of field work. But neither of you must do, say, or even *think* anything which could possibly endanger Miss, ah, Smith. No, no, your mission is merely to deliver the ransom, and then, ah, continue on your way. No doubt, out of sheer interest, you will keep in touch with us in order to discover if and when Miss Smith has been returned to us." He stared at Wilde. "You do understand what I am saying, I hope, Wilde. Now, are there any other points?"

"Yes," Wilde said. "All this talk of money seems to lack a certain reality, compared with the mundane business of making a living."

"I had forgotten your, ah, mercenary streak, Wilde. However, as you are not involved in your usual work, I'm afraid we cannot offer the normal fee. In addition, your responsibility on this occasion is shared. You will each receive one thousand pounds, five hundred down, and five hundred on completion."

"The first thing Paul and I are going to do," Wilde said, "is form a Trade Union. Be prepared for a *very* substantial wage claim before Christmas."

(iv)

Catherine Light sat at her dressing table, brushed her hair with long, slow strokes. She wore a pale green dressing gown over a dark green brush nylon nightdress, looked relaxed, and perhaps a little the worse for champagne. She watched the mirror, and in it the door to the bathroom.

Gerald Light emerged. His dressing gown was scarlet, and his slippers leopardskin. He had the oddest private tastes, perhaps to compensate for his public facelessness. "That was an excellent party, my dear," he said. "I honestly do not think there is a better hostess in England."

"Thank you." She laid down her brush. She had known he would come through that door, tonight, although they slept in separate rooms, seldom engaged in boudoir conversation. But tonight he would wish to. Tonight. She felt a little breathless. Circumstances had made hers an unusually chaste life, so that when sex intruded into her sterilised world she always felt uncertain. Of her own reactions. Gerald was predictable enough. But tonight she had to be *good*.

He sat on her bed, crossed his knees. The dressing gown fell away. Everything about him was neat and unremarkable. This was the result of thought, of planning. His power base was his complete anonymity. So his habits were dictated by choice not vanity. A pot belly, knock knees or bow legs, varicose veins, round shoulders, any of these were identifiable and therefore to be avoided. She supposed he was the fittest sixty-year-old she could possibly know. And she did admire him tremendously . . . Had not Wilde blundered into her life she might even have continued to be happy with him.

And tonight, because of Wilde, it was more than ever necessary to be happy with him.

"How nice it is," he remarked, "to see Zita again. I had no idea she was in the country."

"Neither did I. She telephoned this morning, quite out of the blue. I gather she's just passing, as usual."

"Yes. It's a shame she won't settle down. I do like her, very much. And it would be so good for you to have a close woman friend. Don't you agree?"

She got up, took off her dressing gown, walked slowly to the table on the other side of the bed and poured herself a glass of water. Her figure was illuminated by the light, through the nylon. How ghastly, to be vamping one's own husband after seven years of marriage. But he would talk around the subject all night, if she let him, delighting in the torture he was inflicting. "Champagne always gives me a terrible thirst. And I'm sure you're right, Gerald. I sometimes feel very lonely. And frightened. I nearly died of fright when that man Wilde walked in. Why on earth did you invite him?"

"I wanted to see him on a business matter. I also wanted to introduce him to Fine. I'm afraid Wilde has about reached the end of his career."

The glass clinked against the jug as she put it down. "What do you mean?"

"Well," Sir Gerald said, "he is past forty, you know. He is also a little stale, I'd say. After all, he has been in the field for fifteen years. My God, I never imagined he'd be alive still."

"Yet he is. So he can't be *that* stale."

"On the job he's as good as ever." Sir Gerald lay down, hands behind his head. His gaze never left her. "But he *thinks* too much about his work now. The first requisite for a government executioner is that he should be able to divorce himself from his job except when actually working. I don't think Wilde is any longer capable of that."

Catherine went to the wall, moved a picture of the Thames in mid-eighteenth century, and turned the combination on a safe. She reached inside and took out, after a moment's search through the several folders inside, a black-jacketed file. She sat down in an armchair, crossed her knees. "'Wilde, Jonas,'" she read. "'Born Santiago, Chile, 11 December 1929, of English father—bank manager—and American mother. Family returned

UK in early thirties. Education, grammar school. National Service 1947–49, undistinguished. One year in city, clerk. Volunteer for Korean War, 1950. Decorated, mentioned in despatches. Promoted sergeant three times, reduced to ranks three times for insubordination. Seconded to Elimination Section, B.S.S., 1956.'" She sighed. "I've often wondered what made you select him. He seems to have had a dismal military record."

"Indeed," her husband said patiently. "But he did reveal one remarkable talent, an ability to kill the enemy, with a savage cold-bloodedness which is quite frightening."

"Yes," she agreed, and went on reading. "'Completed training 1957, went to work under command of Ravenspur. Remained Section's field agent until disruption of Section by Russian agent Jola Kieserit (alias Jocelyn Kirby) 1966. Retained as sole agent after decision not to reform Section on former lines. Seriously wounded in 1968 but made full recovery. Taken by Russians in 1969, and severely tortured, but release negotiated. Commended for prompt action during internal crisis of 1971 (the Marston affair).' Do you know that is the last entry?"

"I should. I keep that file myself. Are you coming to bed, my darling?"

Catherine Light closed the file, returned it to the safe, shut the door and turned off the combination. The picture immediately slipped back into place. "It seems odd, to dismiss a man immediately after his most valuable service. He saved your life. Have you forgotten that, as well?"

"Not my life, my dear. I don't think that was ever in danger. My reputation and my career, certainly. And I am grateful. But I cannot help but recall that he had your, ah, assistance in that affair."

Catherine checked at the foot of the bed. She knew her husband well enough to understand that the hesitation he occasionally inserted into his speech was an affectation. He used it when about to play God.

She sat on the bed beside him. "I still shudder when I remember it. And I still think Jonas deserves a medal."

His hands moved up her sides, starting at her thighs. His

fingers plucked impatiently at her nightdress, and she moved sufficiently to free the skirt, and allow the material to rise with his grasp. "Unfortunately," he said, "we don't give our retiring executioners medals."

"What *do* you give your retiring executioners, Gerald?"

She raised her arms above her head, and the nightdress came free. He dropped it on the floor, grasped her shoulders to bring her forward against him. "It is a difficult problem. Especially for a man called Wilde."

Her arms came up between them, her hands flat on his chest. She was strong enough to hold herself there, despite the pressure on her back. Colour flooded her cheeks. "You're going to have him killed. What else can you do with a man as guilty, as knowledgeable, as dangerous?"

He smiled and gently hugged her shoulders. Her arms gave way, and he kissed her mouth. Her face slipped down beside his as he rolled her on her back; so far as he was concerned, any position other than the missionary was immoral, illegal, and dangerous. "You're a dramatist, my dear. If it's any consolation to you, I have not yet made up my mind *what* to do with Jonas. In any event, I want him to show Paul the ropes. It is rather an amusing thought, really: possibly the two most dangerous men in the world setting out from Calais tomorrow morning for a summer cruise."

She submitted, partly because she had to, partly out of relief. And it was very quick. He paid no attention to her requirements as a woman. He regarded Mrs. Pankhurst as quite as dangerous as Marx, and Germaine Greer as far more dangerous than Mao Tse-tung; he reasoned, correctly, that there are far more women in the world, capable of upsetting the established order of things, than all the Russians and all the Chinese put together. And Gerald Light's only deity was the Establishment. Within seconds he was relaxed, lying on his back and sighing, his hand withdrawn from beneath her buttocks.

"But of course," he said, "I should point out that were I to decide that Jonas can serve no useful purpose by remaining alive, and indeed might even be dangerous to the country and the Western Alliance, then he of all people would be least surprised. He must have been expecting such an end to his career for years." He sighed again, replaced his dressing gown, and got up. "And as you have just pointed out, what alternatives do I have?"

He closed the door behind him, leaving Catherine staring at the ceiling.

CHAPTER 3

Paul Fine stood on the dock at the Port de Plaisance, Calais, and carefully placed the heavy suitcases on the ground beside him. He sweated, and not entirely because of the heat, although it was already a warm July morning, even at nine o'clock. "Whew. I suppose we're safe now. I wonder what would have happened had one of these burst open, say at Ramsgate?"

"We'd each have received several years in gaol, for contravening just about every currency regulation they have, not to mention robbing the Bank of England."

"But . . ."

"I suppose your education had better start now." Wilde climbed down the ladder on to the pontoon, reached up for the case. "Except on the occasions when Sir Gerald actually wishes to chat with us, we don't exist."

"Yes, but what about Miss Smith?"

"They'd have collected another boat, another fifty million, and two more blokes. Pass me down those kitbags."

Fine obeyed, and surveyed the fifty-odd craft, varying in size from a hundred-ton motor yacht to several small sailing boats moored alongside the pontoon. "Which is yours?"

"The cat."

Fine placed his hands on his hips, stared at the twin-hulled fibreglass sailing yacht. "We don't have to go out into the North Sea in that?"

Wilde hefted the kitbags into the huge cockpit, then placed the suitcase beside them. "She's all but thirty feet long, you know, and being a cat, she's fourteen feet wide. That means she has about the same accommodation as a fifty-foot monohull and the same seakeeping qualities too. And she's more comfortable."

Fine got on to the ladder cautiously. "Yes, but what about all these cats which capsize?"

"Poor seamanship or freak conditions," Wilde said. "We are likely to meet with neither in the North Sea in July, at least while I'm skipper. And anyway, we're nipping inside the Frisians at the first opportunity."

"Why is she called *Regina B?*"

"Because I used to have a boat called *Regina A,*" Wilde explained patiently.

"And what happened to her?"

"She struck a rock and sank. In the Channel Islands. I had uninvited guests on board at the time and so was doing less navigating than I should." He unlocked the cabin door. The wheelhouse was open astern and the huge plexiglass windshield gave ample visibility forward. Fine stepped on board, looked around the cockpit. "I must say, there is a lot of space out here."

"And equally below." Wilde opened the hatch. "I'm afraid there's only low headroom in the saloon, but there's well over six feet in each of the hulls." He went down the starboard steps, slid the suitcases under the chart table which extended over the berth. "Still, it's more my problem than yours."

Fine ducked his head and looked inside. The saloon was situated amidships, in the transverse section between the two hulls, and so was over a foot above the waterline. It consisted mainly of a U-shaped dinette. On the port side, two steps led down to a spacious galley, forward of which a door opened into a single cabin, while aft of the galley there was another single cabin. On the starboard side, two more steps led down to the single open cabin where Wilde was standing and which had been fitted up as an elaborate chartroom complete with radar and radio telephone. Forward of this was a double cabin. The heads opened aft of the chartroom.

"I see what you mean," Fine said. "Do we have such a thing as an engine?"

"Two, to be precise. Dolphin twelves, nice and light and quiet. And reasonably easy on the petrol. Diesels would be just too heavy for a boat that's meant to sit on top of the water. They're in the hulls, aft. Now let's see; you can have either of the port cabins." Wilde checked his watch with the ship's chronometer. "I think we should get ready; the bridge will be opening in half an hour. Perfect timing, don't you think?"

"If you say so. What bridge?"

Wilde sat down beside the money, changed his loafers for canvas deck shoes. "The one we came over in the taxi, dear boy." He pointed through the open saloon door. "Although you may not realise it, we are in a disused canal, separated from the sea by a lock, so that the yachts will float all the time, because the harbour itself pretty nearly dries at low water. The gates are open now because the tide has reached the level of the water in here. But they only open the bridge one hour each side of high water, and high water this morning is just after ten. Remember?"

"I'm with you." Fine carried his bag into the port cabin. "Looks comfortable enough."

"You're next to the galley, too," Wilde said. "Which you must admit is the ideal place for the cook."

"I'm afraid I'm not very good at it."

"Now there's a shame. I really was hoping."

"I see there's a Mrs. Beaton in here." Fine peered at the bookshelf. *"What* an odd collection. *Modern Chess Openings* next to Brantôme; Keats next to the *North Sea Pilot;* Thucydides next to Shirer; *and* a complete Bierce. They do say that a man's library is the mirror of his character. I'd like to have a look at your home."

"You're doing that."

"You mean you actually live on this thing? All the time? But what do you do? When you're not sailing, I mean."

"I think a little, and I drink a lot. Usually before thinking."

Fine scratched his head. "And how long do you think it will take us to get to Borkum?"

"We'll have six hours of good tide after we come out of here, and there's a very pleasant southwesterly wind blowing, so we should get past Ostend before the tide turns. Then we'll put out to sea and give Walcheren and Schouwen a miss. The tides are weaker as we go farther north, so we'll have less against us. We should certainly be off the Hook by midnight, with the tide again, say Ijmuiden by dawn tomorrow, the Helder by lunch-time, and into the Hubertgat, that's the channel leading into the Ems, by dawn the day after tomorrow. Say Borkum for break-fast on Monday. Unless the weather plays us up."

"Do you carry all that information in your head?"

"No. All I need to work it out is the next high water, where-ever I happen to be, and I can get that from the Nautical Al-manac. Tides are pretty constant things. As a matter of fact, they are about the only constant things, apart from sunrise and sunset, in this world of ours." He went into the cockpit, opened one of the seat lockers, and took out the bag containing the working jib. "Now I'll just bend this on, and we'll be ready to push off the moment the bridge opens." He glanced in the direction of the lock gates; a red light gleamed on the right-hand side, to indicate that opening wasn't very far off.

"But wait a moment." Fine had removed his jacket and tie. Now he came into the cockpit to sit down and change his shoes. "You told his nibs we could be there *by* Monday morning. Isn't this cutting it a bit fine?"

"That's life." Wilde went up on to the foredeck, began hank-ing the sail on to the forestay.

"Well, then . . ."

"What the eye can't see the heart can't grieve over. My job in life and yours, now, I'm afraid, is disposing of people. Not rescuing them. And I don't actually think our Smith female is going to be in any danger if we're a few hours late. They want the money. Of course, if they mean to do her anyway, well then, if we were to show up tomorrow it still wouldn't do her any good."

"I say, old man, that's going it a bit strong. I mean, the odds are that this is Princess . . ."

"Michelle Smith," Wilde pointed out. "But there's a job for you, as soon as we're outside." He tapped the six-man life-raft case bolted to the foredeck. "There's a pot of red paint in the other locker."

"Oh. Oh, yes. I'd rather forgotten that. You know, old man, I rather get the impression that you and Sir Gerald don't get on."

"He despises me, and I despise him. He regards me as a common murderer who should be hanged at the first opportunity, were such things still allowed, and I regard him as a typical bowler hat who's afraid to do his own dirty work. Don't be optimistic. If you happen to be his blue-eyed boy just this minute, it won't last." The sail clewed on to his satisfaction, Wilde tested the fore halliard to make sure it was free, and did the same with the main. "All shipshape and Bristol fashion." He glanced at his watch. "I figure we still have fifteen minutes. Care for a cold beer in the club?"

"But I say, old man, we daren't chance missing the gate."

"We won't. See that red light? It'll change for amber in a little while, which will mean the gate will open in ten minutes. Time for a beer, I should think." He stepped onto the pontoon, climbed the ladder, and checked as his eyes became level with a pair of ankles.

"Why, Jonas Wilde," Catherine Light said, *"what* a pleasant surprise."

(ii)

It occurred to Wilde that this had happened before, the first time they had ever met, in fact, and it had been no less disturbing then. On that occasion it had turned out to be the answer to a prayer, but just because of that, this time had every indication of being a disaster.

Today she was displaying her legs; he supposed that technically they were too slender for her short skirt, but from his angle he was not disposed to be technical. She wore a summer suit in severe black and white stripes, and her hair was loose; over her shoulder she carried a stuffed overnight bag. And she was smiling as brightly as he had ever seen her, but it got no further than the corners of her mouth.

He finished his climb up the ladder. "As you say, Lady Light. You must be a very fast traveller, or was the party a flop?"

She decided he was close enough. "Jonas . . ." she whispered.

Wilde turned back to the steps. "You've met Lady Light, of course, Paul?"

"My God," Fine said. "But . . ."

"Well, hello, Paul," Catherine said brightly. "I bet you never expected to see me again this soon."

"We didn't," Wilde agreed. "Did Sir Gerald send you over to check up on his boys?"

That idea hadn't occurred to her. She glanced at him with her mouth open, and he could almost see the tumblers clicking. "Why, yes," she said, "I suppose you could say that, Mr. Wilde. I happened to be coming across, you know, and Gerald mentioned that you two happened to be in Calais, so I thought I'd look you up."

"Well, that was jolly decent of you," Fine said. "Although I'm not at all sure it's not bad security."

"Oh, is it?" She gazed at him helplessly, and then at Wilde, even more helplessly.

"I don't suppose it matters," Fine said. "On this occasion. But how on earth did you get here so quickly, Lady Light? We've only just arrived ourselves."

"I chartered a plane."

"Lady Light always charters a plane," Wilde pointed out, "whenever she travels. We were just going to have a beer, and I've suddenly remembered that beer doesn't agree with me. I want something a lot stronger. Will you join us?"

"Oh, I'd love to," she said. She peered past their shoulders. "Is that your boat, Mr. Wilde? Gerald has talked so much about it. I believe he secretly envies you, you know."

She was gazing at the cabin in which he had once undressed her, for her own good; the weather hadn't been settled enough for anything more than that.

"We'd better rush," Wilde said.

They climbed the stairs to the bar, and Wilde bought the drinks. Catherine sat on the settee and crossed one knee over the other. Her greatest asset, both as a woman and probably, in her midnight past, as agent, was her coolness. Not just of manner; she always managed to *look* cool, even on a steaming summer morning.

Now she drank her Negroni at great speed. "Were you about to go sailing, or something?" she asked brightly.

"Something," Wilde said.

Catherine sucked ice, turned her smile on Fine. "Do get me the other half, Mr. Fine." She watched him walking to the bar. "Jonas . . ." she said, without turning her head.

"Darling," Wilde said. "Have you gone completely stark staring mad?"

Now her head did turn. "Aren't you pleased to see me?"

"For God's sake. Can you imagine . . ."

"It's all right," she said. "Gerald thinks I've gone to Paris. There is nothing to worry about. Nothing for me to worry about. It's Paul Fine. Jonas, he's . . ."

"One Negroni," Fine said, and placed the full glass in front of her. "I say, Jonas, old man, the light's showing amber, and one or two of the other chaps have cast off."

"Then we'd better rush." Wilde got up. "I'll say good-bye, Lady Light. It really has been splendid, seeing you like this. But we must catch the tide."

Catherine was leaning back, staring at him. She smiled, but her eyes were pools of misery. "Take me for a trip," she said. "Eh?"

"Well, you see," she said, speaking very quickly but with surprising fluency for someone who was obviously making it all up as she went along, "I always take a day or two off after a party, you know, Mr. Wilde, and so I thought I'd pop across to see these friends of mine in Calais. Silly me, I never thought to make sure they'd be home. Well, they're not, and I feel an awful fool. It would be so nice to take a cruise on a yacht. And I do have some sailing sort of clothes with me."

"I'd love to take you for a sail, Lady Light," Wilde said. "But the fact is, we're making north. We won't be back in Calais for three months."

"Oh, that's all right," Catherine said. "I can always catch a plane home from your next stop."

"It really isn't possible, Lady Light," Fine said. "The real truth is, we're doing something for your husband."

Catherine glanced from him to Wilde.

"I'm afraid the man's right, Lady Light," Wilde said. "But when we come back . . ."

"But I won't be in the way," Catherine said, suddenly speaking very loudly indeed. "I know all about where you're going. It's to do with that girl Michelle . . ."

"Shut up," Fine shouted, and turned very red in the face. "I do apologise, Lady Light, but . . ."

"It's confidential," Catherine cried, and went into a peal of laughter. "Everything you do is confidential. But this isn't one of your usual jobs, is it, Mr. Wilde? I mean you usually . . ."

"For Christ's sake, do something," Fine hissed.

Wilde realised that he would have to. For one of the very few times in his life he had completely lost both control and understanding of the situation. Catherine was either stoned out of her mind or she had gone mad. Either way he was the only one who *could* do anything about it.

"Ssssh," he said. "Please, Lady Light. We were only joking about being on a job. If you'd care to come for a cruise, we'd love to have you along. Eh, Paul?"

Fine's mouth opened and shut again, rather like a fish gasping.

Catherine smiled at them, and lowered her voice. "Why, I think that's absolutely charming of you, Mr. Wilde."

(iii)

Although it is not always evident at high tide, the French coast from Boulogne all the way up to the Belgian frontier and beyond, is cluttered with sandbanks which in places extend several miles offshore. But the channels are well buoyed, and navigation in anything but the thickest visibility is perfectly simple. On the other hand, the shallow water means that in fresh winds there is nearly always a short swell, uncomfortable even for catamarans; Wilde had hardly had the time to set the mainsail, with Calais pierheads drifting astern on the flood tide, when Catherine disappeared below. He wondered if she had forgotten, when embarking on this crazy scheme, whatever it was, that she was one of the world's worst sailors. Fine also went below, apparently with the idea of doing something for her; he at least did not seem to have the slightest idea of what this might be all about.

Wilde was quite happy to have an opportunity to think. About a great number of things. He had never been under any misapprehension regarding Britain's shrinking place in the world. As perhaps the strongest of the old-fashioned Great Powers—as opposed to the Super variety—she had had an important part to play during the decade of the Cold War. It had been in the middle of this period that he had been seconded to the Elimination Section, at a time when espionage had been a very deadly affair indeed. Then he had worked with a picked team of experts, commanded by Ravenspur, and consisting of Bulwer, Stern, and himself, who had made the British counterespionage system the envy of the Americans and the terror of the rest of the world.

He did not regret those days; either having taken part in them or their passing. He had been young enough, then, and idealistic enough, then, to see his ghastly profession as no more than a job, sometimes exhilarating, sometimes saddening, but always exciting, and always necessary, and he had been man enough to feel proud that he had been the best of them all, the most deadly, the most feared, the one man who had survived after the Russians, having infiltrated the organisation with extraordinary skill, had destroyed the Section.

In the six years since that terrible day in his London flat—and how long ago *that* seemed—when he had understood the true nature of Jocelyn Kirby, he had been called upon only four times, apart from the two occasions when he had become embroiled in affairs not of his own choosing.

Four assignments in six years was a sign of the times, a sign of that slackening in international tension, of that almost farcical element which had crept into the business of spying, when detection meant a tap on the shoulder and a one-way ticket home, rather as if one had been parking in a restricted area. And he had welcomed this as well. After Jocelyn, and the trail of destruction she had left behind her, he had come to understand more of what he was, of what he had spent his life doing, of what, one day, perhaps, he might have to account. He had lost his own taste for life, as he had long lost his fear of death, had bought this boat and retired into the perfect solitude of the sea, re-emerging only from his self-imposed exile when Sir Gerald advertised for him in *The Times*.

And then had come Catherine Light, blown into his world by a crisis which had involved the entire British Security Services, turning for help to someone she knew only as a name, and discovering far more than that. And suddenly life, and death, had become very important again.

Yet he had continued to work for Sir Gerald. Why? Because only by doing so could he be sure of seeing Catherine from time to time. There was no more compelling reason than that.

So what in the name of God could have happened? Since that night in Philip Marston's flat, they had spent but a single afternoon together, and then she had been the reluctant one. With good reason. But here she was, telling her husband she was off to visit friends, and turning up on Wilde's doorstep. As a wife, in any circumstances, that was embarrassing. As the wife of Gerald Light, that was downright dangerous. And as an ex-agent of the Section, who would have been well aware that Wilde was on a mission, she was breaking every rule in the book.

Was she drunk? Catherine? Incredible. So, then . . .

But what about Paul Fine? Did a nation which had resorted to executive action in the world of espionage only four times in six years really require two executioners? It was far more logical to suppose it had been decided that Wilde had gone on long enough. And far more like Sir Gerald to decide that while it would be disloyal of him to take action against his wife's lover while actually employing him, once the blighter had been placed on the retired list, the situation would be quite different. Oh yes, that was Sir Gerald, all right, and it was difficult for Wilde to convince himself, whatever Catherine's happy dream, that Sir Gerald, who seemed to know everything else that went on in the world, was not perfectly aware of the relationship between his wife and his employee.

On the other hand, it was just possible, now that Britain was a part of a much greater community, with a consequent pooling of resources and expenses, that the counterespionage branch of the new European Security Services had been left in the hands of Sir Gerald Light, the most experienced man in the field, with the most experienced staff. In which case he might well need one or two extra executioners.

But would he choose them from Englishmen, rather than select the best from his partner countries? That was not a very neighbourly attitude.

No matter what was the truth of the matter, Paul Fine would have to be watched, and carefully, the more so as his rather silly-ass projection was patently false; it would have been so whether or not Wilde could forget the feel of those iron fingers around his throat.

All of which, as internal problems, became perfectly irrelevant when compared with the sudden disastrous irruption of Catherine Light.

Fine came on deck, leaned in the hatchway. "My God," he said.

"How is she?" Wilde asked.

"Out," Fine said. "She brought up last week's lunch, I should say, but I managed to get her to hold onto some brandy, and I'd squashed a sedative in it."

"Oh, well done," Wilde said, not sure whether he meant it or not.

"I wish I could think of some reason for all this happening," Fine said thoughtfully.

"So do I," Wilde said, with utter honesty.

"I mean, she was acting very oddly. And what on earth are we going to do with her, old man? Have you thought of that? We just don't have the time to stop anywhere."

"Believe me, I'm brooding on that as well. We may be able to put her ashore on one of the German islands."

"Before, or after?"

"I don't see that that matters very much, as she seems to know exactly what we're about, in any event."

"There's a point," Fine said thoughtfully. "All the same, old man, even if she is a rather gorgeous piece of woman, we don't want to hang onto her for *too* long. Can you possibly imagine what Sir Gerald would say, or do, if he started to worry about her and found out she was along with us?"

"Paul, old son," Wilde said, "you are about the most depressing companion I have ever had. Why don't you nip down into the galley and make us both a drink? I'll have Bacardi and Coke."

(iv)

The wind, a gentle, southwesterly breeze in the morning, freshened all afternoon, and when the tide turned, off Ostend, it whipped up quite a choppy sea. *Regina B* might not roll, but like any ship she could pitch; she surged down the sides of the waves, and then climbed steeply up the next, and although the weather was coming from astern, every so often there was a rattle of spray over the doghouse. The sky had clouded over as well, and the morning warmth had departed with the sun.

Catherine Light had dragged on an oilskin top over her dress, and sat on the lee cockpit seat, gazing sadly at the skyscrapers of Ostend on the eastern horizon. Her hair was scattered by the wind, and her face was pale. But she hadn't been sick since getting up. "Don't you think we should put in?" she asked. "The weather seems to be getting worse. And I know a simply gorgeous little restaurant next to the Handeldokken."

"So do I," Wilde said. "But we're not stopping. This breeze is blowing us along very nicely."

"And you're in a hurry to get where you're going," she said thoughtfully.

"Well," Fine said, "as we are not going to enjoy Belgian food tonight, I had better get on with dinner. I hope nobody will object if it comes out of a tin."

"I'll get it," Wilde said. "In a little while. But I wonder if you'd take the helm, Paul? I'd like to get the weather forecast."

"Oh, sure." Fine stood beside him. "What do I do?"

"You watch this thing here, from time to time. It's called a compass. I'd like you to keep that line, there, roughly on the N. That stands for due north, which is about right for us." He reached into the saloon and brought out a chart. "The point I have in mind is the extreme seaward end of the island of Walcheren. There's a lighthouse on it, but you won't see it for a while. Okay?"

"I imagine so." Fine took the helm, and the catamaran promptly began yawing to and fro. "Oops."

"You'll soon get the hang of it," Wilde said. "And don't worry too much about the odd degree here and there; visibility is good and that's a powerful light. And we have radar, if you get stuck. Just keep the bow between three five five and zero zero five. And keep your eye open for other ships, and also, if you would, floating logs of wood; they won't do our hulls any good at all, at this speed."

"Aye, aye, Skipper," Fine said, and began to concentrate.

"And sing out," Wilde said. "If anything, anything at all, bothers you." He glanced at Catherine.

"Oh, I'm coming below too," she said. "If only to change. It's starting to get quite chilly."

Wilde went into the starboard hull, sat at the chart table with dividers and parallel rule to plot a course for the Frisians after fixing the Westkapelle light, reached out his left hand to turn on the radio. It was six minutes to six. Catherine gazed at him for a moment and then went into the aft single cabin.

"Here is the Weather Forecast," said the announcer, "for seventeen fifty-five on Saturday, the fifth of July. The general synopsis at fourteen hundred . . ."

Catherine re-emerged, wearing a dark blue track suit, and carrying a hairbrush. "I am almost getting the impression that you are afraid to be alone with me," she remarked.

"I am." Wilde picked up his pencil.

"The ridge of high pressure over the Netherlands is weakening and moving away east," said the radio. "As a deep depression, nine seven five millibars, moves into sea area Bailey by midnight tonight; troughs will affect all sea areas before midnight tomorrow. Pressure will remain high over Scandinavia."

"Good old Scandinavia," Catherine said. "Are you finished?"

"Ssssh," Wilde said, busily writing with his pencil.

"Fisher, German Bight, Humber," said the forecaster. "Winds southwest to south force three to five, some rain later, visibility moderate to good. Thames, Dover, Wight . . ."

Wilde switched off the set; Catherine was obviously not going to keep quiet long enough for him to get the station observations.

"What on earth was he talking about?" she asked.

"Those were sea areas," Wilde explained. "We are now moving into the area called the German Bight. So he gave us the direction of the wind, and the force, three to five on the Beaufort Scale, which means somewhere between ten and twenty miles an hour, and the visibility; moderate is from two to five miles, good is anything over five."

"And has what he said sounded all right to you?"

"For the moment. He hinted there'd be a change later on, but we'll make Borkum without trouble. I'll put you ashore there. You can catch the ferry into Emden and take a plane from there."

She was leaning over the back of the saloon seat, her hair hanging down on either side of her face as she brushed. She was only a few inches away. "Do you know," she said, "I once, I really can't remember how, got the impression that you were in love with me."

"Believe it or not, I am still in love with you, Cathy. It is my dream to keep it that way."

"By not upsetting the applecart."

"If you'd care to put it that way." He stood up; their faces almost touched. "Darling, I don't know what brought this on. I'm hoping you'll find an opportunity to tell me some time soon. But under no circumstances must Fine suspect that you are anything else than Catherine Light."

She opened her mouth, and he laid his finger across it.

"Darling, I'm serious. You have my file, right next to your bed. Remember? So I turn you on, and you turn me on. I am also a professional murderer. You take whatever you like from me, whenever you can with safety, and in between times you forget that I exist. Or life is going to become very, very complicated, and it's all going to be sloping down."

She gazed at him for several moments, her face expressionless. Then she said, "Would you like me to prepare dinner?"

"Can you?"

"Of course I can."

"I was thinking of your rebellious tum."

"Oh, that's all right now. I really am disappointed that I was sick at all. Didn't I tell you I've been taking sailing lessons?"

"No," he said.

"Well, I have. And as you're down here, why don't you turn in for a while." She dropped her voice. "You're entitled to, Jonas. You've been on the helm for several hours, and you want to keep fresh. I'm sure Paul can manage for a while."

"And you?"

"While you're eating, I'll tell you why I'm here. There's a promise."

Wilde hesitated. But there was nothing unusual in her at this moment. This was Catherine. So the grimness remained beneath the cocktail party veneer she wore at all times.

He climbed the steps, thrust his head into the wheelhouse. "What do you know. I've a volunteer for the galley. I say, old man, think you could hold her for a couple of hours while I have a nap?"

"Will do," Fine said. "This is rather fun."

"Oh, jolly good." Wilde went forward, took off his sweater, shoes and pants, climbed into the double bunk, and inserted himself into his sleeping bag. He closed his eyes, listened to the slaps of the waves against the hulls. Fine had the makings of a good helmsman. He could sleep easy. But for Catherine. But Catherine . . . he opened his eyes, and there she was, carrying a tray on which was a bowl, a spoon, and two full glasses.

"Upsa daisy," she said. "I've brought you the second leg, as well."

"Fine?"

"Is eating with one hand on the wheel. Is that all right?"

"If he can manage it. Now make it short and sweet, darling, and then off you go to bed."

Catherine closed the cabin door.

"Now just wait a minute . . ."

"It was banging," she explained. "Jonas, you may not approve of my being here. But I am. And I haven't been alone with you for six months. If you don't kiss me I am going to start screaming."

He leaned forward, took her into his arms. "I suppose you think I've had a woman every night, all of that time."

"Yes," she said, and kissed him. He remembered that perhaps the most amazing thing about her to someone like him, at any rate, from a strictly inferior social bracket, was the passion she put into her lovemaking, so apparently at contrast with the cool contempt with which she seemed to regard the world. Their tongues touched, and flicked, and withdrew, and touched again. His hands moved for her shoulders, and found slightly chilled flesh. She had unzipped her track suit, and wore nothing underneath.

"Oh, Christ," he said. "Cathy . . ."

Her mouth sought his again, and she pushed him back on the bunk to make room for herself.

Her hair moved on his shoulder, and she raised her head. "There's not much room for manoeuver inside a sleeping bag, is there?" she asked. "But it certainly warms the old cockles. And everything else."

"Well, you've one of your own, aft," he reminded her. "And my dinner is getting cold."

"Jonas Wilde, you are a cad," she said. "Oh, I know you're trying to be a gentleman. But it doesn't matter. It doesn't matter if Paul Fine were to open that door right this minute. He's just a little problem. Believe me, Jonas." She kissed him. Clearly his dinner was going to get colder yet. "Jonas. I've left Gerald."

CHAPTER 4

"Darling," Wilde said. "Even after an utterly delightful ten minutes, my sense of humour isn't up to yours."

Catherine sat up, handed him his glass, and held her own between both her hands. In the gloom of the cabin she was hardly more than a long-haired shadow, swaying with the ship. "The party broke up about ten," she said, speaking very slowly and distinctly. "Gerald and I went to bed, in every sense, and then he left me for his own bed. In case you didn't know, he likes to talk during the action. So, an hour later, when I was quite sure he would be asleep, I got up, dressed, threw some things into that bag, and left. I drove down to Gatwick and chartered a light aircraft to bring me across here this morning."

Wilde finished his drink and felt slightly better. "You have always suffered from having too much money. The situation isn't irretrievable."

"Before leaving the house," she said, "I wrote a note and left it on his desk. He must have read it several hours ago. And now, I think, you are about ready for another drink."

She took the glass from his nerveless fingers, slowly extricated her legs from the sleeping bag, and leaned across him.

Wilde waited, more or less patiently, for her to come back, listened to the swish of the waves between the hulls, watched the telltale compass mounted in the deck above his head. Suddenly it veered far beyond its normal ten degrees, as *Regina B* went off course for a moment, and he realised that Catherine had not bothered to put on her track suit to walk in front of the wheelhouse. When she burned her boats, she believed in total destruction.

She handed him a full glass, sat on the bunk, facing him,

just beyond the reach of his fingers. "Now. Aren't you going to eat? It really isn't bad." Incredibly, she was enjoying herself.

"I don't think I could keep it down." He sipped. "You promised to tell me why."

"Do you know, apart from being in love with you, Jonas, I almost even admire you? I'd expected the screaming heeby-jeebies by now."

"They're there," Wilde promised her. "I really am rather unhappy."

"Which is no tribute to my feminine charm. I could say that I got tired of living a lie. I read that somewhere, in a magazine."

"Leaving the note was also something of a cliché," he pointed out.

"Clichés always come in threes," she said. "So let's say I wanted to do the right thing by the dear old duck. He has been my lord and master for an interesting ten years, and my husband for the last seven. Things like that make a bond."

"Cathy . . ."

"I am getting to it, in my own way. Please don't interrupt. What do you think he is doing now? About the question in hand, I mean."

"Nothing," Wilde said. "Why should he? And I'm on a job for him, remember. He knows I must come back. And he knows he can do me any time he chooses. I wouldn't have supposed that I would ever have to explain this to you, darling, but I exist suspended at the end of a very long string, and the other end of the string is held by your husband. I am wanted for murder in almost every country in the world, England included. At least, someone is wanted for various unsolved murders. I am reasonably proud of the fact that as I am rather good at my job, no one, with the exception of one or two very senior officials at Scotland Yard, has any proof that I have ever committed a crime in my life, and those one or two officers don't do anything about me, because Gerald Light says they can't. But . . ."

"If Gerald lifts the blanket, it could mean twenty years in gaol." She nodded. "Does that thought frighten you?"

"I really can't say it attracts me."

"Well, if I were you, I'd relax, because it will never happen. It can never happen. I never thought I'd be telling you *this*, Jonas, but in England these frightful events usually take place by due process of law. How on earth could any self-respecting government put the Eliminator on trial, for anything?"

Wilde finished his drink.

"On the other hand, whether I am involved or not," Catherine went on, "the day must come when you have got to go."

"Without your help, I was hoping to make suitable preparations for that day, whenever it looms on the horizon."

Catherine shook her head slowly. "It arrived some time ago."

Wilde remained still, watching her. It occurred to him that in the ten years she had been with Sir Gerald, as right-hand woman and later as wife, she had, naturally enough, picked up some of his characteristics. Attempting to think while listening to her, especially when she was in the nude, was a complete waste of time.

"Hence Fine," she said.

"I had worked that one out for myself," he said. "But it will be a while yet before our boy is quite ready to fly solo."

"If you believe that, Jonas, you'll believe anything. He is as highly trained, and believe me, as competent, as you were when you began. Gerald is a great one for saving money, you know. So he wants the ransom money delivered. After that I don't really thinks he expects to hear from you again. Ever."

Wilde gazed at her.

"He told me so, last night," she said. "Well, just about."

"And you figured to change his mind by pulling this stunt."

"I came to warn you, you great idiot. I really wonder why I bothered."

"Oh, Cathy, I know I'm being woolly. It's all a little much, at the moment. Believe me, I'm grateful. And believe me, to hold you in my arms, just one last time, would even let me die happy. But you could have sent me a telegram. Or something.

I'm a lone wolf. On my own, I can probably cope. But having to look out for you . . ."

"I," she said, "have come here to look out for *you*. You seem to forget that I also received a very thorough training in this business, and seven years of being nothing more than a hostess hasn't encouraged *me* to forget. So you're a lone wolf. You still have a large area of back. Oh, there are other reasons. I love you, Jonas. I really do. Maybe I've been brooding on this for a year now. But if you and Gerald are going to fly into different orbits, I have to make a choice. Now, if by any chance you've been having me on these last few months, and I'm just a good lay, say so, and I'll clear off. He'll take me back. He honestly is fond of me, and he does need a wife, and where can he get one, except out of his own people?"

He leaned forward, kissed her on the nose. "Now you can try believing me. I suspect *I've* always secretly dreamed of a situation like this arising, forcing our hand. And I don't happen to agree with your theories. I think you had yet a third reason for coming, based on your supposition that Gerald is really fond of you: you figure that with you standing beside me he won't do anything about me, just in case you get into the line of fire."

"Oh really, Jonas." She drank.

"That is just the sort of girl-guidish idea you would come up with. And it will probably get you shot. Gerald Light doesn't even love Gerald Light. He's a walking computer, and if he has decided that I am too dangerous to live, he will very rapidly extend that idea over anyone who is too close to me."

"Well, then," she said. "We stand or fall together. I like the idea of that."

"Um. Supposing I decided to do something about my situation right now, what would you suggest?"

"I'd suggest we put in somewhere. After all, it is a pretty dirty night. What about Ijmuiden tomorrow morning? We could take the canal down to Amsterdam, tell friend Paul it's just as quick to get up to Borkum via the Isjelmeer and the

Waddensee, especially in bad weather. After all, you're the navigational expert. He won't argue."

"And in Amsterdam?"

"We just slip off the ship and take a taxi put to Schiphol. There are direct flights to Geneva."

"Why Geneva?"

"Because that is where most of my money is. Daddy put it all there when I was sixteen. We can collect that, and go anywhere in the world."

"While Paul?"

She shrugged, an entrancing sight. "It may be necessary to bop him one."

"And Miss Michelle Smith?"

"Oh, they'll get her back in due course. I caught that tone. You really are like all the rest, Jonas. She is just a very ordinary human being. And she really isn't the one you're thinking about."

"Um. Do you mind if I think about all this for a while? As you have pointed out, we can't be off Ijmuiden before tomorrow morning, and you agree that Fine won't have been instructed to do anything until after the ransom money has been delivered."

"That makes sense. Do you mind if I get back into your bag? I didn't sleep a wink last night."

"Be my guest." He opened the neck for her, and the hatch slammed back in the saloon. "Ahoy, down there," Paul Fine shouted. "Jonas? I see a flashing light dead ahead. Do you think it could be the lighthouse we're looking for?"

Wilde sighed, reached for his pants. "You'd never believe this, but I had also hoped to do some sleeping."

(ii)

It was indeed the Westkapelle light. They were making splendid time, driven north by the fresh southwesterly. "Nice helming," Wilde said.

"I say, that's awfully good of you to say so," Fine said.

"Now you go below and turn in for a while. Relieve me at midnight."

"Ah, yes." Fine hesitated in the hatch. "I say, old man . . ."

"Quite," Wilde said. "The fact is, Lady Light is a raving nymphomaniac. It's one of the things you will just have to get used to, if you intend to work for Sir Gerald."

"You mean this sort of thing has happened before?"

"Several times," Wilde said. "And as she is the boss's wife all we can do is humour her. I have succeeded in doing that, and as she appears to be exhausted, I don't think you will be bothered for a while. I'd really try to get some sleep while you can."

"Oh. Oh yes." He seemed uncertain whether to be pleased or disappointed. But he went below and into his own cabin. Wilde altered course to northwest to avoid the massive shoals of Schouwen, and settled himself down for some hard work; the wind was now on the quarter which made the cat inclined to yaw about, and although the seas were never big enough to be worrying, there was a lot of spray to interfere with visibility.

Navigation was no problem; the row of light vessels that line the Dutch coastal waters, some half-dozen miles from the shore itself, all have radio beacons, which made it a simple matter for him to keep an accurate track of his position. But helming in the choppy seas was a tiring business which required all his concentration; there was no time to do the thinking he felt was necessary.

At midnight he and Fine decided to take two-hour watches. Catherine was fast asleep, and Wilde wrapped himself in a blanket on the berth in the chartroom before also losing consciousness.

Dawn found them in a sea of whitecaps; Wilde had changed his working jib for a number two and taken a reef in the mainsail, half an hour earlier, and *Regina B* was riding the waves quite easily, still maintaining seven knots, although everything on deck was very wet.

The hatch slammed back, and Fine appeared, muffled under his oilskins, stamping his sea boots. "I must say, I'm glad to see the light," he said. "Or am I? Were the seas that big all night?"

"No bigger, anyway," Wilde said. "I've altered course, zero one five. I think we can start closing the coast again."

"Aye, aye, Skipper." Fine took the helm. "About last night. What exactly do we do now?"

"It's quite a problem, isn't it? I think it's about time we had a chat, as I think her ladyship is up." He had come to a decision; it was the only decision he could take in the circumstances. He leaned into the hatch. "Ahoy, below. Would you care to come into the wheelhouse, Cathy?"

"One second," came the reply from the heads. And she was as good as her word. She arrived in her blue track suit, looking like something out of *Vogue*. The night's rest had done her good. "What a frightful morning. Where's Ijmuiden?"

"Roughly south of east," Wilde said. "If you use the binoculars you might just see a chimney or two."

"But . . . isn't that behind us, on this course?"

"I'm afraid so."

"But you said . . ."

"*You* said, darling," Wilde reminded her. "Cathy's idea was that we should nip into the Dutch canal system," he explained to Fine.

"Can't be all bad. Would we still reach Borkum by this time tomorrow?"

"I doubt it. But in any event, she meant to say good-bye to you in Amsterdam, and take me with her."

"Jonas," Catherine said.

"But . . ." Fine said.

"Oh, quite, old man. Mind you, I am strictly on her side. I'm afraid I slandered her last night. She isn't really a nympho. She happens to be my mistress. What has brought our situation into the open is Cathy's theory that this is Wilde's last case. That you are not destined to be my new comrade in arms, but rather my replacement."

"Jonas," Cathy said.

"What utter balderdash," Fine said. "But . . ."

"Oh, quite, old man. But she also suggests that your first brief may be me. After all, you wouldn't want me knocking around, cluttering up your pitch, would you? There's the old historical precedent of there being only one king at a time, and all that jazz. And Sir Gerald did make a rather pointed remark on Friday night, that perhaps you were not actually trying to kill me, at that moment."

"Jonas," Catherine said, "I really do not understand what you are trying to accomplish."

"In any event," Fine said, "it's all a load of invention. I just cannot think what *you* are hoping for, Lady Light."

"She may well be right about you, Paul, old man," Wilde said, "in which case I want you to remember that she is *my* mistress, and that she used to be one of the Section, with all that that implies when it comes to being lethal. I take it you *are* still going for me, Cathy?"

"Oh, Jonas, I wish I could understand your sense of humour. Of course I'm going to back you up. But . . ."

"Whether or not this is the end of the line for Sir Gerald and me, darling, the fact is that he gave me a job of work to do, and I have never failed to complete a mission in my life."

"That's being childish," she objected.

"It's a recognition of the fact that I have to live with myself for a few years yet. And if I can't do that, there won't be much point in your trying to do it, now will there? So, now, we all know just where we stand, and Paul knows that one of us will be watching him at all times. You never know, this way I may even be able to get some sleep from time to time."

(iii)

The wind stayed fresh all Sunday, and *Regina B* made excellent time. By midnight they were off Terschelling, with the swept channel through the minefields immediately in front of them. Wilde handed over to Fine. "There are light buoys every five miles from here on," he said. "With the Terschelling Light Vessel bang in the middle. You couldn't miss this channel if you tried. All you have to remember is that just about every other ship in the North Sea also uses it, and it is just three miles wide.

Now, they *have* to stay inside those limits, because if they strayed they might just suck up the odd mine. Fibreglass doesn't have the magnetic quality of steel, so we're all right, apart from the fact that we only draw two feet. So we'll stay on the seaward side of the channel, three miles out. That way we'll just keep the light buoys in sight to starboard."

"Sounds okay to me," Fine said. "Do you know, this sailing lark could just turn out to be fun?"

"Save your decision until the end of the trip."

Fine watched him go through the hatch. "Right this moment, I envy you. You're sure you can trust me up here, all by myself?"

"You've a date with Miss Michelle Smith, remember? I figure you have no intention of letting *her* down. See you in a couple of hours."

He made his way forward, took off oilskins and sea boots, and heavy sweater, and then the rest of his clothes. Catherine was already inside the sleeping bag, watching him. She did not appear the least sated, but then, neither was he. To have her here, his whenever he could spare the time to take her, to know that she had chucked everything away to *be* here, gave him a feeling of incredible pleasure. And incredible guilt that he should be exposing her to so much more.

"I still think you're a complete fool," she said when he raised his head. "But I'm glad you're going through with it. God, Jonas, I *love* you." She fell asleep.

Wilde lay on his back, her head pillowed on his shoulder, her hair occasionally tickling his nose, her left leg thrown forward across his thighs. She was as warm as toast. But then, it was delightfully warm below deck; only the whine of the wind in the rigging made it seem cold. But the wind and the sounds of the waves against and between the hulls were sounds he welcomed. Familiar sounds, suggesting familiar surroundings. The sea was his real home now. Only at sea could he relax. There was no treachery in the sea. It spoke its mind, declared its intentions openly and without particular emphasis. So, were it deciding to roughen up, first of all the wind clouds would appear, high in the sky, little streaks of white, then the barometer would plunge, and then the wind would come to pile up the seas. But this change would take several hours, and if he chose, or was forced, to remain out in it, that was his problem. The sea, having given him fair warning, would then batter away at *Regina B* with all its might.

But even at sea now the treachery, the uncertainty, with which he existed, hung close about him. Because in this context, Catherine's presence, Catherine's very existence, was irrelevant. It had taken a team of experts six years to make him what he was; he could not believe that it had taken another team of experts less than that time to make Fine whatever *he* now was. Six years. Which meant that the decision to replace Wilde had been taken immediately after the destruction of the old Section. He had been so proud to have been the only survivor of that holocaust, so contemptuous of the new boys, of Mocka in particular. At that time he had not yet met Sir Gerald, although he knew of his existence as the intelligent fly knows that somewhere in the vast web in which he has become enmeshed there must be waiting a monstrous spider.

But if Wilde had not known Sir Gerald, Sir Gerald had known Wilde, and had taken the decision then, that in due course he must be destroyed because his usefulness was coming to an end. And *then* Catherine had been nothing more than a voice on a telephone, receiving his reports, issuing his instructions. The remarkable thing was that she had also known all about him, then, had perhaps even been on the way to falling in love with a voice, and a photograph, and a reputation. Only Wilde had been innocent.

So where did that leave him? It was a very simple matter for Catherine to say, I am virtually a millionairess; with my money and a head start, we can disappear. We can travel the globe, hire guards to protect us, buy an oceangoing yacht and never come near land again. Catherine thought of him as a demigod, a man who killed relentlessly and ruthlessly, who overcame obstacles as a car overcomes a pebble. She had never understood, perhaps, that Wilde drove forward with such momentum only because of his absolute trust in the man behind him. For fifteen years he had trusted that nameless figure; since meeting him he had trusted him even more. The affair with Catherine, a sudden combustion sparked by a unique event, had left him feeling bewildered and guilty, and childishly happy, the woman apart, for having at last done something entirely on his own. Successfully.

Only it hadn't been very successful, had it?

He slept uneasily and dreamed, which was itself unusual for him. Of the girl Michelle Smith, of the face he gave her, which he had seen so often in the newspapers. But whenever he reached for her, the face had disappeared.

He awakened, to hands moving over his body. He reacted instinctively, closed his fingers on Catherine's arms.

"Good morning," she said. "You were muttering."

"I'm not surprised." He rubbed the back of his head, got his brain working.

"Do you realise," she said, "that this is the first time I have *ever* woken up beside a man? Gerald has also insisted we have separate bedrooms."

He swung his legs out of the bunk and reached for his sea boots. He peered through the port. It was well past dawn, but there was fog, and the wind had dropped. "I wish you'd woken me a little earlier."

"There didn't seem any point. It's very misty."

"That is the point, darling. Now, I would like you to get dressed and come on deck. On your way, collect the compressed-air foghorn you will find by the radio, and when you get on deck, start squeezing it. One blast every sixty seconds. It's all we've time for this morning." He visited the heads, pulled on his heavy sweater and an oilskin jacket, and went up to the wheelhouse. "Why in the name of God didn't you call me sooner."

"And interrupt your honeymoon?" But Fine's face was lined with anxiety and fatigue. "I figure we're just about at the entrance to the Hubertgat," he said, "judging by the chart. We just passed a buoy marked E 17."

"That sounds right." Wilde stared astern. The grey mist wall lay on the surface of the sea not a hundred yards away, and they might have been the only people in the world. Visually. All around them there was sound, horns blaring, whistles sounding, competing with Catherine's relentless "Blaaagh" as she settled herself in the cockpit and started pressing the button on the compressed-air foghorn. *Regina B*'s speed had dwindled to a bare three knots as she ghosted along, and he watched a rippling wave, some four feet high, coming towards them out of the mist to port.

"It's these beastly wakes which worry me," Fine grumbled.

"That chap's a good quarter of a mile off. I wish you'd called me while we could still see the buoy, though."

"I recorded the log reading."

"Did you now? We'll make a seaman of you yet, Paul. And maintained the same course since? Oh, well done." He sat at the chart table with a set of tide tables, divider, and parallel rules. "Then we want to steer zero five zero," he decided. "And look out for a red and white middle-ground buoy with HG on it. For Hubertgat."

"That'll mean crossing this traffic," Fine said.

"I'll take her," Wilde said. "You'd better turn in for a while."

"I won't say no to that," Fine agreed. "Have you any idea how our friends are going to find us in this visibility? Even supposing they're waiting off Borkum Harbour."

"I'd say that's their problem. In any event, there is no longer any necessity for us to make Borkum Harbour."

"Of course. I'd forgotten. I say, old man, I've been doing a bit of thinking about this whole setup."

"You do surprise me."

"I don't mean about Lady Light. I mean the real thing. Sir Gerald blithely remarked that he was working on the leak, but I mean to say, even if they had somehow got hold of Michelle Smith's itinerary, these people couldn't have been sure she'd be in such and such a place on such and such a day. It's very easy to slip a day or two behind, in a yacht."

"Very."

"So they must have been tipped off by someone on the spot. Or more correctly, on board. Agree?"

"Oh, certainly. But I still regard that as Sir Gerald's baby."

"Do you really think so? I mean, we have to do *something*, haven't we?"

"We're doing plenty," Wilde reminded him. "Hurrying about the North Sea on a miserable morning when you could be drinking good Dutch beer and Catherine and I could be travelling as fast as possible in the opposite direction."

"Yes, but I have an idea that he really meant us to do more than just deliver the money. I mean, why choose you and me for such a job? Any couple of clerks from his office could have done it. I don't believe a word of all that nonsense about you being conveniently on hand with your boat. You could have had her down in the south of France or somewhere."

"Quite," Wilde said. "But my advice would still be, don't look a gift horse in the mouth. You seem to forget that we're on half pay for this one. Less than half pay, come to think of it."

"That's a bloody mercenary attitude," Fine remarked. "I really must say, old man, think of that poor girl . . ."

"She's probably having the time of her life. And I hate to sound like a granddad, old son, but in our business there is absolutely no place for heroics or idealism. Do what you're paid to do, and count yourself damned lucky you're breathing at the end of each day. Now turn in. We'll negotiate the channel." Wilde put the helm to starboard and hardened the sheets. Coming more on to the wind, *Regina B* increased speed. "Keep your eyes open," he told Catherine.

"Then you want to avoid that chap," she suggested, pointing at a huge, rust-streaked black bow looming out of the mist perhaps fifty yards to starboard, and at the same time giving her foghorn another long squeeze.

Wilde hastily put the helm back to port, and *Regina B*'s boom swung across in a gentle gybe as the stern passed through the eye of the wind. "Gybe-ho," Wilde muttered.

"Thanks for nothing," Catherine said. "That thing nearly removed my head. What's he saying?"

The freighter surged by, her horn blaring. Now she stopped
that noise, and instead an officer appeared on the edge of the
flying bridge, shouting through a megaphone.

"Do you speak Greek?" Wilde asked.

"I'm afraid I don't."

"Just as well. Most of that lot began with b's and s's, except
for the odd f. In English, I mean."

He thrust two fingers into the air, the back of his hand towards the big ship. The officer put away his megaphone and
shook his fist instead. The huge vessel was past now, and the
little catamaran bobbed in her wake like a toy.

"Mind you," Wilde said, as he altered course again, "that
chap was absolutely right. In weather like this, and in a channel
this narrow, yachts are just bloody nuisances. We should be in
port."

"Isn't that what I've been telling you, all along?" she asked.

"Oh, go and cook breakfast," he suggested. "Give me the
horn."

Half an hour later he picked up the Hubertgat buoy dead
ahead. At least his navigation was still as accurate as ever. And
now the traffic had thinned, was merely a hoot in the mist. He
even thought he could hear the groan of the Borkum lighthouse, just where it ought to be, on the port bow, and there
was a yellowness about the mist which suggested there was sunshine around, somewhere.

So the seagoing crisis was finished for the time being; the
real crisis was about to begin. Time to forget about Catherine
and Paul Fine, except as members of a team of which he was
the head. Time to think about what came next, however much
he had talked down at Fine. How would they make the collection? Obviously by boat. But what sort of boat? Because afterwards, what? A yacht would not be difficult to trace. And
whatever precautions they took, they must anticipate that the
people who delivered the ransom would be in touch with the
police almost immediately. Presumably they would wreck his
radio telephone, but even if they also wrecked his engines and
made off with his sails, inside the islands the odds must be all in

favour of their being picked up within an hour or two. So they would have something else up their sleeves. What, for instance, would happen in a normal kidnapping? He frowned, and leaned on the wheel to peer into the mist. Had Sir Gerald thought of that? Oh, you could bet your last penny that Sir Gerald had thought of that. Thus Wilde. Sir Gerald wanted as speedy a solution as possible to this business. But he also wanted Michelle Smith alive and unharmed.

Or did he? Did Sir Gerald Light really give a damn about royalty? Any royalty? He doubted it. Sir Gerald was far more concerned with the threat to the orderly world he controlled. This could not rank as espionage or counterespionage. But it had been dumped in Sir Gerald's lap, so he would handle it in his own way, even if, as a sop to governmental and perhaps, eventually, public opinion, he could not issue the orders in so many words.

And if Wilde acted overzealously, and had to be sacrificed as a result, what difference did it make? Wilde's head was on the chopping block, anyway.

"Don't tell me that's bacon frying," Paul Fine remarked, emerging on deck. "This sea air gives you an appetite, eh?"

(iv)

By mid-morning the mist had thinned. *Regina B* moved up the Ems on the tide, pushed by the ever lightening southwesterly wind, while the dark shape of Borkum loomed on the port bow. "I've always wanted to visit the German Frisians," Catherine said wistfully. She had changed her track suit for a bikini, sat on the coach roof smoking a cigarette and drinking coffee from a pint mug; it occurred to Wilde that no one was likely to notice the brilliantly red life raft on the foredeck in these circumstances. "Why don't we stop and have a civilised lunch?"

"Maybe tomorrow," Wilde said. "You take her, Paul." He unhooked his binoculars, focussed on an approaching motorboat, coming downriver from Emden.

"Is it true that one of them is a nudist camp?" Catherine asked.

"There is a nudist colony on Spiekeroog," Wilde said. "Or so I believe."

"I read somewhere that the most beautiful girls in the world come from Juist," Fine said dreamily. "Isn't that the island just beyond Borkum?"

"Your geography is spot on. As a matter of fact, the two used to be one island, way back when. But the sea is always nibbling away at them. But you're wrong about the girls. The most beautiful girls in the world come from Samsoe."

"Where's that?" Catherine wanted to know.

"One of the Danish islands in the Kattegat. Just luff up a point, Paul."

"Aye, aye, Skipper. Think this could be our friends?"

"Maybe," Wilde said. But this was far too conspicuous a yacht, in too popular a stretch of water. Now the mist had definitely lifted, there were two patrol boats coming out of Borkum Harbour just astern of them, a sailing yacht on the far side of the channel and two freighters surging upriver on the tide; the far side of the huge estuary was out of sight.

"Ah," Catherine leaned through the doghouse window to set her empty mug on the steering console. "I wondered what we were doing. You mean we're rendezvousing with somebody."

"I never knew there was such a word," Wilde said. "And somebody is rendezvousing with us. But not this bloke." The motor yacht, a forty-footer, he estimated, and newly built, flew the Dutch flag; she zoomed past, making a steady fifteen knots. Her name was *Carissima*. The man in the wheelhouse waved, and Catherine waved back.

"Now that's a shame," she said. "I would call that a yacht and not an ingenious exercise machine."

"What do you figure now?" Fine asked. "Do we keep on up-river for Emden?"

"The orders were, Wangerooge and back. We turn off for the watts. If they don't contact us today, we'll put into Langeoog for the night. We can wait for the tide at Nordeney."

"You mean we go through *that* lot?" Fine gazed to port.

Borkum had slipped astern into the mist, and the channel was now marked by a long brown line of sand, slowly covering as the tide rose.

"There's a main channel about five miles farther on. Just follow the buoys. The Germans are almost as buoy-conscious as the Dutch. Mind this fellow."

Close to the banks, a fishing boat moved slowly along, huge nets extended on either side by overhead arms, sweeping through the shallow water.

"Is that how they do it?" Catherine asked. "They look a little top-heavy to me. What happens if one of those nets collects something more solid than fish?"

"I believe they turn over." Wilde glanced astern. "Here's another prospect."

The motor cruiser was just inside the line of buoys instead of just outside them, moving at a good twenty knots, he figured. She was white, perhaps fifty feet long, and had a flying bridge. He also had the impression that twenty knots was nowhere near her maximum speed.

"He's watching us through glasses," Fine said. "And is that a dolly bird on the helm?"

"Long black hair and all. She's nearly as spectacular as ours." Wilde reached for the binoculars. "There's something . . ." but the woman with black hair had handed over the wheel and gone below. "Pity. Off they go." The cruiser gathered speed, and disappeared into the mist. "Still, I'd better add her to the list." He went into the cabin, wrote the name *Nemo* beneath *Carissima*.

"Where do you figure that one came from?" Fine asked. "Because here's another."

"Out of Borkum, now the mist is lifting." Wilde brought the binoculars on deck for another look. "There's our turnoff. Just beyond that next port hand buoy."

"I don't know if we'll make that," Fine said, as the mainsail gave a warning flap. "This sun isn't only burning off the mist; it's doing for the wind, as well."

"So we'll motor. Our instructions were to keep moving."

. "Can I help?" Catherine dropped into the cockpit with a bump which shook the entire boat.

"I thought you said you'd been taking lessons?" Wilde demanded. "You just have to tred lightly on these things. That cost us at least two knots." He lowered himself into the starboard engine compartment, switched on the petrol and the extractor fan. "Try that."

Fine turned the key in the ignition, and the engine hummed gently. "Pretty good."

"We'll have them both on," Wilde decided, climbing into the port hole in turn. "It makes steering easier."

"And what kind of speed would you like?" Fine asked.

"Quarter throttle will be ideal. They didn't say anything about hurrying, and it'll save petrol."

Catherine prepared a lunch of cold ham and Russian salad to go with beer, and Wilde smoked a cigar as he surveyed the placid brown waters about them. Now they had left the Ems proper and were in the first of the watts, and already the traffic was limited to a barge, coming upstream, and another motor cruiser. The names duly went into the log book.

"I must say, this is the life." Paul Fine sat in the steering chair and rested his feet on the wheel. "Incredible to think that only a few hours ago we were bouncing around the North Sea."

"It would be so much more fun if we were doing it for fun," Catherine pointed out, collecting the dishes. "Do you mean you really have no idea how these people mean to collect, Jonas?"

"I've one or two ideas," Wilde said. "But I should think they'll let us get a little warm under the collar first. And also to a less popular piece of the sea. Around here there's always liable to be a couple like those two."

"If you hadn't told me there was land all about, I'd say they were crazy," Fine remarked. The open boat was anchored on the edge of the sandbank to starboard, and the two men on board each had a line out. "Suppose a gale blew up?"

"It's not likely at the moment. The glass hadn't started to drop when last I checked." Wilde ducked his head to look at the barometer. "Hello, it's started now, by God. It's fallen a good five millibars. Still, they'll be home long before the wind arrives."

"They must have a barometer of their own," Fine suggested. "They're getting underway."

"Wise fellows," Wilde agreed. "Well, old son, I'm going to have a kip. All you have to do is follow the buoys, and when, as will happen soon enough, they stop being buoys and become branches stuck in the mud, leave them to port. Give me a shout if anything untoward, or even interesting, comes up."

"Must be a Borkum boat," Fine mused. "They're coming this way. Hey, Jonas, who gives way, seeing that we're both under power?"

"He's approaching us from our starboard side," Wilde said patiently, sitting down to pull off his sea boots. "So we keep out of his way."

"Oh, right ho. Then I'd better reduce speed. Hey, whatever is the matter with the fellow? He's altering course towards us."

"He is, you know," Catherine remarked, peering through the window as she washed the dishes.

Wilde sighed and went on deck. The fishing boat was now quite close, and the man in the bow was kneeling to face them.

"I'd say he wants to chat." Wilde climbed out of the cockpit, made his way forward. "Can we help you?" he asked in German.

The man in the bow smiled and waved. "We are admiring your ship, Captain," he said. "Would you mind if we came alongside?" He also spoke in German.

"Normally I'd say, help yourself," Wilde said. "But today we're in just a little bit of a hurry. So, if you'd like to take a rain check on that . . ."

"I'm sorry, Captain," said the man in the bow, suddenly speaking English with an American accent, "I must insist. Johann."

The man amidships sat up and presented a Thompson submachine gun at Wilde's stomach.

CHAPTER 5

Not for the first time in his life, Wilde wondered why it was that whenever a gun was pointed at him, his hackles rose. And on this occasion the whole thing was so unnecessary. Were they meaning to resist, a simple turn of the helm would run the little boat down, and the man would scarcely have the time to fire a shot. While if the kidnappers had correctly identified the red life raft, there was no need to show a weapon at all.

But they were both very young and dressed with quite ludicrous self-consciousness as yachtsmen, blue peaked caps, blue sweaters, and blue canvas trousers, while around each chest was strapped a bright orange life jacket.

"Come alongside," Wilde suggested. "We never argue with guns. Cut your engines, Paul." He crossed the foredeck and let go the anchor. *Regina B* snubbed her chain, and came to a halt, the tide flowing past her hulls with a gentle swish. The outboard had also ceased chattering as the fishermen came into the side of the cat, and Fine was there to take their painter. By now the young man with the tommy gun was looking somewhat embarrassed, and kept moving the barrel from Fine to Wilde and back again, with the occasional hesitation at Catherine's midriff.

"What strange friends you have, Jonas," she remarked.

"You," said the spokesman, "get down here."

"You're not serious," Catherine said. "I don't even like boats *this* size."

"Get down," the young man said again. "We are not playing games."

"I think you should do as the man says, darling," Wilde suggested. "Otherwise we'll be here all day."

"Oh, cheer me up," she grumbled, and carefully sat on the deck, extending two long, pale, exquisitely slender legs over the side.

"There," said the spokesman, the one called Johann, pointing to the bow of the dinghy. For that second, as Catherine lowered herself from the deck, neither man was looking at the catamaran. Paul Fine, standing on the cockpit seats, propelled himself into the air and landed on the gunwale of the dinghy, tilting it onto its beam ends. There was a single shot from the tommy gun, lost in the splash and the scream from Catherine as she dived into the water. Then the dinghy hit the surface again, upside down.

Wilde sighed and made his way aft. For the moment all four had disappeared beneath the sea, but now Johann's head reappeared. He still held his tommy gun, and was waving it around while he tried to clear water from his eyes. Wilde removed the boathook from its rack, gave it a slight twirl, and brought it down on the young man's head. Johann gave a gulp, and sagged in the water. Wilde turned the boathook, inserted the hook itself into the lifeless sweater, and brought him alongside. A heave, and Johann was tumbled into the cockpit, to lie unconscious on the deck.

"Help me," Catherine was screaming, splashing about not six feet away.

"In a moment," Wilde promised, and made sure that the dinghy remained tied to the yacht; it floated on the cushion of air it had trapped when capsizing; the outboard propeller shaft stuck straight in the air, and the red propeller still gently rotated. "Catch a hold of this."

She splashed violently; apparently she was not an expert swimmer. Farther aft, a good twenty feet behind the yacht, Paul Fine's head broke the surface. His arms struck the water, and then he went under again. Clearly he was engaged with the other young man.

"Jonas," Catherine shouted. "I need a life belt."

But now she had drifted within reach. He inserted the boathook into her bra and pulled; the bra promptly came away.

"For God's sake," he commented, but now she was into the side of the yacht, and he could lean over and give her his hand.

"Oh boy," she gasped. "Oh boy. Lift, Jonas. Lift."

Another heave, and she sat on the deck beside him, water draining from her hair and her bikini. "I am going to commit *murder,*" she promised.

"Help," Fine was shouting. He was now fifty feet astern. "Help."

Wilde sighed again, and pulled off his sweater as he kicked off his shoes. "If Johann opens his eyes, bop him one. But for God's sake don't murder him until I get back."

He dived in, reached Fine in a few strokes.

"He's a tough one," Fine gasped. "I've got my legs round his neck, but he's still fighting."

Wilde dived deep, almost to the bottom of the watt, his ears ballooning as his feet touched the sand. The young man stared at him, his hair rising above his head and his eyes wide. His neck was gripped in a scissors lock by Fine's thighs, and his hands clawed into Fine's waist. Wilde drew his seaman's knife, cut the cords securing the life jacket, and drew it clear. Then he kicked, and regained the surface. "I'd let him sink, if I were you," he said. "He's quite dead."

"Oh," Fine said. His whole body seemed to slump in the water. "Good Lord."

"Your first?" Wilde inquired, and gave him the life jacket. "I suggest you get back on board and pour yourself a stiff brandy while I see if I can get that tommy gun back. We might just need it, in view of everything."

He swam back to the yacht, kicked up his heels, and dived to the bottom once again. The current kept trying to sweep him backwards, which made searching the sand difficult, and the weed kept driving into his face. On the other hand, it was conveniently sweeping the dead body out to sea, he figured. He fumbled in the gloom, swept his hand to and fro, marking himself by the shadow of the cat above him, and found nothing. His head broke the surface, and he tossed hair from his eyes as he reached for breath. *Regina B* was again receding as the current pulled at him. He swam back; it seemed to take all after-noon, while Fine anxiously watched him from the cockpit.

"You all right?"

"I've lost the goddamned gun. And there'll be no getting it back now. Where's Cathy and the other bloke?"

"She's giving him the kiss of life," Fine explained. "Says she doesn't know any other method."

(ii)

Wilde righted the dinghy, and then scrambled on board. Cath-erine lent him her towel. She had dried her hair and was sitting on the other side of the cockpit breathing deeply; her bikini trunks seemed to have shrunk, but she had added a shirt in place of the lost bra—not that the damp nylon made a great deal of difference. The rescued man lay on the deck and gazed up at her with a petrified expression; he also was breathing deeply.

"I must say, I'm in a bit of a fog," Wilde confessed. "Our or-ders were, no violence."

"Our brief is to bring Michelle Smith home," Fine pointed out. "And it strikes me it's now or never."

"I'm glad you think so. And as I'm rather dense, you'll have to explain it all to me. Beginning with the idea behind nobbling this pair."

"Well," Fine said, a little less certainly, "it occurred to me that these blokes wouldn't be all on their lonesome. There has to be a mother ship around somewhere pretty close."

"Good thinking," Wilde agreed, and gazed at the mist. Al-though much better than at dawn, and quite clear overhead, visibility was not much more than a mile on the water. "Where, do you suppose?"

"That's the idea," Fine explained. "I thought one of these fellows might like to tell us."

"One of these fellows has just *got* to tell us, now," Wilde pointed out. He put down the towel, leaned forward. "Good afternoon."

The young man stared at him. He was a solidly built fellow, not bad-looking, Wilde supposed. And distinctly frightened.

"Maybe he doesn't understand English," Fine suggested.

"He spoke English, didn't he?" Catherine demanded. *"And* got fresh." She still seemed annoyed over her unintended swim.

"Maybe he's suffering from shock," Wilde said. "After all, things have suddenly got very out of control. There's another bottle of brandy in the galley, Paul. Try him with that."

"Me too," Catherine said. "That water was cold."

Fine went below, and Wilde addressed the young man again. "I think you should know that your friend is still at the bottom of the watt," he said. "And we have a saying in England, in for a penny in for a pound."

Fine returned on deck, with a tray on which were the brandy bottle and four glasses.

"I think this is very civilised," Catherine remarked, as she emptied a glass.

The young man on the floor also drank deeply; then he sat up and looked around him.

"So why don't you try to be friendly," Wilde suggested. "Like telling us your name."

"We'll have to get a move on," Fine said. "Wherever they came from, they'll be expected back soon."

"Quite," Wilde agreed. "Skip your name, if you wish. I want to know where your ship is exactly, and how many people are on board, and who the principals are, and where Miss Smith is now. And I would like the answers now."

The young man gazed at him.

"We are going to have to persuade him," Fine said.

"Yes," Wilde said doubtfully. "He looks a somewhat tough young fellow. Or have you been learning new techniques?"

"They told me you usually got the answers."

"Hm. Well, I tell you what we are going to do, my lad. If you don't tell us what we want to know, we are going to tie you up and then push off and leave you alone on this boat with this young lady here. She is *very* angry at having been dumped into

the water just now, and what she is likely to do to you doesn't
bear consideration."

"What are you talking about?" Catherine had been pouring
her second brandy.

"I know we don't have your usual equipment on board, darling," Wilde said. "But I'm sure you'll find something you can
use. I mean, it's not as if the marks mustn't show, is it? I say,
old chap, I suppose you've read about Arab women? They
taught Cathy all she knows."

Catherine gazed at the young man, and the young man gazed
at Catherine.

"Okay," Wilde said, and shrugged. "We'll go for a ride in the
dinghy. Bring the bottle, will you, Paul. Cathy, you'll find everything you need in that locker. Knives, pliers, screwdrivers, a fret-
saw. Oh, and an axe."

"I say," Catherine said, but she was interrupted by the young
man.

"Johann," he said urgently. "Johann."

"That figures," Fine said. "That's what his friend called him."

"And then," Wilde said helpfully. "If you want electrics, there
are four batteries in that locker over there. You'll need tape, of
course; you'll find it in the drawer. Tell me what I've forgotten."

"The ship is over there," Johann gabbled. "It is called the
Nemo. A big white motor yacht. It is a mile and a half east of
here, in the mist. On the other side of the sandbank where we
were fishing. Please, that is the truth."

"I think you should check it out, Paul," Wilde said. "Take a
look in the radar."

Catherine finished her second brandy. "I think you made a
very sensible decision," she told Johann. "From all our points
of view."

Fine went below and switched on the radar, cut the range to
two miles. "There's a blip over there, all right. I say, this does
make life very easy, doesn't it? All we have to do is follow
them."

"Oh, for God's sake," Wilde said, "don't you think they're
going to get upset when their boys don't come home? Didn't

you think of that before you went into action? We're committed to paying them a return visit."

"How?" Fine asked. "They'll see the cat coming while she's still a mile away, even in this fog."

"So we won't use the cat. You never told us how many people are on board, Johann."

Johann continued to stare at Catherine, like a rabbit confronting an outsize snake. "Three," he said. "The captain, Zita, and Yves."

"Did you say Zita?" Catherine asked.

"A plague of Zitas," Wilde said thoughtfully, and frowned as he remembered the long-haired woman on *Nemo*'s bridge.

"That idea just has to be absurd," Catherine said. "After all, she's . . ."

"Your oldest friend," Wilde agreed. "What's the captain called, Johann?"

"Dave."

"He hasn't told us if Miss Smith is on board," Fine said.

"No," Johann said.

"And what about Mr. Weber and Inspector Parks?"

"And Miss Weenink?"

"No," Johann said. "No. They are on the other boat."

"Another one? You are just going to have to tell us all about it," Wilde said. "Give the boy a drink, Catherine."

She obeyed. Johann stared at her. Catherine climbed on to the coach roof and lit a cigarette.

"There is another boat," Johann explained. "For the getaway. The idea is to pick up the money and then go to sea, at speed. Out there we will rendezvous with the other ship—it is a small trawler—scuttle the *Nemo,* and just disappear. The North Sea is full of trawlers."

"So simple it's almost ridiculous," Wilde agreed. "So what about Miss Smith and Miss Weenink and the men? Are they to be scuttled too?"

"Oh yes." Johann's tongue circled his lips. "Dave said so."

Wilde smiled at him. "You know, Cathy, I'm almost inclined to give you carte blanche with this character. But you'll have time. Now, let's see, we'll take their own dinghy. We're wearing roughly the same garb as these two. Blue canvas trousers, Paul. You'll have to borrow a pair of mine. You can roll up the legs to fit. Then the life jackets, of course. Mine are the same pattern, and they're as good as bulletproof vests. And peaked caps, pulled well down, and bobs your uncle."

"Yes, but . . ."

"So when we get within a hundred yards of them we'll start working on the outboard. Everyone looks alike when crouching over an outboard. And we'll have the suitcases. That'll fill their eyes. I wish to God we also had that tommy gun, though."

"Try this." Catherine uncoiled her legs, went below, and produced a Browning Automatic pistol from her overnight bag.

"Well for crying out loud," Wilde said. "You know I don't allow firearms on board my ship. Why on earth do you have that along?"

She shrugged. "Habit, I suppose. I just never travel without it. I mean, you never can tell when someone may make an attempt on Gerald's life."

"I never thought of that. Do you mean that in addition to being his secretary and his wife you are also his bodyguard? I have a feeling that despite everything, I really don't know you well enough. The gun's all yours, Paul. I'm going to see if that outboard will still work."

He got into the dinghy, took the cowl off the engine. "You can bail this thing for me," he told Catherine.

She squatted beside him, started mopping up the water with a sponge. "What do I do in this assault? Won't they think it odd, having a woman along?"

"I imagine they will. So we won't have one."

"Oh no," she said. "Oh no, no, no. I'm not staying here all by myself."

"You won't be by yourself, darling; you'll have Johann."

"That's what's worrying me."

"Oh, I'm sure you can take care of him. I imagine you could have a very jolly afternoon. He's obviously fallen madly in love with you."

"And suppose something goes wrong and you don't come back?"

"You've been taking lessons, you say. Start the engines, raise the anchor, and motor to the nearest harbour. Or use the radio telephone and call Borkum lifeboat. Tell them your boy friends went swimming and disappeared, and you're getting worried."

"Which will be the understatement of the year."

"And not a word more than that," Wilde reminded her. "Or I'll come back to haunt you."

Fine returned on deck, wearing Wilde's spare pants and carrying the suitcases. "I hope you know what we're doing. We could just be costing that girl her life."

"You started the play, dear boy, and as Johann has just told us, once they get that money, Michelle Smith's life isn't worth a hole in the ground, anyway. If we can get on board before they have the time to send a message to the trawler, we may just swing it." He bent over Catherine, kissed her lightly on the lips. "Take care," he whispered.

"You can't leave me alone with her," Johann protested.

"I'm glad you mentioned that," Wilde said. "We nearly forgot to tie you up."

(iii)

The outboard chattered gently, and the dinghy nosed between the shallows at the side of the watt. In another two hours these would dry into sandbanks, but for the moment there were several feet of water available. Wilde carried his hand-bearing compass, to steer a course for the boat he assumed to be their destination. He *assumed*. But they'd gone and done it now. It was all or bust. An attitude he very rarely adopted. As a rule his every move was carefully calculated, carefully planned, with his entry reconnoitred, his target isolated, his retreat covered, and his eventual exit from the vicinity, invariably by the anonymity of public transport, booked and waiting.

Today he was setting off on a commando mission, with one death already behind him and God knew how many waiting in front of him, with a target whose identity was unbelievable, and no certainty that he was even travelling in the right direction, with no guaranteed exit, and an untried aide whom he did not even know if he could trust, leaving the only person in the whole world who really mattered alone on his boat with a potential murderer, stuck in the middle of nowhere.

All for the sake of an overprotected and overwealthy young woman whose sole reason for existence was that her father had existed before her, and his before him, and so on and so on for a few hundred years.

It was a bloody stupid world.

But it was the name Zita which hung in his mind, which was, in fact, the reason for his being here at all. The name rang a bell, and the woman on the bridge had also rung a bell. Zita Richmond? Zita Richmond, Cathy's oldest friend? Cathy, who had left her husband and coming chasing behind them, a truly irrevocable step. Because the man she loved was in danger. Did she love? Was she capable of loving a man like Wilde?

But she had given them a gun. And as for her love, surely he had sufficient proof of that. But he had had sufficient proof of so many things in the past. Or thought he had.

He glanced over his shoulder, but the catamaran was already fading into the mist. Perhaps Catherine was standing on the foredeck, he couldn't be sure.

Fine, sitting in the bow of the dinghy, his blue yachting cap pulled low over his eyes, was looking anxious. As well he might. His problems must be just as great, Wilde supposed.

"I don't imagine there is any way of doing this without bloodshed," Fine said. "I mean, without more bloodshed."

"I'm afraid I don't see how there is," Wilde pointed out. "We have got to take over that ship before anyone there pulls the switch on our Miss Smith. And as we won't know who's on deck and who isn't, it's a matter of shooting first and asking questions afterwards. I'd hate you to let me down on this, Paul, even if we haven't yet had the time to work out a system of signals."

"Um." Fine faced forward again, one hand resting on the pistol in his waistband. "This thing only has nine bullets."

"That's a lot of lead; there are only three of them. There she blows."

The water was changing colour as it deepened on the far side of the sandbank; *Regina B* had now quite disappeared behind them, and in front of them was the long, low hull of the motor yacht.

"That's a lot of boat," Fine said. "Recognise her?"

"She's one of those that passed us this morning. *Nemo*, remember?"

"For crying out loud," Fine said. "That woman on the bridge. I've just remembered who she reminded me of. That good-looking female we met at the Lights on Friday night."

"And Johann referred to her as Zita," Wilde agreed. "As the poet would say, the plot thickens. But I think we're coming to the last act."

The mist hung above the yacht, anchored at the side of the watt, but now they were inside the curtain, and the afternoon was almost bright. Wilde tried to decide what her below-decks layout might be; there was a row of small ports forward, suggesting a fairly extensive crew's accommodation, large windows in the wheelhouse-saloon amidships, and another row of large ports aft, to indicate at least one stateroom, and perhaps more.

"Company," Fine muttered.

A head showed on the flying bridge, and then immediately disappeared again.

"Calling the others," Wilde said.

"So hadn't we better open the throttle?"

"We don't want to excite them," Wilde said. "We'll hold this speed until we're close enough to be identified. Stand by with your suitcases, and let me have one."

Fine passed the second suitcase forward. "I wonder if we shouldn't have emptied these first."

"Always keep an alternative in hand," Wilde said. "We may still have to bargain. Besides, stuffed with banknotes they'll make useful shields."

A woman came on deck with a pair of binoculars.

"Raise your suitcase," Wilde said. "Triumphantly. But be sure it covers your face."

Fine held his suitcase at shoulder level, peering over the top. Wilde himself bent forward as though looking at the engine, so that the peak of the cap obscured his features. At the same time he eased the throttle slightly more open, and the dinghy gathered speed.

The woman waved her hand and returned into the wheelhouse. The man was again standing on the flying bridge, and he leaned on the wheel, gazing at them.

"I say," Fine muttered, lowering the suitcase and turning round to present his back to the onlookers, "do you want them *all* killed?"

"No. So long as they don't get around to killing us. But we'll want to have a chat with at least one of them afterwards. Preferably Mrs. Richmond. And start now."

The yacht was only fifty feet away, and the man on the bridge had straightened. In the same movement he slapped the hatch cover back and shouted into the wheelhouse. Fine turned, still sitting, the suitcase held in front of him, and brought up the automatic pistol. He squeezed the trigger, and the man on the bridge ducked and seemed to tumble to the deck.

"He's not hit," Wilde muttered, and started slewing the tiller to and fro. "Get the windows."

Fine fired again, and splinters flew. But now someone on board the yacht threw back the big windows in the wheelhouse, and there was the crack of a rifle, which developed into a burst. Spurts of water flew beside the dinghy.

"That's an M-16," Wilde bawled, bringing the helm round again. "Didn't they teach you how to shoot?"

"Well, hold the goddamned boat steady," Fine shouted, and dropped the suitcase to wrap both hands around the butt of the pistol.

But they were too close. Wilde had to straighten the tiller and cut the throttle to allow the dinghy to coast under the accommodation ladder, and the next *crump* of the rifle seemed to blow him out of the water. Two holes appeared in the bottom of the dinghy, and green sea water welled through. Fine dropped the suitcase and charged the ladder, firing again and again, and the afternoon filled with the sound of shattering glass. He reached the top of the ladder as his hammer clicked on his last spent cartridge, and hurled the pistol itself at the opened window as the rifle roared again. Wilde was immediately behind him, carrying the hand-bearing compass as a possible weapon—it was a heavy, well-weighted piece of metal on the end of a wooden haft—but as he reached the deck Fine came staggering backwards into his arms; there was a surprised look on his face and his life jacket was exploding kapok mingled with blood. Wilde dropped him to the deck and hit the door with his shoulder as it slid back. The man with the rifle was coming out, and received Wilde on his chest. The rifle exploded again, and the bullet whined into the mist. The man fell aside. There were two other people in the wheelhouse; the man, tall and thin, with pointed features and a long nose, who had been on the bridge, and Zita Richmond, wearing sailing clothes like her companions, and with her hair loose. Both were armed with pistols, and Wilde suspected that his life jacket was also going to prove inadequate. He checked and smiled at them, while great waves of dismay seemed to well up from his belly. This had been a forlorn venture at best. But just how forlorn he had not even suspected.

"Well, hi there," he said. "This is a surprise." And the coach roof fell on his head.

(iv)

The engines growled, ceaselessly and tunelessly; their thrust travelled the length of the ship from the engine room, seemed to develop maximum power immediately beneath him. He was in the aft sleeping cabin.

He lay on the port bunk, gazed at the deck immediately above his head. He felt uncomfortable and physically sick. Uncomfortable because his hands and wrists were bound, his hands behind him. Sick, because his head seemed to have no scalp; perhaps not even a skull. It responded to every throb of the engines, every movement of the ship, made keeping his eyes open next to impossible. But shutting them didn't help much either.

He figured they might be making twenty knots. It helped to figure something, to allow his brain to wander across an area he knew well, to try to convince himself that in time the pain would recede.

And he felt sick with despair. How he had ever let himself be conned into something as crazy as this . . . although once Fine had attacked the two men in the dinghy there had been very little alternative left. He felt very inclined towards a good old-fashioned murder, with Paul Fine as the victim. If the poor bastard wasn't dead already.

So then, think about the ship. He could do that with pleasure. The mattress on which he lay was softer than anything on board *Regina B;* the varnish with which he was surrounded was smooth and even. There was a bookshelf above him, just below the closed port. It contained a few paperbacks. Beyond this bunk a door was open, slapping to and fro as the *Nemo* developed a slight roll, and in there he could see a bathroom. The word was carefully chosen. No heads on this gin palace. No doubt there were several bathrooms.

To his right was another bunk, and between the two a dressing table. At the foot of the starboard bunk there was a hanging cupboard, the door closed. And between the two bunks was the door out of the cabin. This, surprisingly, was also open, also flopping to and fro; beyond was a corridor. Occasionally he caught a glimpse of another door, to another cabin. This was a *ship*, all right. And she was travelling at speed. Where? To gain the open sea, of course.

And he was naked. This came as something of a shock. The cabin was so warm, his head was so painful, he had up to now been feeling rather than seeing. Naked, and very, very exposed.

To Zita Richmond. Catherine Light's best friend. But they were no longer close friends. So Cathy had said. And Zita had just drifted in to the party, from the Seychelles or New York.

There was a thought. An implication. Why, if she was involved in something like this, should she choose to drift into England and pay the Lights a visit? Only because she knew something about Sir Gerald. And there was only one thing worth knowing about Sir Gerald.

And how many people were there in the world that could have given her such information about Sir Gerald?

This seemed to be rather a mess. Into which, thanks to his blind following of Paul Fine, he had jumped with both feet.

He watched her approach, along the corridor. She smoked a cigarette, moved with a looseness he found unusual in a woman. She entered the cabin, closed the door. "Welcome back to the land of the living."

"Is that where it is?" he asked.

"Oh, witty." She sat on the opposite bunk. "For you, temporarily, at any rate." Her gaze drifted over him like a cold wind.

"What were you looking for?" he asked.

She shrugged. "I could say, anything. Identification, you know. But actually, I was just looking. Did anyone ever tell you that you are a quite beautiful man?"

Wilde started to shake his head, and hurriedly changed his mind. "I'm afraid not."

"Painful? Yves is terribly enthusiastic, and he was also a little annoyed at the way you tossed him around. I thought for a dreadful moment that he had split your skull."

"That would have bothered you?"

"Oh yes," she said. "I suspected from the moment I saw you that you were going to be nice to know; and if Yves was upset, I was most impressed. You don't *look* quite that strong. I suppose you practice. We met at Catherine's party, remember?"

"I remember," he said.

"And I also suspected, even then, that we were going to get to know each other, Mr. Wilde. Or do you mind terribly if I call you Jonas?"

"Be my guest. You're wading in very deep waters, Zita."

"Oh, but it's such fun."

"So where do you get your information?"

"Ah," she said, "there's a point. Don't you think, in our circumstances, that I should be asking the questions, instead of you?"

"I expect you will. But as I suppose you do mean to kill me, in any event, I thought you mightn't object to telling me where the ship is leaking. It would appear to have a hole in its bottom the size of a bucket."

Zita Richmond got up, crossed the cabin. She bent over him, scooped his legs into her arms, and moved them against the hull. Some of the ash fell from her cigarette onto his thighs, and she raised her head to watch him as it burned. He sucked air through his nostrils slowly.

Zita sat beside him. "A large hole, yes," she said. "People are too impressed by position, by rank, I always feel. They never trouble about what goes on in the mind underneath. In the belly."

"Let's see," Wilde said thoughtfully. The pain had stopped. It had, in fact, been only the slightest twinge of pain. Not even a starting cocktail, in fact. More like a preliminary pretzel. "Commander Mocka?"

"Now, what on earth made you choose poor Rodney? Why not Catherine?"

"Because I know Catherine." But the sickness was back, eating at his belly.

"Of course you do, Jonas. Very well." Her hands came up his body slowly, pausing here and there, her fingers probing for sensitivity. "And she knows you. I find that almost incredible. Catherine, of all people. I would have described her as a prude. And I used to know her very well."

"The operative word would appear to be used." He watched, getting his breath in first, this time, as she took the cigarette from her mouth, looked at it for a moment, and then pressed it into his navel. She had surprised him again. His legs came up before he could stop himself, and he knew he made a noise, whether a grunt or a gasp or a squeal he couldn't be sure. His knees cannoned into her back, and she leaned against them to force them down. "I don't know what you're on at, anyway," he gasped. But perhaps talking had been a mistake. Once his mouth was open, air rushed out in an uncontrollable mass, mixed with saliva.

Zita Richmond cleaned spit off her jeans, with a preoccupied air. "I'm a woman, darling. I know how a woman looks at her lover. So maybe she wouldn't let you down. Then why not Sir Gerald? He must bear you a slight grudge. You're not going to pretend he doesn't know what's going on?"

"I'm sure he does," Wilde agreed. "Bear me a grudge, I mean. But I don't think he bears anyone else a grudge. Particularly royalty. He thinks they are important."

She leaned back, still gazing at him. "The invitation was from him. Delivered to my hotel. Tell me about him."

"As you say, he's the husband of my mistress."

"And also your employer. And a hell of a lot more than that. And he knew I was in England and invited me to his party. So that his hatchet men could look me over?"

"You're doing the talking, Zita. By now you must realise you can't get away with this crazy scheme."

"I am getting away with it, Jonas. Gerald Light or no Gerald Light. What happened to Johann and Wilbur?"

"Wilbur managed to drown himself. Johann lived a bit longer."

She took a cigarette case from her hip pocket, tapped thoughtfully.

"Think about it," he begged. "How else could we have known you were here?"

"How did Gerald know, not only that I was in England, but where I was staying? *Why* should he know that? As for now, didn't you recognise me this morning when we passed you?"

It occurred to Wilde that she was almost as confused as himself and also that she hadn't seen Catherine this morning. Which was just as well. But she was placing a cigarette in her mouth and flicking the lighter.

"If I had, Zita, you'd be behind bars by now, instead of merely next week. Believe me. I'm only the messenger boy."

"Who thought he'd try a commando stunt? Oh, ha, ha, ha. But whoever's idea it was, it was plain crazy. I'd be quite entitled to kill the little pest."

"According to Johann, you were going to follow the best examples and do that anyway. Hence we felt we had nothing to lose."

Once again that frightening stare. But the cigarette remained in her mouth. On the other hand, the pain was still seeping through his belly, and the cigarette still lay in his navel. It had, at any rate, removed some of the beauty she seemed to find so fascinating.

"Instead of which," she said at last. "You both got yourselves into a jam."

"Where is Paul?"

"I'm afraid he's dead. I don't think Yves's bullet did more than nick him, but he must have decided things weren't going his way, because he rolled overboard. Silly fool. He just disappeared. The current is very strong around here. Tell me, Jonas, who else was on board your boat?"

"Not a soul," Wilde said. "Not even Johann, now. We weighted him and dumped him in the watt."

Once again the stare. Then with a quick movement she hit him sharply in the groin. This time he did scream. Her actions were always unexpected, always deadly. Once again his knees came up, and once again she leaned against them to force them flat. Now her lips parted, as she watched him writhe on the bunk. Her face seemed to hover above his blood-filled eyes. Talk about chickens coming home to roost, he thought desperately. Oh, Johann. No doubt Catherine was at this moment making him a cup of coffee.

The pain was subsiding. Breath escaped between his clenched teeth.

"Listen," she said, "you think you have problems? There is no reason for anyone to connect me with this affair. So I go to England, and I'm promptly invited to the Lights. There I meet a couple of handsome boys who only three days later are trying to fill me full of holes. Are you trying to tell me that you were just sent out on your lonesomes, with no cover?"

"You shouldn't have gone to the party," Wilde whispered. "Old Gerald moves in a mysterious way his wonders to perform."

Her fingers were back. Not squeezing yet. Caressing. "Tell me about Johann again."

"At the bottom of the watt." His voice seemed to be coming from the deck. "And you want to be careful. If I'm to stay beautiful."

She smiled. "Oh, you *are* beautiful, Jonas. In every way. I never knew Gerald employed such magnificent men. I thought, in his business, they were all seedy civil servants, who wandered around with binoculars and tape recorders, and called in the Special Branch when the going got rough."

His breathing was almost normal again. But shafts of pain still drifted through his groin, and some of them were caused by anticipation. But now she released him, leaned across his legs, propped on her elbow. Trouble was, this brought her teeth into the firing line as well.

"Talking about the Special Branch," he said. "What have you done with my friend Olly Parks?"

She watched him for a moment, then reached for another cigarette. "I would say you are unharmed, Jonas. Wouldn't you?"

"Olly Parks," he said.

"He told me you and he were acquainted. Oh, you'll get Olly back, darling. And Carl Weber. We're in this thing for the money, you know. Not for blood. And think of it, you can spend the rest of your life wondering which of them, or of all your crowd, pulled the fast one."

Wilde's shoulders flexed before he intended.

She smiled. "That got to you, didn't it? Oh, we worked this one out very carefully, Jonas. Would the condemned man enjoy a last fling?"

"Be my guest."

Zita Richmond got up, and sat down again as the *Nemo* struck a wave and lurched. It had come very suddenly, so still had been the sea for the past half an hour. "We must be in the gap," she said, and took off her sweater. Like Catherine, she had little-girl breasts, but hers somehow managed to droop, where Catherine's stayed erect. No doubt she had seen a lot more of life. Or perhaps she was just unfortunate.

"Has it occurred to you to look at a barometer recently?" Wilde asked.

"So it'll blow tonight. A ship like *Nemo* will take anything." Her jeans joined her sweater on the deck, and she kicked off her canvas shoes. She wore sheer pink briefs, a remarkable touch of femininity. And she was thin. Bones ridged her belly, made a crater around her pubes. A hungry woman. And now she was sitting beside him again. He watched her hands. For the moment they were again stroking, but his belly muscles remained tensed.

"Where did you say your boat was?"

"Anchored at the side of the watt back there."

"And your instructions?"

"Were to hand over the money and make ourselves scarce. Didn't you get the money?"

"Oh, we did. Dave fished it out of the dinghy before it sank. So why did you disobey?"

"Believe me," Wilde said, "it wasn't my idea. Paul was all set up to be a hero. He's the idealistic half of the partnership."

"And you're the realist. I suppose, if I kissed you, you'd bite off my tongue."

"I love tongue. Particularly devilled."

She stroked her nails up his body, reached his nipples, scoured them. "Sometimes," she said, "sometimes, I get so worked up I'd just like to tear someone to pieces."

Wilde worked on his breathing. He had a distinct feeling that he was tied up inside the lioness's cage at feeding time.

"But you *are* a partnership?" she asked. Her pants slipped down her legs slowly.

"Oh yes. Sir Gerald's boys, don't you know?"

She lay on the bunk opposite, on her stomach, her chin on her hands. She gazed at him. Well, he was gazing at her. It was extremely warm in the cabin.

"Shall *I* tell *you* all about it?" she asked.

"Oh, please. I love a good story."

"I'm talking about Sir Gerald," she said, and rolled on her back, to stare at the deck above her. "Sir Gerald is the commander of the British Security Services. As such, his activities cover a very wide range of subjects, and he employs a very wide range of hatchet men, go-betweens, couriers, and what have you. Almost a private army. As we expected, when Michelle Smith was lifted the powers that are went to him. And in due course, our instructions went to him as well. I also went to him, just to see what was going on. He didn't invite me to that party, Jonas, and neither did Cathy. I crashed it. I like to be where the action is. I hope that doesn't depress you too much."

"In one way it quite relieves me," Wilde said. "I would hate to think that Sir G was two-timing on *me*. At the same time, I will confess that it depresses me to realise that he isn't really God, that we really aren't surrounded by the entire NATO fleet, just waiting to pounce. It makes the future a trifle grim."

"Um," she said. "But I did find out one thing about the old bastard at that party. I met Jonas Wilde. Because one of the most secret departments under Sir Gerald's personal control is the Elimination Section. A section composed of just one man: Jonas Wilde. Her Majesty's Executioner. Oh, you are nominally supervised by Rodney Mocka, and there's that dumb little girl, Melanie. And now, it seems, there's Paul Fine as well. Or there was, up to this afternoon. But the man who matters after Sir Gerald, is Jonas Wilde."

Wilde also gazed at the deck. He felt he was floating through the air, and none of it was the motion of the yacht. He was dreaming, obviously. That he should be lying here, trussed like a chicken, listening to a woman he had only met the previous Friday recounting some of the most secret material in the world with an air almost of boredom. But who? How? When? Zita had told him so many lies this afternoon he didn't know where the truth ended and fantasy began, as she intended. He did not think he had ever been interrogated quite so skilfully. But everything she said needed a great deal of thought. About Sir Gerald?

About Catherine? About Mocka? About Melanie? A girl trained almost from adolescence for the role she played? Mocka, who had been in charge of the Section for six years? Catherine? That did not bear thinking about. And Fine was dead. The bullet might not have killed him, but even in a pool it would have made swimming pretty difficult.

Sir Gerald? But there was an incredible supposition. And where did it leave him?

"I must say," Zita Richmond remarked, "I was a bit disappointed when you came on board like some reincarnated pirate, waving a hand-bearing compass. And accompanied by a man with a gun. I was told that Jonas Wilde always acted with great quiet and finesse, that he never used weapons, and that he killed with his hands. How do you kill with your hands, Jonas?"

"I hit people in the right place."

"You mean some form of karate?"

"No, I do not mean some form of karate."

"Anyway, I'm relieved to hear you say so. I was beginning to wonder if I had the right man. Isn't it amusing? I was also told that you're high on the wanted list in a dozen countries, not all of them officially our enemies, either. And here is a little amateur like me going to do the job for them. If you'd just tell me one little thing, we could part friends."

"All you have to do is ask. And I really would not describe you as an amateur, Zita."

"You are a witty man. Why did Gerald send *you* after me? I made it perfectly clear that any interference of that sort would cost him the little beauty."

"I happened to be on the spot, with a boat. Your instructions might almost have included the name Wilde." He wondered why they hadn't.

But maybe she hadn't heard; her eyes were glazing. He watched a large bead of sweat trickle out of her hair and down her forehead. She was, after all, far more interested in herself than in him.

"Do you know what I think?" he asked. "I think you are a pervert. In the nicest possible way, of course."

She lay on her back, her hands still, and gazed at the deckhead. "He shouldn't have sent you," she said. "Not you, Jonas. Not that nice boy, Fine. He was breaking the rules. Nobody should have got hurt. I didn't want that."

"If we omit Olly and Weber. And Ilse Weenink. You haven't told me how she died."

"She isn't dead," Zita Richmond said. "None of them are dead. I didn't *mean* anything like this to happen. Christalmighty, can't you *understand?*"

Her legs flailed the air as she turned violently, sat up on the bunk. She moved from side to side, hair, shoulders, nipples trembling as the engines grew louder and the yacht plunged to the waves. They were in the shallows off the island now. Outside the islands, with a rising sea. And a rising wind, too, he thought. He could hear it whistle.

"*Nothing* like this should have happened," she said. "It was all so *simple.* Mind you, we had to wait for the right moment. But it was an idea I had had for a long time. Kidnapping is in, nowadays. But it's all so petty. So you lift a plane and collect five million or you nab a diplomat and get a friend out of gaol. Because that's all the market will allow, isn't it? Because nobody has the guts to think big. On a scale where the sky's the limit."

"But you did," Wilde said.

"I had to." She began to dress herself. "So I'm Zita Richmond. Do you know what that means, what that always meant, Jonas? Not a bloody thing. My mother ran off with the dustman when I was four. Dad always had a lot of money, and a lot of connections. So I got to the best schools, met all the best people. Like Cathy. Now, she really did have money. Still does, I suppose. And being a simple soul, she thought I was likewise equipped. We were at the same school, weren't we? It wasn't until after I'd left that I discovered Dad lived with a pair of dice in one pocket and a pack of cards in the other, was broke at least as often as he had ten cents in the bank, had merely had one sensible instinct in his life; he took out an endowment policy when I was five, to see me through school. Seems that year he backed a Derby winner. But that was it. Not another centime, my friend. Not a bloody thing."

"So you got yourself a millionaire."

"I decided to be conventional. But me, I always had this weakness for picking losers. Richmond's bank balance looked good. But it didn't stand up. It was all in Australian mining shares, and the fool wouldn't sell when they were each worth pure gold. He waited until they weren't worth dirty paper, and committed suicide. He left a note, you know. Said he'd had a jolly good life. The exact words. And thanked me for everything. For Christ's sake, what did I have to thank *him* for?"

"You'll have me weeping in a moment," Wilde said.

"Yeah. So I had to start living the way Dad did. But I always kept my eye on the main chance. I made friends where it mattered. Thanks to my old school chums I had quite a few already, where it mattered. The world is full of long shots, but into everyone's life there comes a long shot which is going to pay, sooner or later. If you have the sense and the guts to grab it. I know that, because Daddy always said so. So I waited. And at last that stupid little girl elected to take a boat trip. Incognito."

"And one of your friends got in on the act," Wilde said thoughtfully.

Zita Richmond stood above him, her mouth smiling. "One of my friends, Jonas. So I recruited a few more. Nowadays I go for the kids. I'm not saying they're better than anyone else; they just haven't had the time to turn into losers yet. And they do what they're told, if you can give them sufficient reason. So I'm the lucky one. Maybe, if I'd met someone like you a few years back I'd have settled down to motherhood."

The door opened, and the man Yves looked in. "Got what you wanted?"

"Oh yes," Zita said. "He's the delivery boy for the British Security Services who got ambitious. Like I thought. What's happening on deck?"

"The trawler is signalling," Yves said.

"Anything else around?"

"A couple of ships on the radar screen. But well out of visual contact."

"Good. Let's get it done and go home. This motion could just make me seasick."

The cabin door was left open, swaying more regularly now as the *Nemo* began to slow and thus rolled the more. Now the wind was loud, whining through even the scanty rigging of the motorboat, and every so often *Nemo* stopped dead as she ran into a solid wall of water. A night not fit for man or beast, in the North Sea.

The pain in his gut was subsiding. But the ropes round his wrists were as tight as ever, no matter how he sawed. Time was running short. It was time which he did not think he was going to beat. As Zita Richmond had said, the whole thing was just too simple. Provided one had the patience, and the sheer gall to think big, there was almost nothing unattainable. And a friend in the right place. A friend was the most important thing of all.

Now the ship was almost stopped, rolling in the trough of each sea. And now there was a more solid jar, and the rolling stopped for a moment. The trawler had come alongside.

There were voices on deck, cutting across the howl of the wind, the squeaking of the fenders as the two hulls scraped together. And feet clattering above his head. Then, in the corridor, coming towards the open door. Two very young women. One was a short, stocky blonde, handsome rather than pretty. She gazed at Wilde with wide, frightened eyes. The other was taller. She too gazed at Wilde, with an expression of mingled contempt and dismay.

"My God," she said, "he's *naked*."

"It's my best feature," Wilde pointed out. "Michelle Smith, I presume?"

PART TWO

THE REALIST

CHAPTER 6

Nemo gave a lurch, and Michelle Smith nearly fell over. She caught herself on the bulkhead and turned her gaze on Zita Richmond, who stood in the doorway with Dave by her side. Dave carried the rifle.

"Is this another of your tasteless jokes?"

"I've given them up," Zita said. "And I haven't even asked you to undress as well. But Jonas and I had some business matters to discuss. If you'd kneel down, you won't go falling around all over the place. After I tie your hands."

"After you . . ." Michelle Smith gave another glance at Wilde. "You mean we're being left in here? With him?"

"How rough can life get?" Wilde asked at large. "And you're not even the one I thought you were. Ma'am."

Zita smiled. "You may not believe this, Michelle, but he tried to rescue you. Kneel."

Michelle Smith hesitated, glanced at Wilde again, and knelt, her back to the door. Her shoulder brushed his arm as the ship rolled, and he turned his head to study her face. As he had said, it was not the one he had anticipated, but it was none the less regal. She had now, apparently, been in the hands of these people for a week. She wore no make-up, but her hair was remarkably tidy, although he guessed that she had done her combing with her fingers. He wondered if she had been allowed a bath in all that time. It was fine hair. She had fine features. But her jaw was so tightly clamped there were hard ridges of muscle at each base, and there was a combination of sleepless shadows under her eyes and red rims within. He wondered what they could have done to Michelle Smith to make her weep so much and so often. More often than Ilse Weenink, who sat on the port bunk, her face expressionless. She too was untidy and unwashed. But she had not wept recently. No doubt she was the better trained of the pair.

"His name is Jonas Wilde," Zita said, tying Michelle Smith's hands behind her back with great expertise. Clearly she had done a lot of sailing. "He works for the British Security Services. For Gerald Light, as a matter of fact. You must remember Cathy? We were all at that ball in Monaco together, oh, three years ago, now. Gerald is her husband."

Michelle Smith stared at the bulkhead, spread her knees to prevent herself falling over, and did fall over as Zita pulled her legs back together to tie her ankles. She made a sound as she hit the deck. It might have been a grunt of pain, or it might have been a sob. Wilde rather thought it was a growl. Two lionesses. But one was tame. And trussed.

"I think we'll leave her on the floor, Dave," Zita said. "That's the best place for princesses. Would you lie down on that bunk, Ilse."

Ilse Weenink lay down on the starboard bunk without a word, turned her face to the bulkhead. Tying her up took no time at all.

"Now," Zita said, "we have to say good-bye. Jonas, I know you are interested in technicalities. You are all bound, quite securely. I am sure you know a great deal about knots and how to get out of them, but it will still take you at least half an hour to do that. Once you *have* released yourselves, the cabin door will have to be opened. We have had it specially strengthened for this part of the voyage, and I may say it is built of steel with four bolts on the outside. I don't think even you will be able to slam your way through that, Jonas. The cabin ports are fitted with screw-down caps from the outside, so you will be hermetically sealed in here. Oh, you won't die of suffocation; there is the ventilator over there. Dave will set the automatic pilot on a course of three hundred degrees magnetic, which should eventually take you well south of the Faroes, and out into the Atlantic. In about three days you will run out of fuel. But by then I'm sure you will have been rescued."

"You mean you don't intend to kill me?" Michelle Smith asked in surprise. "Despite all this?"

"Oh no, Michelle. Despite all that has happened, I didn't want any bloodshed. And now we have the money, and it's not marked. We'll get a message to old Gerald Light, giving him your last known position and your course. And a description of the yacht. He won't find it difficult to track you. Of course, he won't get the message for two days, but you shouldn't find that too inconvenient. By then, in fact, you should have succeeded in breaking out of here; you'll be able to surprise everyone and turn up in some Scottish port. Jonas is very good at navigating and that sort of thing, I'm sure."

Wilde gazed at Dave. The yacht captain smiled at him coldly.

"Do you think it won't work, Jonas?" Zita asked. "It will be dark in a little while. You will be showing all the necessary navigation lights, and be a yacht proceeding on her legitimate way. Rather carelessly, with the weather deteriorating, but none the less legitimately. By dawn you'll be outside the shipping lanes, and in the loneliest part of the North Sea. And then the ocean. No one is going to do anything about you until we tell them to. And in two days we can be on the other side of the world. No one has any reason to chase behind us. And I'm sure, Michelle, that you will use your authority to dissuade anyone from such a foolish act. I have kept my word, so far. I will continue to do so, despite the behaviour of the British." She glanced at Wilde. "And their hatchet men."

Michelle Smith made no reply.

"What about Carl Weber and Olly Parks?" Wilde asked.

"They too will be returned in due course," Zita said. "You are dealing with honest people, Jonas."

Wilde nodded thoughtfully. Johann had said that Dave intended them to die. With the weather as it promised to be, *Nemo*'s survival chances on automatic pilot were slim enough. But to point that out to Zita might just make matters worse; Dave held the gun.

"We'd better go," Dave said. "There is a ship on the radar, only five miles off. We do not wish to be seen together."

Zita remained gazing at Wilde. "It really is a shame," she said, "that we won't be able to get together again. Ah well, there'll be others. Tell Michelle your life story, Jonas. You've time." The door slammed, and they listened to the bolts being pushed home. She hadn't been kidding, after all. Wilde counted four.

A moment later the cabin light went out.

(ii)

The darkness was immediately Stygian; the ports had already been clamped into place. And stuffy, for all the howling wind outside. *Nemo* rolled and bucked, scraped against the fenders protecting the trawler's sides. Wilde listened to the clumping of feet overhead, snatches of conversation lost in the wind. The engines, for the past half an hour no more than idling, suddenly gained in power, and there was a last hurried scamper of feet on the deck. Dave would have had to hurry. A moment later there was a huge bump and a twang; one of the restraining warps had parted. And *Nemo* was away, plunging to the northwest, with the wind and the sea on her port quarter, causing her to pitch and roll at the same time. The trouble with this entire business, Wilde realised, was that none of Zita's crowd were deep-water sailors.

"God," Michelle Smith muttered. "To spend two days, like this. God."

"Then it would be a good idea to get ourselves free as quickly as possible," Wilde suggested.

"We can't," Michelle said. "She knows that. We can't get out of the cabin."

"We'd better," Wilde said. "I don't think this ship is going to stay afloat for two days in this weather. Certainly not if it freshens up."

"Oh, God," Ilse Weenink groaned. "Oh, God."

"Prayer is a long-term arrangement," Wilde pointed out. "I've always understood that the time-honoured way of coping with our situation is to use our teeth. But I happen to have recently had a filling, so I'm asking for a volunteer."

"Just who *are* you, anyway?" Michelle demanded.

"I sometimes wonder."

"I mean, do you really work for Gerald Light? I don't see how he comes into it at all."

"Sir Gerald comes into everything, darling. Ooops. I meant, ma'am. *Do* you think we could save the chat? Ilse, how's the cavity problem?"

"I can try," Ilse said. There was a rustling, bumping sound from the far side of the cabin, shrouded in the creaking of timbers and the slapping of the waves against the hull. "Oh, God," Ilse said. "Oh, God." She retched.

"She's not in very good shape," Michelle said. "They beat her up. Horribly. I'm terribly worried about her."

"Why did they beat her up?" Wilde asked. "And not you?"

"To . . . does it matter?"

"I'll tell *you*," Wilde said. "It was to make you do what they wanted. And when you did what they wanted, they photographed you."

"I have no idea what you're talking about," Michelle said.

"Which is why Zita is quite sure that you are not going to follow the matter up. I was brooding on that."

"Does it matter, now? It's all over."

"It is just beginning," Wilde said. "And you, ma'am, have good teeth in addition to a strong stomach. I have no doubt at all."

"What a horrible thought," she said. "You have nothing on."

"You're a big girl, now, Michelle. I think the best thing for you to do is to kneel. That way you can brace yourself against the bunk, and I can turn my back on you."

He did so and waited. The wind gusted, and *Nemo* did a very deep roll and even seemed to hesitate before coming up again. Ilse Weenink vomited, and Michelle Smith muttered something under her breath as she fell over.

"I suppose there's no chance of this tub capsizing?"

"I would say there is every chance in the world, ma'am. A

ship like this should be steaming slowly into the seas in these conditions, not charging along with the waves on her quarter. Which is why I'd like you to hurry."

She grunted and panted as she got herself straight. "Yet you seem perfectly calm."

"It's my business to be a realist. Yours too, I would imagine. And after all, drowning is better than the guillotine."

"Are you trying to be funny?" Hair flopped across his thighs, and he felt her breath on his back.

"As a matter of fact, yes."

Teeth scoured his arm, began working down his hand. They gave a few perfunctory tugs at the rope, and then vanished again as the ship lurched. There was a bumping sound, and some more muttering from Michelle Smith.

"Try saying it aloud," Wilde suggested. "It really does help."

"Well then, God damn and blast this bloody ocean," she said, and her breath was back. "Look, even if I can get you free, we can't get out of here."

"I prefer to die on my feet. Come on. Up the blues."

Tug, tug, went her teeth, and one gave a slight crunching sound. Ah well, he thought, she can always have them capped.

"Try dreaming about what you'd like to do to Zita Richmond."

His wrists were covered in royal saliva, and she paused for breath. "I'd like . . . oh, never mind."

"Ma'am, if I may offer another opinion, you are repressed," Wilde said. "Now come on, what *would* you like to do to her? Think about it."

Tug, tug, tug. Lurch went *Nemo,* and there was a sudden rattle of spray across the deck above them. Ilse Weenink vomited again and groaned.

Michelle Smith sighed, and he heard her bump against the lockers. "I have the strangest wish to be playing polo," she said. "With her as the ball. But not the ball, if you see what I mean. Just to be riding round and round her with a polo stick, swinging whenever I felt the urge. My God. What a thing to say."

"Interesting," Wilde said. "Don't give up now. A couple more tugs might just do it."

"I've broken a tooth," she said. "I'm sure of it."

"Now's not the time for worrying about the bridgework," he said. "Just a couple more tugs."

"Just let me rest for a moment." She sighed. "Zita said you should tell me your life story. Is it that interesting?"

"Not really."

"But you're a Secret Service man. Or Special Branch, like Oliver?"

"Secret Service, I suppose." He wondered how much she knew about the way a country was run. If anything. His Irish sense of humour was putting forth endless temptations. "I kill people."

"You *what?*"

"Occasionally it is necessary, you know, ma'am. Abolitionists notwithstanding. There are some people who are just too dangerous to live. For the good of us all."

"Politicians?"

"Heavens, no. Political assassination is not on my agenda. Nor Sir Gerald's. No, people in our game. You know, for every spy who can be arrested with a fanfare and television cameras present and personal interviews to the newspapers, there are at least two shadowy figures who we dare not arrest, simply because they know too much about us. Oh, the Russians and the Chinese and all our other various rivals and even our allies have the same problem. Just say I work in a sewer, and it's my job to make sure all the dirt stays there, so that people like you don't have to wrinkle your nostrils."

"I suspect you don't like me very much, Mr. Wilde."

"I'd love you forever, ma'am, if you'd finish my wrists."

The mouth was back at his flesh, the tongue licked his fingers, and she gasped.

"Try that."

He forced his wrists apart, brought them together again, ignored the biting pain of the rope sawing into his hitherto unnumbed flesh, repeated the operation again, and felt the rope slip. A moment later he sat up, and was able to look at his watch. It was seventeen minutes past six.

"Michelle?" he asked. "Where are you?"

"Here," she muttered, from the vicinity of his knees.

He thrust his hands down, found the cord securing his ankles, searched for the knots. How long had she been at his hands? A good hour, at least. So the trawler would be half a dozen miles off, at any rate. And he still had to get through the door.

In time. There was a factor, now. *Nemo* found her way into another big one, this time apparently curling up from behind. There was a whoosh of solid water crashing onto the cabin roof and the cracking sound of something carrying away. Drips of water fell on Wilde's face, and Ilse gave a squeal of terror in between gasps. "We're sinking," she wailed.

"Not yet," Wilde said. "But she won't take many more of those."

His ankles were free. He pulled himself up, tried the light switch, without success. Desperately he fumbled for the bathroom door, half fell in as the ship lurched the other way, and again swept his hands over the bulkhead, looking for a useless light switch.

"She's disconnected all the after lights," he said. "Ah, well, where did you say you were, ma'am?"

"I haven't moved," she pointed out.

He stumbled back into the cabin and over her, fell to his hands and knees.

"You *are* a clumsy beast," she said.

He found her shoulders, pulled her round, and slid his hands down the sleeves of her sweater. From beneath him there came an ominous slurping sound rising above the grinding of the screws.

The ropes came loose. "I think," he said, "if you try moving your wrists, you'll get a pleasant surprise. Now, I'm going to lift you onto the bunk. Will you look after your own ankles, and then see what you can do about Ilse?"

"While you do what?"

"I'm going to take this cabin apart." He scooped her round

the thighs, rolled her onto the bunk, heard her head bang the bulkhead.

"For what?" she asked.

"I want to get out, ma'am. Nothing more ambitious than that."

He slid his hands over the door, found the lock easily enough. He could pick this, he supposed, even in the dark; it was part of his training and one of the girls would be sure to have a hairpin. But would that help matters? He could feel the rivets holding the brackets for the bolts. There seemed an awfully large number of them.

The noise was tremendous, the surge of the engines competing with the steady blast of the wind and the consistent chatter of the waves.

Michelle Smith grunted as her ankles came free. "Can I help?"

"Do something about Ilse," he suggested again, and tried the bathroom once more. He could tear out the plumbing, but as a weapon against steel it was useless. It occurred to him that he was stymied, that in all probability he was going to drown, right here. With a princess. The wind was getting up all the time.

What made it so absolutely absurd was that at this moment no one was actually *trying* to kill him. Officially.

"Come on, Ilse," Michelle said. "Get your head up. God, you do pong."

"We're going to die," Ilse said. "Oh, God, after everything, Michelle, we're still going to die. Oh, God . . ."

There was a crisp sound in the darkness as Michelle swung her hand. Ilse gave a gasp, and was joined by Michelle as *Nemo* seemed to leap out of the water, corkscrew between two waves, and come down again on her bow. Wilde lost his balance and went cannoning down the cabin, bumped into Michelle and tumbled her over against the door, while on the next roll Ilse fell off her bunk to land on top of them. From above there was an endless cacophony, together with the shattering of glass. Wilde realised that *Nemo* might well have taken a death blow. This was no weather for even a big motorboat; she had never been intended to face a full gale, unless expertly manned and steered.

And she was operating on automatic pilot, blindly following a course without any regard for the shape or size of the waves.

"Get off my stomach," Michelle begged. "What happened, Mr. Wilde?"

"I'd say we took two big ones at the same time," Wilde said.

"Ugh," Ilse shrieked. "Water. Water."

Wilde bundled her out of the way, reached the cabin door. A thin trickle of water came from beneath the bulkhead, overflowed into the already full bilges. Oh yes, that one had got in forward, all right.

And suddenly nothing was right. *Nemo* took the next one exactly on the beam, rolled over on her side. Ilse gave another despairing shriek and vanished up the bunk. Michelle gasped, reached for something solid, and found Wilde instead. Her arms went round his neck, but she only succeeded in pulling him over as well, and they found themselves sliding down the lockers on the side of the bunk as the ship slowly came upright again.

"My God," she said, "what's *happening?*"

Wilde fell away from her. He knew what had happened, what *had* to have happened. He reached downwards, pulled up the carpet, plucked at the floor boards. *Nemo* was struck broadside by another tumultuous wave; this time she went the other way. A leg caught him behind the ear as he struck the port bunk, and for a moment he was dizzy. Now there was water flooding out of the bilges; it had found its way along from the engine room, he thought.

His fingers caught at the floor, and he thrust his hand under the bunk. As he had supposed, the steering cable hung limp.

"Mr. Wilde?" Michelle called from the darkness, her voice faint above the tremendous crashing of the waves.

"Steering's gone," he said. "Zita really doesn't have a clue."

"Which means what?" She was panting.

"That we're probably going round and round in circles in a big sea. I don't know how much of this the tub can take."

Even as he spoke, *Nemo* seemed to stand on her bows. He slid forward, bumped into Ilse Weenink as she fell off the starboard bunk, and was thrown back again as the ship came up, tossing her head like a frightened horse. A solid wall of water struck Wilde on the chest, hard enough to send his breath cascading away, and to hurl him against the dressing table between the bunks. Ilse's scream was lost in a gargle as she swallowed, and Michelle's voice rose above the roaring.

"Mr. Wilde? The door's open."

(iii)

It was light enough to see, as Wilde dragged himself up. Zita had miscalculated on at least two points, but if they didn't hurry, it wasn't going to do them much good. The after cabin was three feet deep in water in which the two girls splashed as if swimming, hair matted to their heads and faces white with fear. The wave must have come straight through the wheelhouse and down the after companionway like a team of wild horses; not even four steel bolts had been able to keep it out.

Correction. His fingers clawed at the bulkhead as he dragged himself forward. The bolts were still in place, bent into right angles, but the door had been torn from its hinges on the other side.

Ilse started to scream in a high-pitched voice.

"Can you shut her up?" Wilde bawled. "And get her up, as well? Come on. This ship is sinking."

Even as he spoke, another wall of water moved down the corridor from the saloon, and this time *Nemo* did not toss her head; she hardly moved at all, settled sluggishly into the next trough, like a boxer out on his feet, kept from going down by sheer instinct.

Wilde reached behind him, grabbed Michelle's sweater. "Come *on*."

She splashed to her feet, sat on the port bunk. "Ilse," she gasped, held onto the Dutch girl's shoulders, and fell into the water again. "Aagh. I can't breathe."

He plucked her back to her feet, pushed her to the shattered door and through it, and then reached for Ilse. The Dutch girl struck at him angrily, and he closed his fist and drove it at her face. He missed her chin, and hit her on the cheek; she gave a moan and fell backwards. He grabbed her before she could disappear under the water, tossed her over his shoulder, forced his way through the shattered door, and received Michelle in the stomach as she staggered backwards.

"Hurry," he begged, and pushed her away again as he reached for the stairs leading into the wheelhouse. At the foot another wave came down, and he slipped on his knees beside the galley; in there was a complete shambles, with crockery and plastic bins floating about and the door to the fridge hanging open, while water slurped in and out. Ilse Weenink slipped off his back and he had to stretch after her with one hand, while holding on to the grabrail with the other. Michelle had disappeared, but as he got back to his feet and struggled to the foot of the ladder, she was there again, waiting to help him.

"God," she said, "what a mess."

The evening was surprisingly bright. The mist had been blasted away by the wind, and although the solid ceiling of black cloud, certainly well under a thousand feet, hid the sun, there was a sharpness in the air which gave a horrifying accent to one of the most terrifying scenes even he had ever witnessed. Wherever he looked there was tumbling green water, towering above the yacht on either side, in front of her and behind her, streaked with white foam and with massive white crests curling over like closing fists. As he reached the top of the ladder a wave came in from the side, struck him a hammer blow, and swept his feet out from under him. He lost Ilse again, found himself floating across the wheelhouse, and came to rest against the dinette. Something to grab; its steel legs were still anchored to the deck. The still deck, because the engines had cut out, no doubt swamped. There was no surprise. The windows of the wheelhouse were shattered, and the starboard door had been blown in, leaving a gaping hole roughly six feet square through which every wave slammed unopposed. The yacht was so low in the water her scuppers were awash, and he figured it was a miracle she still floated at all. But even miracles don't last forever. Although here was another; he discovered that he had company under the table. The six-man life raft had been torn from its mounting immediately aft of the wheelhouse and had come through the windows like a bomb, and wedged itself under the dinette. And its release cord was still attached, still unpulled.

He saw Michelle hanging onto the top of the stairs with one arm, while the other clutched Ilse round the waist, and left the safety of the table to crouch beside them. "Listen," he bawled in Michelle's ear, "I've found a raft. Tie this round your waist."

He reached past her, lay flat on the after window sill, while jagged pieces of glass sliced at his naked belly, and tugged the holding line towards him as he searched for the shackle. His fingers reached it as the next wave approached. He looked up seconds before it hit, saw it towering above the suddenly tiny boat, high, high, blotting out the clouds for a long moment, realised that here *was Nemo*'s death blow.

"Take a breath," he yelled, and threw both arms around the two girls. His hands met behind them, and he locked his fingers.

A tremendous force descended on his back, and he listened to a crack as the hull was torn apart. Then there was nothing but a gigantic roaring in his ears, and a series of tugs at his body. Something struck him on the left thigh and paralysed the leg, and water was battering at his nostrils, demanding entrance to his lungs.

He turned over, and looked upwards, as strands of hair caught around his head. There was a pale blue up there, and then a darker darkness. After all, he was drowning. Drowning, with a princess still crooked in his arms. Because now he had to breathe. Maybe she also breathed and was already dead. So where was the point in maintaining the struggle, continuing to kick, continuing to fight for life?

But she was still tied to the raft, and the raft was free, even as *Nemo* gave a lurch, and seemed to utter a scream of her own, as the next wave struck her, or rather strangled her, for she was too low in the water to present a target and the sea merely slurped down the companionways and through the shattered ports.

But he was gulping air, his arms still locked around the princess, and rising above him, on the next wave, he saw the canopy billowing above the already inflated life raft.

His hands came up, sliding across the sodden sweater to get her chin up. "Michelle," he shouted. "Michelle. The raft. Pull yourself in."

Her head moved, from side to side, her mouth open as she choked and vomited sea water. And then she too saw the raft, and her hands clawed at the rope. And slipped again.

Wilde realised that his other arm was empty. He turned his head, left and right, was swamped by a huge curling wave which seemed to drop on his head. It took another eternity for him to come up, and by then even the yacht had disappeared. To search for Ilse Weenink in this holocaust would be to lose Michelle Smith once again.

"I can't," she gasped, and vomited. "I can't."

"Then keep afloat," he told her. "That's all you have to do, keep afloat. Don't forget now. It'll only be for a few seconds."

She nodded, gasped, and took another mouthful of slurping water. Wilde pulled himself round her and went up the painter, hand over hand, timing his breathing to fit in with the constantly flying spray. His body was turning numb with the chill of the water, and his muscles were losing the last of their power with the constant buffeting. The evening seemed to be darkening, and the entire ocean was torn into white spray as the wind gusted up to gale force and the waves took on that long, hanging formation he knew so well.

But always in front of him was the life raft, and warmth, and shelter from the wind and the waves. Just in front of him now. It seemed to climb above his head on the next crest, and hang there, and he thought it was going to turn over. No problem, theoretically. There were loops underneath for standing on and righting it. But to do that required strength.

The painter was only thirty feet long. His hands were at the raft, tucking themselves round the safety lines, reaching up to release the vent, anxious now, for he didn't want a wave to break on board as he opened the canopy.

The plastic zip slid down smoothly and easily. Thank God for life rafts; and thank God Dave had at least enough seamanship to see that it was serviced.

"Wilde," Ilse Weenink screamed. "Wilde."

She was not twelve feet away, rising on the crest of a wave as she surged past him.

Wilde hesitated. To release the raft now, when he was almost on board, required a real act of will. But she would never get back on her own. He sighed, let go of the warp, and swam after her. She was at least to windward.

"Wilde," she shrieked.

Wilde clutched at her wrist, found flesh, slipped, got hold of her sweater, and swung her round. She gave a cry and bumped into the raft. "Grab it," he bawled.

Her fingers locked in the life lines, and a moment later Wilde was beside her; he reached into the water, seized her by the thighs, and heaved her into the raft. Then he kicked, pulled himself upwards, got his elbows on to the rubber gunwale, and fell forward into the soft bottom beside her, listening to the endless water slurping about him. How good, how soft, how immediately warm, to shut himself off from the wind and the sea and the cold.

But Michelle Smith was still out there. He turned frantically, panting, leaned out of the entrance and watched a breaking crest rushing at him. He threw himself backwards, clawed at the vent, and was struck in the face by flying spray. Only spray. The raft coasted up the tumbling water and down the other side. Wilde fell forward again, reached for the warp, and brought it in, hand over hand. Now he could see the girl, lying in the water, but still using her hands to keep her head above water. She had a lot of guts. More than he would have thought possible; a will to live commensurate with his own.

She came up to the raft, surging on the next wave, and he jerked the rope towards him, caught her shoulders, made a gigantic heave, and tumbled her into the gloom beside him. His fingers clawed at the inner lip, and the canopy closed on the howling white outside.

"Oh, God," Michelle Smith said. "Oh, God. I think you have just saved my life."

(iv)

There was water in the bottom of the raft. Nearly as much as outside, he figured, squelching and moving to and fro as the bottom itself squelched and moved to and fro. And suddenly it was cold. Not so cold as outside, but still a deadly, numbing cold, increasing the exhaustion of his muscles, the numbness of his brain.

His lifeless fingers fumbled at the survival pack, and found the bailer. He crawled across the raft, sat next to the flap, released the zip a few inches.

"What are you doing?" Michelle gasped.

"Getting this water out. Come over here."

She lurched towards him, on her hands and knees. "It's so thin," she said. "The bottom. It can't last. Surely."

"It'll last," he promised her. "It has a double skin. Just relax."

She lay down beside him with a slight splash. But the addition of her weight brought the water down to their side of the raft, and he was getting on top of it.

"Oh, God," she said. "I'm going to be sick. Oh, God."

She vomited in time with Ilse.

Wilde bailed.

"I'm sorry," Michelle said. "I really am sorry. I thought I was a good sailor."

"This thing has a motion like nothing on earth," he told her. "Put your hand out to your right, and you'll find the survival pack. There's a torch in there."

She scrabbled across the soft rubber, and Wilde's bailer found nothing. There was a click, and a glow of light illuminated the inside of the tented raft.

"My God," she said, "Aladdin's Cave."

"Couldn't be more accurate. Let's have a look."

The torch swung round, illuminated him, and hastily moved away again.

"Darling," Wilde said, "you have just got to grow up. Ma'am, I mean. On the bottom first."

She shone it downwards. The raft was indeed no more than damp. He could do nothing more about that right now.

"And now me," he told her. "I took a wallop before we left the ship."

"My God," she said, "you're turning blue. Literally."

"That could be just cold. Aren't you colonel in chief of some nursing organisation or other? It's my thigh that's hurting."

"Well . . . hold the torch." He took it, played it over his shoulder, and watched her kneeling there, swaying as the raft swayed, her bra straps showing through the sodden sweater, her water-darkened hair plastered to her head and cheeks, while her fingers, long, slim, with surprisingly still manicured nails, stroked over his back and down to his hip. "It *is* nasty," she said, and prodded.

"Ow."

"Mmmm." Another prod, and a stroke. "I don't think anything is broken, Mr. Wilde. But it is going to be a horrible bruise. On the other hand, I don't see what else I can do about it."

He turned the torch on her, watched her teeth chatter. "Then you'd better do something about yourself."

"I don't see what I can do about that, either."

"You have got to get warm, ma'am. Would you like to take off your wet clothes?"

"I would not."

"Oh, for God's sake. What the bloody hell is the use of rescuing you if you go and die of exposure? I'll wake Ilse up." He crawled across the swaying, slurping rubber, gripped the girl by the shoulder. "Oy."

"Leave me alone," she whispered. "Oh, God, I just want to die."

"You had your chance, you know," he pointed out. "And muffed it by shouting for help. Now I'm afraid the only dying you can do is by a long and painful process called hypothermia. It really isn't worth it. Don't go back to sleep." He shook her shoulder, released her to give her two crisp slaps across the face.

"Ow," she screamed, and swung back, "you . . . you bastard."

"She's alive," Wilde informed Michelle. "Now listen, darling, you have got to go over there and warm the young lady up. Take off your clothes and I'll hang them up to dry. They will, you know."

"You . . ." she gazed at him, but he had already placed the flashlight on the rubber deck and was untying her soaking shoes. "I can't. Do you know who she really is?"

"You can and you will. Duty before pleasure. And if you both won't behave, I'll keep the light on you."

Ilse hesitated, looked at Michelle Smith.

"Oh, come *on*," Michelle said. "I suppose he is right."

Ilse took off her sweater, crawled past him into the gloom at the other end of the raft. Wilde sat with his back to them, waited for their clothes to arrive, and spread them out on the deck. "Tell me about the hijack."

"It was all rather casual," Michelle said. She was breathing more heavily. "The *Nemo* forced us out of the watt and on to a sandbank and then came round as if to offer us help, but they all had guns."

"And what did you do? I'm thinking of Weber and Parks."

"I made them do nothing," Michelle said. "They'd have been shot."

Wilde nodded. "And who were on board the yacht?"

"Zita Richmond. And Dave. And three others. Yves, Johann, and Wilbur."

"That tallies. What happened afterwards?"

Michelle Smith gasped, and Ilse Weenink sighed. "They . . . they made us go on board," Michelle muttered. "Ilse and me. Johann and Wilbur went on board the *Fair Winds*. For the rest of that day the two ships sailed in company. But by Tuesday morning *Fair Winds* had disappeared."

Wilde checked through the emergency pack. "And you haven't seen either Weber or Parks since?"

"Well, we were both kept in some kind of hole right down in the hull of the trawler." There was a scrabbling sound. "Carl and Olly could have been on board as well. We never saw them. But I was sure they'd been killed."

Enough water for six men for two days meant, by his reckoning, enough water for three people for four days. In the middle of the North Sea that should be more than sufficient. "Zita really doesn't seem keen on the bloodshed bit. Tell me about the trawler."

"I can't," Michelle said. "They blindfolded us before taking us off *Nemo*. And again before bringing us on board this afternoon."

Biscuits and vitamins. And at the bottom, what he really wanted; a package of parachute flares. "But they didn't put either Olly or Carl on to *Nemo* with you. Inconsistent." He crawled towards the vent in the canopy, was struck in the ribs by a flailing set of toes. "Easy," he said. "You're not supposed to be enjoying it."

He reached the vent, waited for some seconds, listening to the howl of the wind and the sloshing of the waves. There was less noise now. Did that mean that the wind had gone down after that brief, fierce squall? Or, more likely, that as there was nothing for the waves to hit down here they only sounded smaller? But there were six flares. He could risk two now; no matter how hard the girls were working, they were going to get cold again, and pretty soon.

He opened the vent, and a burst of spray came in.

"For God's *sake*," Michelle shouted, "what's the use."

"You'll have to start all over again." He released the trigger, watched the rocket disappear into the darkness, counted slowly. A few seconds later it burst high above the raft, a glowing ball of incandescence which slowly, beautifully slowly, settled towards the water.

"What in the name of God was that?" Michelle demanded.

"I want the world to know we're here," Wilde said. "How are the girls doing?"

"I suppose we're warm," Michelle said. The flashlight played across his back. "Did you know that you have turned blue all over?"

"It's the fashionable colour this year."

"I suppose we should do the same for him," Ilse suggested.

"Mmmmm," Michelle agreed. "Well . . ."

"Just let me set off one more flare," Wilde said. "Not that I'm a prude, mind. It's just that we shall probably get bored with each other's company if we hang about out here for too long."

"You had better let me do it, Michelle," Ilse said.

Wilde sighed, and closed the vent. "Bang goes another happy dream."

But she *was* warm. He took her in his arms, leaned against the rubber gunwale, relaxed, his head against the underside of the canopy, allowed the girl's hands to wander over his body, followed by her own body; he wondered if she had ever trained as a masseuse, or if she was just doing what came naturally.

"What a way to die."

"Don't tell me you believe in bed talk as well," Michelle said from the darkness. She sounded displeased. Of course, she always sounded displeased. But he wondered if she was jealous, or just frustrated. "Oh, damnation," she cried. "What's that?"

The noise seemed to come from very close, a high "blaaagh" from just outside the canopy.

"Probably a seagull," Ilse said dreamily. Her lips were moving up his cheek. "Do you know, Mr. Wilde, I don't feel seasick any more?"

"I must be the most unlucky bloke on the face of the earth," Wilde said. Because he *had* recognised the sound. Gently he removed Ilse, crawled across to the flap, and pulled down the zip. The seas were still very big, but the catamaran rode them beautifully, under storm jib and triple-reefed mainsail, now shooting some distance north of the raft, but coming about with hardly a splash. Clearly there was an expert on the helm. An expert wearing sheer red nylon oilskins, and with long black hair flowing in the wind.

CHAPTER 7

"You do seem to have friends in the oddest places," Michelle Smith remarked. But she crowded against him in the vent, apparently forgetting her nudity.

The catamaran surged past, while Catherine shouted something.

"What did she say?" Ilse gasped. She leaned on Wilde's back; she seemed reluctant to let him go.

"I think she wants us to take a line. Would you girls mind moving back a bit?"

There was a man on the foredeck, wearing a safety harness over oilskins and looking very much at home on the heaving surface. Now he swung a rope, and Wilde decided there was no point in brooding on his identity at this moment. That Catherine was here was sufficient.

"Are these more of Gerald Light's people?" Michelle asked.

"I am assuming that." Wilde sucked air into his lungs as the warp came flying through the air. It was a superb throw, struck the canopy immediately above the vent, and slid down into his hands. Hastily he made it fast to the raft's life lines, just before the tug came. When it did it was violent. The raft seemed to leap out of the waves, and the two girls were scattered across the rubber deck.

"Godalmighty," Michelle cried. "What's happened?"

Wilde had received a mouthful of water and was choking. Catherine had put the helm up again, and her assistant was dragging on the sheets as the catamaran came round into the wind, this time to heave to, dancing down the troughs and racing up the crests, while Catherine sheeted home the main, and then left the helm to join her friend in winching in the hawser.

"Hold on, girls." Wilde had cleared his nostrils. "There is going to be a bump."

"But we can't be seen like this," Michelle said. "Our clothes . . ."

"Are so wet it'll take you half an hour to get them on," Wilde pointed out. "Whereas not twenty feet away are blankets, and soft mattresses, and hot coffee diluted with brandy. Just keep looking to the future, ma'am."

The catamaran loomed above them now, high on a crest, and then slid down the other side with a tremendous rush. "Grab something," Wilde shouted, and a moment later the life raft tilted on its side as the fibreglass hull ploughed into the rubber. It came down again as they threw their weights towards the lifting gunwale, but now there was a hiss of escaping air as the floats were punctured.

"Come on," Wilde snapped, and grabbed Michelle by the arm. He thrust her into the opening, and she hung there, a long sliver of shuddering white flesh looking up at the catamaran, where Paul Fine and Catherine were both peering down at them while the seas slurped around them and a rattle of spray flew across the foredeck.

Paul Fine? Wilde assumed he had been knocked unconscious and was dreaming.

"Give us your arms," Catherine shouted. "My God, you didn't let him take your clothes off?"

Which was a rhetorical question. "I beg your pardon, ma'am," Wilde muttered in Michelle's ear as she still hesitated, placed one hand on each buttock, and pushed. She gave a startled exclamation and shot upwards, was grabbed under the armpits by Fine, and landed on the deck.

"Cathy Light," she said. "Cathy *Light?*"

"It's a small world," Catherine said. "I suppose I had better follow the prevailing fashion and call you Michelle. But welcome on board anyway."

"Can we have the small talk later?" Wilde begged. "Here's another one."

Fine set Michelle on the cockpit sole and released her reluctantly, turning back to do the same for Ilse.

"Now you, Jonas. He's very heavy," she confided to Fine.

Wilde's hands closed on the shrouds, and he pulled himself up, got his knees on to the deck.

"You really are an amazing man," Catherine said. "I had just about given you up for good. Now I'm wondering if you *wanted* to be rescued. But God, it's good to see you, Jonas." She kissed him on the mouth.

"The feeling is entirely mutual, darling." He sat in the cockpit. How good it felt. His own ship, and a ship which could take the worst that the North Sea could throw at it. Properly handled. But he no longer doubted that he was being crewed by experts. "You are just going to have to put me straight about one or two things," he said. "But first, blankets and hot coffee."

"All waiting," Catherine said. "I think you can cut that life raft free, Paul. After all, we don't want to be lumbered with two of the things. And it's nearly flat."

The girls had already gone below and wrapped themselves in the blankets which waited on the saloon table. They sat together, both looking slightly dazed. Wilde found himself a blanket and joined them.

"Coffee coming up," Catherine said from the galley. The catamaran jumped and heaved, dipped and plunged, and Catherine remained as steady as a rock, swaying with the boat, placing cups of coffee on the table without spilling a drop. "And here's the brandy."

Michelle Smith poured her own. "I don't suppose you are going to tell me what you are doing here," she said.

"I'm with Jonas," Catherine said.

"Yes," Wilde said. He gazed at Fine, standing in the hatchway dripping water, smiling at them. "When last I heard of you, the patient was ill."

"As you said, Jonas, those life jackets are almost like bulletproof vests. I've a nasty wound in the chest, but it's only skin deep."

"So?"

"So I realised that we'd had it and hopped over the side. I didn't think it necessary to mention this before, but I'm an excellent swimmer, and while I was under water the tide took me a good distance away from *Nemo*. When I surfaced she was gone in the mist. But by then I was on the edge of the channel, and I found myself amongst those branch things sticking up out of the sand. So I held onto one of them. As a matter of fact, only about half an hour later I was standing up. Of course, I was a bit cold, but . . ."

"You didn't have long to wait," Wilde said.

"Not really. I heard *Nemo* take off, and it wasn't very long after that that Catherine came along."

"Well, it was very lonely, on the other side of that sandbank," Catherine explained. "And Johann kept staring at me."

"I was hoping you'd get around to him."

"Yes," she said. "Well, it's all your fault, really. You didn't do a very good job of tying him up. And you see, because he *was* staring at me all the time I thought I'd change into something a little more decent, you know, and while I was doing that, he got himself free."

"And conveniently jumped overboard."

"Well, no," Catherine confessed. "He seemed to have something else on his mind. Took me quite by surprise."

"You can't stop now, darling."

"Well," she said again. "I used judo, and that sort of thing, and we sort of flopped around and found ourselves out there, and . . . well, to cut a long story short, I *threw* him overboard."

"You threw him overboard," Wilde said.

Michelle Smith was staring at her friend with her mouth open.

"I didn't *mean* to, Jonas. The thing is, he didn't come up, either. Just like Paul, I mean. Do you think he's hanging onto a *boom* somewhere as well?"

"There aren't any in that particular channel," Wilde said.

"Oh. Well, I never saw him again. And by now I was feeling pretty upset. I mean, you can *imagine*." She turned her gaze on Michelle, who nodded and then stared at Wilde, as if uncertain why she had.

"So I started the engines, raised the anchors, and followed the channel round," Catherine said. "I was becoming a little worried about you as well, by now."

Wilde added more brandy to the last of his coffee. "You started the engines, raised the anchor, and motored round the channel," he said slowly.

"I told you, I've been taking lessons. All last winter, in the freezing cold. I wanted to be useful to you, Jonas."

"You managed to conceal the finished article rather well."

She shook her head. "You never gave me a chance. Do you know, you have not offered me the helm once since leaving Calais?"

"You got seasick."

"So did Nelson," she said, quite irrefutably. "And I got over mine quicker than he did. Anyway, to cut a long story short, I heard this shouting, and there he was. Paul I mean." She came as close to giggling as Catherine Light had ever done. "I had quite a shock when I first heard it. I thought it was Johann."

"And the two of you just happened to find your way out here."

"Well, it wasn't too difficult, keeping tabs on *Nemo,* even if she was bursting along. Paul had made a note of the direction in which she had disappeared, and I looked it up on the chart and realised that she must be making for the open sea. I was terribly worried, because we didn't really know whether you were alive or dead, but when Paul told me that the woman on board *was* Zita, I felt sure she wouldn't kill you unless she had to. I mean . . ."

"She's your old school chum," Wilde said.

"Well, yes, she is. I really don't know what can have changed her like this. Mind you, last Friday . . ."

"No girlish gossip right this minute, please, darling. You still haven't caught up with us."

"Oh. Well, I laid a course through the gap. We lost the big boat soon after she made the open sea, but we kept on coming under both engines as fast as we could, and soon we picked up two ships very close together. So, remembering what Johann had told us, we made for them. A gamble, really, but it paid. And then I thought we'd lost you forever when one of the ships turned back for Germany, and the other one started straight out to sea. I decided that the second one was our best bet, so we kept coming in this direction, but we only just managed to stay in radar range. It was blowing up by then, and we set sail. I must say, Jonas, this thing of yours can really travel; even reefed we were knocking back a steady ten knots. But even so, we were no motorboat. I was beginning to worry."

"And then you suddenly stopped and started coming back towards us," Paul said. "Well, not exactly. You seemed to be trying to go in every direction at once."

"The steering cable burst," Michelle said. "Mr. Wilde says it was because we were held on the automatic pilot, beam on."

"I'm so glad," Catherine said, "that you're still calling him Mr., I mean, after all of this."

"Well, my clothes got wet, you see," Michelle explained.

It occurred to Wilde that he was in for a tiring night.

"And then, the blip went and disappeared altogether," Paul said. "And we figured you had had it. But Cathy wanted to keep on for a while, and suddenly we saw that parachute flare."

"And next thing, there you were. Accompanied as usual. But I really am glad to see you, Michelle, safe and sound." Catherine gathered the cups, lurched against the bulkhead as *Regina B* slid down a trough.

"We were rather happy with your appearance, as well," Wilde said. "Now, darlings, I suggest you both retire forward and have a lie-down. Neither of you is looking terribly strong at the moment, and we have the problem of discovering something for you to wear."

"My clothes," Michelle said sharply.

"Were cut adrift in the life raft," Wilde said. "Cathy is good at things like that. I'm sure we shall be able to sort something out. But first thing a good warming nap. Cathy will even lay on some hot soup and a sandwich or two."

"So it's back to the galley," Catherine sighed.

"Up front," Wilde said, as neither Michelle nor Ilse seemed

capable of movement. "You'll find a couple of sleeping bags. And stay there until I call you."

Michelle Smith started to slide out from under the table, and checked. "While you do what?"

"While I get dressed," he said. "I do have clothes, you see."

"I mean, what are you, we, all of us, going to do now?"

Wilde looked at the barometer. The glass was stuck around the nine-ninety mark, suggesting that the drop in the wind might only be temporary. "I'm going to call Norddeich Radio and get a forecast and also see if I can book you a passage home tomorrow morning by the best available means. Then, providing the weather doesn't mean to blow up again before tomorrow morning, we'll close the land. We should be back inside the shelter of the islands by dawn, and you'll be on a plane by lunchtime. That I promise."

Michelle frowned. "What about Zita? And that lot?"

"My business is to get you home."

"Oh no," she said. "Oh no, no, no. I want Zita. I want what Zita has on me. I want to be there when you catch up with her, Mr. Wilde."

"That might take some time. And it wasn't in my contract."

"Then I'll change your contract."

Wilde gazed at her. Certainly she was used to giving the orders; there could be no doubt about that. And equally certainly, providing he could keep Michelle out of trouble, Zita Richmond was very high on his list at this moment; she knew too much, and there were too many unanswered questions floating around her head.

There were also Carl Weber and Oliver Parks, very much on his mind. Piecing together what Zita had said in the cabin of the *Nemo* and what Michelle had told him in the life raft with certain obvious facts about this whole caper, it was very important to discover just what had happened to those two; quite apart from the fact that they were his colleagues.

And how could he face the future with Cathy, which promised to be fairly exciting anyway, without *knowing?*

"I won't get in your way," Michelle promised. "You'll be in

command, Mr. Wilde. Another thing; you don't want to forget that she has fifty million English pounds. That's a lot of the taxpayer's money." She went down the steps into the starboard hull, switched on the radar. Of course, he realised, apart from being colonel in chief of her local ambulance brigade she was probably colonel in chief of the anti-aircraft regiment as well.

He gazed at Ilse Weenink. Ilse shrugged.

"To tell you the truth," Catherine said, "I wouldn't mind a word with Zita, myself."

"If it's what Miss Smith *wants*," Fine said.

"This *is* a busy bit of ocean," Michelle muttered. She leaned forward, elbows on the chart table, the blanket slipping from around her shoulders. "But I think that's an interesting blip."

Wilde leaned over her. His chin touched her hair, but she didn't seem to notice. There were several blips all around them. "Why?" he asked.

"Because when I first spotted it, it was just moving up and down slowly."

"Trawling," he said. "So is that one."

"But now it's suddenly turned for the east, and at a good speed," she said. "They must have decided that we've sunk."

Wilde frowned at the set. "But they didn't mean us to sink. At least, Zita didn't."

"That's what she *said*."

"And I believed her, oddly enough. Anyway, I agree that's the one we should track. On condition you go up front and lie down, ma'am."

She turned her head and then hastily remembered the blanket, and gathered it round her shoulders. And then yawned. "I would like to lie down for a while. Just to relax . . ."

"There's the cabin." Wilde escorted her in. "And I really will try to rustle you up something to wear. But you'll be as snug as a bug in a rug inside that sleeping bag."

Michelle hesitated for a moment, and then shrugged off her blanket and crawled into the sleeping bag. She really was a surprisingly good-looking young woman. But a moment later she was cocooned to the neck. Wilde wrapped a blanket round her.

"You won't forget Ilse," she said.

"She'll be here in a moment."

"She was wonderful," Michelle whispered. "All the time . . . every time . . ."

"You must tell me about it."

The huge eyes opened again suddenly. "You've been pretty wonderful, too, Mr. Wilde," she said, and fell asleep.

(ii)

"Must be nice to be a hero," Catherine remarked. Michelle hadn't realised that the cabin acted as a natural echo chamber.

"Your turn next, Ilse," Wilde said, "before you get the collywobbles again."

Ilse nodded. "Do you really intend to go after the trawler, now?"

"I certainly intend to keep it in radar vision until we can obtain some help," Wilde said. "But just in case we happen to get closer than that, I don't want you to forget that Michelle is strictly your problem."

"I know that, Mr. Wilde. I am sorry I was not more use on board that ship. I have never been so seasick before. I was not sick at all on board *Fair Winds*."

"So in future stick to sail," he suggested. "Off you go."

He saw her into the forecabin, then opened the locker in the chart room and began to get dressed. Catherine leaned on the back of the seat and watched him. Paul Fine leaned in the hatchway and stared at him. And *Regina B* bucked and danced, up and down the waves, constantly running off to windward under the impulse of her mainsail and being brought back again by her backed jib.

"What exactly happened, anyway?" Catherine asked.

"Nothing very dramatic," Wilde said. "But Zita and I did manage to have a chat." He pulled his sweater over his head; how good it was to be warmly clad again. But he never took his gaze from the radar screen. Michelle's choice of blips certainly seemed to be their best bet; it was now forging steadily for

Borkum. "She was willing to trade a little information to put me in the right frame of mind for answering."

"What exactly do you mean?"

He raised his head. "Who invited her to your party?"

Catherine shrugged. "She just turned up. Well, I wasn't going to throw her out. She's . . ."

"Your oldest friend. When last did you see her?"

Again the shrug. "A couple of years, I suppose. You know how easy it is to lose touch. Jonas, would you mind telling me what you are getting at?"

Wilde pulled his nose. "She knows a hell of a lot about our organisation," he said. "In fact, she knows as much about our organisation as any of us do."

Catherine stared at him, a frown slowly gathering between those marvellous eyes. "And you think . . ."

"I don't *think* anything. My business is putting things together. Suppose we list one or two facts. Paul and I have been sent on a very secret mission, which, although we didn't know it at the time, involved your old school chum. So what happens? You appear at Calais and insist on accompanying us."

"I could point out that I not only gave you a gun just now but that without me you'd still be floating around the North Sea," Catherine said rather coldly. "But I won't. I will merely point out that if that's the way you think, you can bloody well get knotted."

She went down the steps to the galley. Wilde gazed at Fine, who obligingly shrugged, and then went behind her.

"Cathy . . ."

The door of her cabin banged in his face. But fortunately there were no locks.

"Would you mind leaving me alone," she said.

He sat beside her on the bunk. "Cathy. I told you when you came on board I'm on a job."

"And the job ranks above everything else. Even if the end of it is kaput for you. You are a fool, Jonas."

"Darling, would you love me if I wasn't that sort of a fool? Wouldn't that just make me a common murderer?"

Her head turned reluctantly.

"So in a situation like this, I'd suspect my own mother, if I had to," Wilde said. "Of course you wouldn't have come chasing behind me if you were working with her. But someone is. Think about it."

"To kidnap Michelle Smith? It just isn't possible, Jonas. We've had ideological defections in the past. You know that as well as I. But that Rodney or that little girl Melanie would do something like this for money . . ."

"And there is nobody else, except Sir Gerald."

"Now, Jonas, that *is* . . ."

"Being absurd. Oh, quite. But keep thinking." He kissed her on the lips. "And believe that I love you. That if you'd been in with Zita, I would have changed sides myself."

She stared at him from a distance of six inches. Then she shook her head slowly. "Not you, Jonas. Not you."

"You believe it. We'd better get on with it. Whatever it is." He got up, opened the door.

"You know," she said. "There *are* other people who know enough about the Elimination Section to do a lot of damage. One or two in the government, one or two in the police . . ."

Wilde hesitated, frowning. "Yeah," he said thoughtfully. "I'll keep that in mind."

He went up the steps into the saloon.

"Now, let me get this straight," Fine said. "You are proposing to track a trawler full of armed baddies, so far as we know, in this fibreglass greyhound."

"We'll keep within radar range," Wilde said. "No closer. Until we're inside the islands. Then we'll try to close them. We'll have to, or we'll lose them. But amidst the islands they'll have to be careful how they react."

Catherine was in the galley, washing coffee cups, back braced against the bulkhead as the ship tossed her head. "I don't remember that they were so very careful last time we were inside the islands. How many would you say are on board?"

"Three left *Nemo*. And there must have been at least two on board the trawler. But I'd say probably one or two more than that."

"Let's settle for six. You are going to wind up with your lovely yacht and all the lovely people on it being shot full of holes. That wasn't what Gerald had in mind. At least for Michelle."

Fine was peering into the radar screen. "The blip is getting towards the edge. We have to do something, or we'll lose them. I don't see that we can come to any harm, just tracking them from a safe distance."

"Well then, you watch the screen," Catherine said. She was still a little bad-tempered. Understandably, Wilde acknowledged. "Jonas and I will do the deckwork."

She meant him. He sighed, pulled on his oilskins, strapped a safety harness around his chest, and went up forward. Catherine took the helm. The seas had definitely moderated with the wind, but they were still breaking, and there were clouds of spray coming over the bows. Still, he supposed the trawler would be making similarly heavy weather of it.

He sheeted the storm jib home on the starboard tack—the wind was still south of west—and joined Catherine in the doghouse. "Wet. I've had enough salt water today to last me the summer."

"Take the helm and I'll make you a drink," she offered.

"Can't be bad." He checked the compass, leaned into the hatch. "How's that blip bearing?"

"Zero one five off the ship's head," Paul Fine called. "But I'm afraid we're losing her."

"She'll be getting into the shelter of the land, and increasing speed a little. Could you look at the chart and see just what she has in mind, old man?" He brought the ship round onto the correct course just south of east. "She has a choice of several gaps."

"She's making south of Borkum," Paul said.

"I think that once she gets beyond the islands we've lost her for good." Catherine propped herself in the hatchway, a mug in each hand. "You'll be out of radar range for a couple of hours, and in that time she could go anywhere."

"So we'll just have to play it by ear."

"If there is one thing about you I admire more than any other, it's your confidence. Here you are acting as if everything is under control when you don't really have a clue. And before, I always thought that everything really *was* under control where you were concerned."

"I'm an optimist," Wilde said. "You'd be surprised how often people do just the thing they shouldn't, but you'd like them to, just because you are upsetting them."

"I say," Paul Fine called up from the chartroom, "do you know that blip we're tracking? It's turned round. It's coming straight back for us."

(iii)

They gave him the helm and huddled in front of the radar screen. There was certainly a ship approaching them on a reciprocal compass bearing. "As they say in the Navy, range fourteen miles and closing," Wilde said.

"So we're making eight knots, and they're probably doing about the same, as they're going into the seas," Catherine said thoughtfully. "Do you realise that's only an hour?"

Wilde looked at his watch. "It's just past midnight."

"Unless we get the hell out of here. I don't want you to think I have cold feet, Jonas, but I have cold feet. Like you said, that's a North Sea trawler with all sorts of iron bands and thick wooden timbers, not to mention, I bet, enough fire power to start a war. We have half an inch of fibreglass. And Michelle. Her safety does come first."

"I wonder what's bringing them back," Wilde said, half to himself. But it certainly wasn't part of his plan to expose Michelle Smith to Zita Richmond's friends all over again, especially out here on the lonely ocean. On the other hand, would closing the coast with the wind about to come back from the opposite quarter be any less dangerous?

"I can tell you what's bringing them back," Catherine said. "They were watching *Nemo* on their screen and she suddenly disappeared, and all they have is this other ship in the area. That could be coincidence, so they hold their course for a while. So this other ship makes every alteration of course they make. So they chat about it and decide that this is worth looking into. After all, you can bet their bottom dollar that they have their radio tuned to two one eight two kilocycles all the time and they know you haven't called any shore station. So they figure that if this *is* you, you're still not interested in making this affair public. They can also see that this isn't a very big ship."

Wilde nodded. She was making sense and even more sense when he added it to his private information. He could imagine quite an argument in the trawler's wheelhouse. Maybe more than just an argument. From the start it had been clear that Dave did not have the faith in a couple of obscene photographs that Zita did, and whatever idealistic plans she may have had, he had no doubt at all that Dave had been well aware that he had been sending *Nemo* into disaster. So whereas Zita might have become upset at the thought that they might have sunk, Dave would be upset at the thought that they might have survived. But from either angle Zita would go along with him now; even her photos wouldn't be much good if Wilde caught up with her before she could use them.

And then there was the other person also in the wheelhouse, who he suspected would know Wilde better than either Zita or her skipper, who would be telling them that they either stopped him now, while he still had to look out for the safety of Michelle Smith, or they didn't stop him at all.

"That seems a reasonable reconstruction," he said. "I think we will alter course just a little, Cathy." He looked up into the wheelhouse. "Come about ten degrees to starboard, will you, Paul? You keep an eye on the screen, and I'll adjust the sheets," he told Catherine.

"Ten degrees isn't going to make much difference," she objected. "They'll still pass us close enough to spit, if they want to."

"It'll help to prove they mean us," Wilde told her. "If they do mean business, they won't want us to close the shore, or even the shipping lane up the banks. Let's give it a few minutes."

He returned to the doghouse, got his binoculars, and swept the horizon. Everywhere he looked there were whitecaps, but now breaking regularly, and no wave seemed much above ten feet, which was rough enough, certainly, but a long way from the huge curling greybeards of a few hours before. Of course they were entering shallow water, and the wind had already shifted; it was about due west, he saw from a look at the compass, and not much above Force Six. Still, were he sailing for fun he'd be much happier turning round and staying out at sea for a while.

There were ships all around them now; they were within twenty miles of the islands and over the shallow bank known as the Borkum Flat; on the port bow he could pick out the flashes of the buoys marking the swept channel up to Denmark, and dead ahead he could see the loom of the Borkum Riff Light Vessel dipping into the waves but coming closer every second. Once south of the light vessel, they would have left the shipping behind.

"She's turning to close," Catherine called.

"Right," he said, and went down to the screen again. Now the light vessel was large. "Course one hundred," he called up to Paul Fine. "Come on, Catherine. We'll loose that mainsail."

Fifteen minutes later *Regina B* was racing along, the wind now on her port quarter; she surged up the waves and seemed to take off on the crests, surfing down the far sides with the needle of her speedometer hovering around ten knots. After the first of these, when the stern of the cat waggled dangerously, Wilde relieved Fine on the helm, sent him down to watch the screen, and asked Catherine to prepare coffee and sandwiches; he didn't want to risk their broaching to in these seas.

"I wish I knew what was going on inside that funny brain of yours," Catherine grumbled. "So now we might just get past them. But they'll alter course again, won't they? I think you *want* to close them."

"On my own terms," Wilde said.

"Um. If we knew her name or her call sign, I'd ring them up and say boo." But he no longer doubted that she was enjoying herself. "Ah well, three coffees coming up."

"You'd better make it four," he suggested, as he watched a blanket-shrouded figure appear in the doorway of the forward sleeping cabin, looming above the concentrating Fine like some reincarnation of Lady Macbeth.

"Oh yeah," Catherine muttered, her bad humour reappearing, and she disappeared into the port hull from whence there immediately came a crashing of crockery. Wilde realised that he was several kinds of a fool; she was probably not the least upset at his appearing to suspect her relationship with Zita—she had been in the business long enough herself. But she was upset at those hours he had spent in the life raft with a nude princess.

Fine allowed Michelle past, and she slowly climbed into the saloon to remain within the hatch, but stood in the doorway, so that she was only a few inches from Wilde as he hung onto the helm.

"I can't sleep," she said. "I suppose I'm just wound right up. I wish I had Ilse's capacity for going out. She's snoring, believe it or not. But I suppose she's exhausted."

"And you're not?"

"Exhausted?" She considered. "Physically. But I'm . . . I'm angry I suppose. With myself, mainly, for causing all this to happen."

"You couldn't have expected it to happen." *Regina B* ducked her bows, and a rattle of spray clouded the windows. Wilde leaned on the helm, and she eased off again.

"Couldn't I? In my position? Oh, there were some very long faces pulled when I told them what I wanted to do this summer. But I felt . . . God, I felt I was being strangled. Can you understand that?"

"No," Wilde said. "My world has necessarily to be an intensely private one. But I can imagine."

"I shouldn't think you can, Mr. Wilde, any more than I can understand yours. I suppose this is just a job of work to you."

"Yes," Wilde said.

"And do you expect to come this close to death every time you go out on a job?"

"That's the job."

"My God. What a way to live. And I thought I had a hard life. I'm surprised you stick at it. How long *have* you been at it?"

"Fifteen years."

"Fifteen *years?*"

"Coffee," Catherine said, appearing beside her. "And sandwiches. Look, Michelle, if you like, Paul and I will look after the ship, and you can take Jonas up front and explain a thing or two."

"I have no idea *what* you're talking about," Michelle remarked.

"Haven't you? Then let *me* try some explaining. You have obviously developed a terrible crush on my boy here. I know, it's not hard to do. It's not that he's particularly good looking. And I can tell you that he's not the loving kind himself. I suppose he touches the mother instinct in all of us women. That's the male's great advantage, you know. His fatherly instincts have to be dragged out of him, in most cases. But if you want so desperately to go to bed with him, now's the time. You'll never have such an opportunity again. And while we're on the subject, I can tell you that he's quite good in bed. Disinterested, you know, but he does all the right things. Puts his hands in all the right places."

"You," Michelle Smith remarked, "seem to be a little upset, Catherine. I wish I knew what you were doing here, anyway."

"That," Catherine said, almost viciously, "is the whole point. Ma'am." She shouldered her way past the princess, went down to the chartroom, and looked over Fine's shoulder. "Target bearing zero six five, range twelve miles, and closing."

"What does she mean?" Michelle asked.

"Our friends are coming back to look for us. I'm afraid they've come to the conclusion that there may be something wrong."

"Oh. Oh, my God."

"Didn't you want to go after them?"

"Well, yes, I suppose I did. But I meant to track them. Until we could call the police or something. I mean, won't their ship be bigger than ours? And there'll be more of them than of us, too."

"Very likely there will. Unfortunately, the police are not on, or I'd have called them long ago. Not only are you supposed to be tucked up in bed in your little palace, but there is the small matter of those photographs. If you really wish it, I can alter course."

"And go where?"

"Name it. If we were to turn out to sea, just for example, we'd be in Harwich by tomorrow morning."

Michelle Smith nodded thoughtfully. "And what alternative do you have in mind?"

"Well, I'm taking what appears to be evasive action. I'm heading south of east, crossing the shipping lanes and making for the empty waters just off the German Islands. It's shoal in there, and no big ship is going to come in. Supposing we get back towards dawn, especially with this wind blowing, it's going to be a *very* empty stretch of water. I could well appear to be making a mistake."

"And you're not? I am glad to hear that. But you think she'll follow us in there?"

"I think the trawler will. I don't think *she* is any longer the operative word."

"And once we're in the shoals, what happens?"

"Let's say I've a hunch I'm a better seaman than Zita or any of her friends. And I'm pretty sure I know these waters better than they do."

Michelle turned, gazed through the spray splattered windshield at the seas. "What's that light?"

"The Borkum Riff Light Vessel. It's about ten miles away."

"Do you know all these lights by heart?"

"Most of them."

"Must be nice to feel so at home in such alien surroundings."

But she wasn't really paying him a compliment, just as she had not really been interested in the name of the light. Michelle Smith, princess, conversing with Jonas Wilde, executioner. He wondered if, incredibly, Catherine in her jealous anger could have made an accurate summation of the situation.

And if that were so, what was he going to do about it? Fortunately, he doubted there was going to be enough time to do anything about it.

"You mean to wreck them," she said, half to herself.

"It's one way of getting them to stay put."

She continued to gaze at the seas. "These will be worse, close in to shore. Somebody could be drowned."

"Somebody probably will. These are not very nice people, Michelle. I'd have thought you'd understand that, by now."

"And that . . ." she sighed. "Do you think I could have another cup of coffee?"

"Just give Cathy a shout. Even if her eyes are shut, she'll be awake."

"I can make my own." She hitched up her blanket, went down the steps to the galley. Wilde checked his compass course, although with the loom of the light vessel showing clear on the port horizon it was easy enough to tell which direction he was taking.

"How are our friends doing?" he called down the hatch.

"Bearing zero three five, range seven miles," Catherine said. "Oh, they're coming behind us, all right. They're altering course to try and cut us off, as a matter of fact."

"They won't make that," Wilde said.

"Maybe not. But I certainly hope we can see what's happening when it happens. What time is sunrise, anyway?"

Wilde looked at his watch. It was just past one. "Another three hours and it'll be twilight." He unhooked his binoculars, leaned his weight on the wheel, and looked to the north. There were endless lights out there. But most of them belonged to merchant vessels making north for the Elbe and Hamburg.

"How." Once again Michelle Smith wedged herself in the hatchway. "I'm trying to say something, you know."

"So shoot."

"I wish you wouldn't use words like that. What I'm trying to say is, I'm sorry, really sorry, to have involved everyone in a mess like this. To have caused the deaths of Carl Weber and Olly Parks. And you say there were two other men as well."

"According to Zita, and I believe her, Olly and Carl are still around. The other two knew what they were risking."

"Oh, how marvellous," she said, with heavy sarcasm. "Oh, God, I don't know why I should be rude to you. It's just that I'm bloody well sick of the whole thing. I mean, if I hadn't been me, I mean, *what* I am, this couldn't have happened. No one would have died at all."

"If you hadn't been what you are, ma'am, you wouldn't have been kidnapped."

"That's what I'm trying to say, stupid. That maybe there's something in real democracy, after all. You know, what a waste of time, kidnapping the secretary of the Russian Communist Party."

"It would cause a stir."

"But would it cause as much of a stir as this? Aren't there always a hundred, a thousand, men waiting to step into his shoes?"

"Don't sell yourself short," Wilde said. "There is only one man, at any time, for any job. And believe me, Michelle Smith, you are not the least bit relevant to the issue. Even if you were a queen instead of just a princess, *you* wouldn't be relevant. It's the principle we object to. Sir Gerald Light objects to. There are ways of doing things, and there are ways not to do things. If you follow me."

"Oh yes." She sighed. "I don't think you've made me feel any better, Mr. Wilde."

"Then I apologise. It's not really my forte, making girls feel better by talking to them."

Her head came up. She really did have very fine eyes. "No, of course it isn't. Your forte is killing people. Isn't it?"

"I'm afraid it is." Wilde studied the compass, glanced over his shoulder. The light vessel was now astern of them. Ahead, in the darkness, there were more lights. But these were still a long way off the land. It was a very clear night. And between even the lights and *Regina B* there was still a lot of water. Relatively shallow water, filled with sandbanks, and the wrecks of ships which had ventured or been driven too close to those sandbanks. He wondered if Michelle Smith really understood the risks he was taking with her life.

"Have you ever killed a woman?"

"Several. Ma'am, your old-fashioned outlook is showing. I'm a liberationist. If they want to be my equal, I'm happy about that. So when it comes to killing, they have to take their chances."

"And of course, they're the more deadly sex. Isn't that what the novelists say?"

"Only when you make the mistake of assuming they're inferior, ma'am. A dangerous man will always be more dangerous than a dangerous woman, so long as you recognise that they are *both* dangerous. It's a plain matter of physical strength."

She nodded. "A very simple point of view. And what do you feel like, Mr. Wilde, when you are killing a woman?"

"Same as when I'm killing a man, ma'am."

"My mistake. Well?"

"*When* I'm doing it? I hate them. I need to hate, to kill. Because I use my hands. Hands are silent, and quick, and clean. And sure, ma'am. But to use your hands, you have to hate."

"My God," she said, half to herself. "And afterwards, Mr. Wilde?"

"Afterwards, ma'am? Afterwards I hate just as much. Only then I hate myself."

"Target now bearing three five five," Fine called. "And range two and a half miles. If you take a look, skipper, you might just pick up her lights."

CHAPTER 8

"Douse those cabin lights," Wilde said. "And the navigation lights, Catherine."

"Isn't that illegal?" Michelle asked.

"You tell me one thing about this business that isn't illegal," he said. "Here. Take the helm for a moment."

"But . . . oh, all right." She removed the blanket from her shoulders, wrapped it round herself under her armpits, like a sarong, and tucked it in between her breasts. Then she took the wheel, with a relieving assurance, while Wilde unhooked his binoculars and studied the horizon behind them. The wind was now definitely north of west, still not more than Force Six, he estimated, which was quite strong enough on this coast. The seas were smaller than earlier, but they were several feet high, and almost every crest was breaking white. To the left he could still see the loom of the light vessel's powerful lamp, and dead aft he thought he could make out a darker shape, occasionally showing as it topped a large wave. In front of the catamaran lights winked from every quarter; the buoys marking the approaches to the Frisians.

"See them?" Michelle asked.

"I'm not sure. But if the radar says they're there, they're there." He leaned into the hatch. "You'd better close that down now for a while, Paul. Just what it's doing to my batteries I hate to think; we've been under sail for too long. Okay, Michelle, I'll take her."

"I must say, I have goose pimples." She leaned against him for a moment. *"Do* you think I could have some clothes to wear?"

"I can let you have a couple of sweaters," he said. "That'll keep out the cold. But the blanket suits you."

"I'll take the sweaters," she decided.

"They're in my locker. Under the chartroom bunk."

"And a brush? Or do you have dandruff?"

"You can borrow Cathy's."

"I'd rather not, right this minute. I'll risk yours."

She went down the steps. Like some sort of one-woman quick-change act, the moment she disappeared Catherine reappeared.

"Seasick again?"

"I don't think she gets seasick very often. Tell Paul to try the box again and see if he can pick up land."

"You know," she said, "you are acting just a little bit anxious."

Fine was studying his screen. "It's there," he said. "Twelve miles."

"Close it down again." Wilde looked at his watch. It was after two, and the night had assumed that utter darkness which means an imminent dawn. With the ship now also in darkness, he could hardly see Catherine's face.

"We'll get there at first light, all right. Any luck astern?"

Catherine used his binoculars, swept the horizon. "Not a goddamned thing. But I'm sure they're there."

"Who isn't? Scared?"

"Apprehensive. You're going to try to mess them about in the shallows? Suppose they don't play?"

"They'll play just long enough, I hope. But when things start to happen, they'll happen quick. It might be a good idea for you to rustle us up some coffee now; we may not have time later on." He leaned into the hatch. "Can you take the helm for a spell, Paul? It's time I did some navigating."

"Will do." Fine pulled on his oilskin jacket, came on deck, took a sweep of the horizon with the binoculars. "Something *there*. I say, that'd only be a couple of miles."

"Less. I thought I saw something too. But they must be just as worried as we are. Anyway, keep your eyes open."

He went below, leaned on the chart table, switching on the low powered chart light, and spread the Admiralty Chart of the area Friesche Zeegat to Die Jade in front of him. The starboard single bunk was situated half under the table, and Michelle Smith knelt beside him; she had removed her blanket and put on his sweater instead; it came just below her thighs.

"Where are we?"

"That's what I mean to find out, exactly. It's rather urgent at this point, wouldn't you say?"

He plugged in his direction finder, turned to three hundred and eight kilocycles, and almost immediately picked up, very loud and clear, the dash-dot-dot-dot, dot-dot-dash-dot signal of the Borkum Riff Light Vessel. "Bearing zero four five magnetic," he muttered, turning the aerial until the signal faded.

"I'll do it." Michelle scribbled on the scratch pad. "I make that zero four zero true." She laid it off with the parallel rule on the chart. "What's next?"

"The Texel Light Vessel and the Elbe Number One Light Vessel in this sequence. But we'll skip them." His fingers drummed on the table. "We want the Terschelling signal."

Michelle studied the line she had drawn; *Regina B* was somewhere on it. "That's an awfully messy-looking piece of water. Are those *all* wrecks?"

"I'm afraid so. Mostly left over from the last war. We're bang in the estuary of the Wester Ems. Should be crossing the Emden shipping lane in a few minutes. Here's Terschelling." Dash-dash-dash-dot went the signal. Dash-dash-dash-dot. Wilde turned the aerial slowly, waited for the bleeps to fade, kept on turning until they started again, brought it back until they faded once again. "The null bears two six zero magnetic. Hello, we're closer in than I thought."

"That's two six five true, near as damn it." Michelle drew another line and then marked a circle where the two lines crossed. "We are there."

"That's not quite good enough for this one, ma'am. We have to be dead sure. There's another beacon on Ameland Island." He turned his frequency control. "Two nine four kilocycles, if I remember rightly."

"There," Michelle said.

Dot-dash-dash-dot-dot went the signal.

"Two zero zero magnetic," Wilde muttered.

"Two zero five. I say," Michelle said with some pleasure. "What a perfect bearing. We *are* there." Her third line neatly bisected the circle, leaving only the smallest of cock hats in the centre. "Ugh."

The chart was nothing but a mass of light buoys marking the positions of the various wrecks.

"It is a pretty gloomy prospect," Wilde agreed. "And inside that there is a mighty sandbank called the Wierumergronden. But there's a passage through it, called the Friesche Zeegat." He placed his finger on the chart. "There."

"How nice," Michelle said. "It doesn't seem to be lighted, except for the bay buoy."

"And that light tower. It's unmanned, but it gives a good signal. Once we pick those two up we'll be all right. It'll be daylight in another hour."

"I wish I could look forward to that," she said, half to herself.

He turned, his shoulder brushing hers. Their faces were only inches apart.

"Chin up," he said. "And you have the chin for it."

She smiled. "It's a family characteristic." She put her left hand on the back of his head and brought him forward. Her mouth was open, and her tongue was strong and eager. And surprisingly experienced.

Her eyes remained open and wider than ever. Her head moved back an inch or two. "For God's *sake*," she whispered. "Don't just sit there."

"Did anyone ever tell you," Wilde said, "that you are a first-class navigator?"

"No," she said.

His hands slipped on the sweater as she came back to him; a moment later they touched bare flesh. But this was of course impossible. At this moment she was nothing more than a frightened girl.

"Coffee and sandwiches," Catherine said from above them. "If you can spare the time to eat."

"And a lot of shipping dead ahead," Fine called.

"That's the Terschelling Swept Channel." Wilde released her

reluctantly. "You'd better put the navigation lights on again, Cathy."

"Won't that help Zita to pick us up?"

"She's got us on her radar anyway, darling. And if we choose we can lose her again amongst those ships. Michelle, do you think you could get Ilse up? There's another sweater in there she can wear, and I want you to add life jackets. You too, Cathy. And Paul."

"You think it's going to be that dangerous?" Catherine asked.

"From here on in, anything can happen." He put on an orange life jacket himself and relieved Fine on the helm. Another sweep aft revealed nothing but the flashing light buoys astern. The trawler could be anywhere behind them. But she was there.

And now there was the shipping lane ahead to be negotiated. A steady stream of coasters and small merchantmen making their way north on the tide. They were perhaps twenty miles west of the Hubertgat; amazing to think that they had been here just twenty-four hours before as well. Then there had been thick mist and an almost holiday atmosphere. And he had never met Michelle Smith.

A gust of wind threatened to tear the wheel from his hands. This was no time for day-dreaming; they were almost amidst the ships, and he had to alter course to starboard to get around the stern of the first of them.

Catherine joined him in the doghouse. "There," she said.

He looked over his shoulder. Amidst the forest of flashing light buoys there had appeared three more lights, fixed, a red and a green separated by a white steaming light in the centre. Zita, or whoever was in command of the trawler at this moment, was also obeying the rules.

"Take her for a moment," he said. "Mind that chap over there."

He focussed the binoculars, but it was still too dark to make out anything much beyond the darker darkness of the ship. She was painted in a dark colour, as well, which made sense. But when he replaced the glasses in their case, and again looked to the east, it was to see the blackness become streaked with faint threads of pink.

"How utterly beautiful," Catherine whispered. "I love dawn, at sea. Jonas, were you and Michelle really necking down there?"

"She's a little overwrought."

"There's an understatement," Catherine said. "But my God . . . I mean, I knew what she wanted. But it never occurred to me that she'd do something about it. Or that you would let her."

"I won't and she won't," Wilde said. "You may take my word for it."

"I'm glad you said that. You don't want to forget that I'm a little overwrought myself."

The next freighter gave a poop-poop on her horn to indicate that she was going to port, and Wilde altered course once again. Then they were on the far side of the channel, with nothing but the pink-streaked blackness ahead of them, except for a single flashing light on the port side.

"That'll be the tower," he said. "There should be another light just beyond it, marking the entrance to the gap itself. The buoy is marked VMG when we get up to it."

"There," Catherine said.

There was another gust, and *Regina B* seemed to shake herself. The wheelhouse suddenly became full of people; Michelle and Ilse, both wearing life jackets over their sweaters, and Paul Fine, also life-jacketed and for the first time looking a little nervous.

Wilde glanced over his shoulder. The trawler was through the line of ships as well now and forging steadily on, but not at this moment really closing, as the wind freshened. And the ships were vanishing into the darkness as the winking passage buoys came closer ahead. Presumably Zita's friends could see them as well as anyone else.

"Okay, folks," Wilde said. "I think it's time for action stations."

(ii)

"What do you want us to do?" Michelle asked.

"I want you and Ilse to go below, retire up front again, and sit tight. Only come up if one of us three calls you. I'm serious about this, Michelle. All hell is going to cut loose very shortly, and I won't have time to worry whether you are in the line of fire or not."

"Yes." She hesitated. "I wish we could be of more use."

"You're not dressed for it." He waited for them to duck down the steps, and then closed the hatch and the doorway.

"Ugh," Catherine said. "It's cold out here. I say, do you realise we're holding them?"

"Drawing away, if anything," Fine said.

"And that we don't want," Wilde said. "They still have time to change their minds and pull out, and we want them to feel that they have a chance of catching us and running us down. Paul, release your mainsheet."

"Eh? But . . ."

"It's not light enough to see properly yet. They'll think we've parted something." He closed one eye. "But keep the end in your hand, old son, will you? We don't want to lose the mast."

"Aye, aye," Fine agreed. He moved aft, flicked the sheet out of the jam cleat, and let it run. The mainsail boomed away to starboard as the wind suddenly discovered it was free. *Regina B* gave a leap through the water, and the boom crashed against the shrouds.

"Hold onto it," Wilde bellowed, and put the helm up. The catamaran sluiced round through the next wave and came up into the wind, facing the trawler. "Now get out there and fuss," Wilde told Catherine. "But don't bring her in yet."

The noise was suddenly tremendous. The wind howled in the rigging, the seas slapped against the hulls and thumped in between, and came flying over the doghouse as rattling spray, and the mainsail was making a noise like a gigantic ouija board. He was taking a risk that it would tear a batten pocket and perhaps split the sail itself, but there could be no doubt that *Regina B,* now practically hove to, was giving every indication of a ship in trouble.

The trawler came surging out of the north, suddenly enormous as she approached, showing no lights, revealed principally by the bow wave she was carving through the slurping green water.

"All right," Wilde told Catherine. "Bring it in."

The catamaran was falling away on the starboard tack. Catherine leaned on the rope, and the boom started to come in. Wilde put the helm down, and *Regina B* began to turn, about to commence one of the most difficult and dangerous of all manoeuvres in a strong wind, the gybe.

"Easy now," he told Catherine. "Easy. Bring her in."

Round went the ship, slapped on the beam by a larger than usual wave, which heaved her up but could not upset the basic stability of the big cat.

"Get your boom amidships," Wilde shouted.

Catherine tugged harder, now assisted by Fine, and the boom came in, while the sail, now again filled with wind, ballooned above their heads and the ship trembled as every inch of standing rigging hummed under the strain.

The stern swung into the wind, which came roaring through the doghouse and whistling into the cabin. *Regina B* plunged forward, dipping her bows into the seas, suggesting a real possibility that she would trip and somersault.

"Let her go," Wilde yelled, and the mainsheet raced through its blocks and through Catherine's fingers as well. The stern continued on its way through the eye of the wind, and the catamaran gathered way again, seeming to leap forward as if propelled from a gun.

And at that same moment, from behind them, there *was* the explosion of a gun, carried forward on the wind. Wilde glanced over his shoulder in time to see the flashes of two more reports.

"Ow," Catherine said. "Now that is not very nice. Especially as we can't return."

"We're not quite bereft," Wilde said. "Paul, nip down into

the chartroom. You'll find a Very pistol and a box of cartridges. Bring them up."

"A Very pistol?" Fine demanded.

"A signal gun, stupid. It's better than nothing. Hurry, now. Cathy, belay that sheet and get below. I want to know if we were hit."

"Aye, aye," she said, and hastily cleated the mainsheet. Her oilskin cap had come off and her hair streamed in the wind; her face was wet with a combination of flying spray and sweat. She lurched past him and half fell down the steps into the port hull.

Paul reappeared, clutching the thick-barrelled pistol and the box of red and white flare cartridges. "I don't see what I'm supposed to do with this thing," he grumbled. "It doesn't have any sights."

"You'll have to use the big-gun technique. But don't aim too high; we don't want to attract a lifeboat."

Once again the explosions drifted dimly across the water, but this time they were met with a *pfft* from close at hand, as Fine, holding the Very pistol in both hands, returned fire.

"Well?" Wilde asked.

"It sort of nose-dived under their bows," Fine said. "I'll have to raise the trajectory."

"So get on with it," Wilde suggested. "What you want to do now is pop one through the wheelhouse windows. That'll shake them up."

By now *Regina B* was gathering way again, and the flashing lights of the bar buoy and the tower were close at hand; in the steadily improving light it was even possible to make out the grey shape of the tower itself. Land was only a few miles away beyond the curtain of ending night and already there was a suspicion of a mist creeping across the water.

Catherine reappeared in the hatchway. "Nothing wrong down there that I can see. They must be pretty poor shots."

"Pretty optimistic shots," Wilde said. "At least one of those big noises is an M-16, which isn't really very effective beyond three hundred yards. But they'll get closer."

Paul Fine placed another cartridge in the breach of the Very pistol, snapped it shut. "Too high," he said. "But we're losing them again."

"Take a look in the echo sounder," Wilde said.

"Nine fathoms," Fine said.

"And we're in the channel. That'll mean at least twelve feet over the banks at this moment. Get on those sheets." He put the helm to starboard, and *Regina B* gybed once again to leave the channel and go screaming on a broad reach across the sandbanks. Now the motion was entirely different, a series of short, steep, crashing wavelets, every one crested, splashing around the bows. They could almost feel the sand beneath them.

"They're coming," Fine said. "And cutting the corner."

The light tower was very close now, a solid grey mass rising out of the waves. *Regina B* passed it not fifty yards to windward, and Wilde glanced over his shoulder. The trawler had altered course the moment he had and was considerably closer. It was almost light now, and he looked at a high-bowed, black painted vessel, her sides streaked with rust to make her exactly like any other hard-working fishing boat, with a huge windowed bridge deck and a steadying sail aft. She leapt and plunged through the waves, but even as he watched there was a flash of light from one of the windows, and he thought he saw the splash not twenty yards astern. But perhaps he was dreaming; the entire morning was a mayhem of green and white waves, tumbling here and there, confused by the sudden alterations in the sea bed which left them thundering against each other, leaping around the light tower and dragging the channel buoys over onto their sides. In the strongest contrast, the sky above was a solid wall of grey which seemed to extend down to the surface of the sea in every direction, like a celestial curtain. Wilde figured visibility was already down to four hundred yards, and closing.

As was the trawler on this course.

"Gybe," he bawled, and round went the helm again. *Regina B* responded with all her usual life; Catherine and Fine brought the sheets home on the starboard cleats, and away the catamaran boomed on the port reach, gaining speed again as she hurtled northwards. But as she did so there was another flurry of red flashes from the bridge of the trawler, and they could feel the ship shudder.

"Oh my God," Catherine said, "we've been hit."

From below there came a cry of alarm from Ilse Weenink.

"Take the helm," Wilde snapped, and brushed past her as he pulled open the door and ran down the steps. "Keep her as she is." The galley was on the port side, and he saw the damage immediately. The bullet had ripped through the outer fibreglass skin, ricochetted through the larder underneath the sink, and torn open the sliding doors before embedding itself in the inner fibreglass hull. With the ship on her present course the hole was several inches above the boot topping, but water was spurting through with every slapping wave.

"What's happened?" Michelle Smith peered at him through the windows leading to the forecabin.

"We stopped one. But it's not too serious right this minute. Stay put." He went up to the wheelhouse. Catherine leaned on the wheel, but her face was pink with exertion. Fine watched the trawler, which was coming round behind them. Now the buoys once more rushed towards them; they were inside the tower and crossing the channel at right angles, and a glance to the east showed him a dark line of sand perhaps a mile away, with a ripple of white surf breaking on the beach. At least, so far as he remembered, there were no rocks over there. And the tide was falling.

"What happens now?" Catherine asked.

"Keep her as she is." He went below again, checked the chart; the water was shallower on the north side of the channel.

"I don't like this, Jonas," Catherine called. Her voice actually trembled.

He popped his head into the hatch again; there were steep waves ahead, and the crests were flying. But the trawler was closing again, and again there were the red flashes. From above his head there came a tremendous crack, and pieces of broken glass shattered on to their heads and shoulders.

"Oh my God," Catherine cried, "the windscreen's gone."

"Better visibility," Wilde pointed out. "Discourage them, Paul."

Fine fired, reloaded, and fired again. The glowing rockets arced through the air and disappeared into the waves beside the trawler; he had the trajectory right at last, even if his aim was off.

"Give me that thing." Wilde took the pistol, reloaded, and watched another burst of flame explode from the bridge window, now not three hundred yards away. Instinctively he half ducked as Fine gave a cry of agony and hit the deck.

"Oh my God," Catherine said for the third time. "Are you all right?"

"This just isn't my week," Fine groaned.

"Hold on." Wilde fired, reloaded, fired, reloaded, fired again. He was too far away to see what he had accomplished, but for a few short seconds the trawler was bathed in light, and he was sure at least one of the rockets had landed on deck. For the moment, at any rate, there was no more firing.

He stuck the pistol into his waistband, and dragged Fine into the cabin. This time he had stopped the bullet in the right thigh; it was a nasty wound, and there was no question of his walking for a while, but Wilde did not think it would prove fatal, providing the bleeding could be stopped.

"If this keeps up, you are going to resemble a sieve," he remarked. "Come on, Michelle. You too, Ilse. Back to the nursing bit. But for God's sake keep out of the doorway."

They came scrambling aft as there was another crunch from hull. Below decks it sounded very loud and was accompanied by a nasty crackling sound.

"Jonas," Catherine wailed, and *Regina B* did a series of leaps as she found herself back amongst the sandbanks.

Wilde hurried on deck. The trawler seemed very close. Far too close. But she was still in the channel, and he could see without using the echo sounder that the catamaran was in very shallow water.

"Stand by to go about," he said. "Now. Put your helm down. Gybe."

The bows came round as Catherine twisted the wheel. The boom came amidships, was held there by Wilde's straining muscles, and then released as the wind began to fill the sail from the starboard side. *Regina B* gathered way again.

"Stay in the shallows," Wilde said. "Make for the beach."

"The beach? But . . ."

"Do it." Wilde watched the trawler. She had crossed the channel, was altering course to close them again. Now he could see three heads in the wheelhouse, although, as they were all wearing oilskins and southwesters, he couldn't identify anyone. But one of them was bracing his elbows on the window, holding the rifle to his shoulder. Wilde reloaded the Very pistol, propped himself against Catherine, gripped the gun in both hands, sighted down the barrel, raised the trajectory to allow for the curve of the rocket, and squeezed the trigger. The rocket sizzled away and burst on the wheelhouse windows. "A hit," he yelled delightedly.

Certainly the marksman had disappeared, and there was a great deal of movement on the bridge.

"Jonas," Michelle called, "we're making an awful lot of water."

Wilde ran below. The galley was a mess where three more bullets had sliced through the fibreglass and smashed into the wooden cupboards. The catamaran was heeling very little, even pushed by the strong wind, but she was plunging enough to keep the bullet holes awash, and steady streams of water were forming on the decking.

"And she's such a lovely ship," Ilse commented. She had at least got over her seasickness.

"She'll survive," Wilde said. "I can fill all those holes in half an hour. When I can find the half an hour."

"Jonas." Catherine had switched on the echo sounder. "There's only six feet of water."

"So we won't sink very far."

Behind him the rifle was cracking again, and a series of holes appeared in the boomed out mainsail.

Wilde climbed into the wheelhouse and reloaded. "Either he doesn't have an echo sounder himself, or they're too wrapped up in us. It would be a good idea to keep it that way."

He fired, reloaded, and fired again. Now he had the range just right; both rockets burst in front of the wheelhouse, showering the trawler with sparks, and she turned to port, away from the channel. But suddenly she seemed farther away, as she reduced speed. Someone *had* noticed the depths. Wilde sent another rocket screaming across the water, threw the pistol in the doorway. "Michelle, reload that for me, if you will. Give me the helm, Cathy."

"I won't say no to that." She held onto the bulkhead. "I feel as if I've been through the wringer. Jonas. That's a beach."

Although he figured the mist had thickened—the tower was already out of sight behind them—there was brown sand appearing everywhere ahead. Presumably there was land somewhere behind it.

"Dive into that stern locker," he told Catherine. "And you'll find the kedge anchor. There's twelve fathoms of warp already attached. When I say the word, you heave it over. Make the warp fast to the cleat first, mind you."

"Oh, marvellous," she said. "I've been taking lessons in seamanship, remember? Although I must say, dropping anchors is supposed to be man's work, according to my instructor."

"Get on with it," Wilde suggested.

She stepped out of the wheelhouse, was driven back by another fusillade of shots. Holes appeared all over the cockpit.

"Aaagh," Catherine squealed. "They mean business, Jonas."

"So drop that bloody anchor," he bellowed; the echo sounder was showing four feet. They coasted up the next wave and down the crest on the farther side, and touched the bottom with a jar which shattered crockery in the galley and brought a cry of alarm from the girls. Catherine crawled across the cockpit, pulled open the aft locker, took a turn on the cleat with the warp, and threw the plough anchor over the side. Wilde listened to the deadly chatter from astern, but now was no time for looking or worrying where the bullets might be flying. The beach was not fifty feet away, and shelving steeply. He sucked air into his lungs. "Catherine," he shouted, "drop the mainsail."

"Oh, for God's sake," she cried, but she clambered on to the coach roof, crawled forward, and released the halliard. Wilde left the helm for a moment, ran aft, and heaved on the mainsheet to bring the boom amidships and spill some of the wind. The catamaran grounded again, bounced, and settled, held by the straining warp as the kedge anchor bit deep into the sand. But the mainsail was clouding down and Catherine, revealing some more of her recent training, had also released the jib halliard; she was completely obliterated by collapsing sail.

Wilde had time for another quick look over his shoulder. The trawler had realised her danger and turned away, but fractionally too late. As her helmsman put the wheel hard over and she swung broadside to the rollers, a larger than usual wave caught her amidships and she lost way for an instant. Her stern swung round, and even across the howl of the wind Wilde could hear the crunch as her rudder and propellers hit the sand. She shook, lifted, and was then thrown sideways again, heeling onto her port beam while he watched people tumbling across the wheelhouse like scattered ninepins. She was there for the day.

(iii)

Wilde scrambled forward, leapt over the bows with the main Danforth anchor in his arms. He landed in waist-deep water, unpleasantly cold, which promptly filled his sea boots and made movement difficult. But he scrambled up the beach clear of the water, and stamped the anchor into the sand. The cat was safe for the time being, and as he had told the girls, patching holes in fibreglass was a very simple business, supposing he could settle with the crew of the trawler before the tide started to rise again.

He stood for a moment gazing up the beach into the mist.

He *thought* he could see bushes some distance to his left. But the tide went out so far over these sandbanks it was difficult to decide, and it would be highly dangerous to walk in the wrong direction.

On the other hand, it would hardly be as dangerous as remaining within range of the trawler's fire power unnecessarily. He turned to look at the stranded ship. She lay on her side, battered by each wave. It would be half an hour before the sea would have gone down sufficiently to let anyone fire from her decks with any accuracy. Thirty minutes. But then, with both ships still, *real* accuracy would be possible.

He ran back to *Regina B.* Catherine was just emerging from beneath the mainsail, puffing and scooping hair from her eyes. "My God," she said, "what a trip. If I had known . . ."

"Get the girls up," Wilde said. "The oars for the dinghy are in the aft locker. Bring them on deck." He held onto the stanchions of the handrail, swung himself back on board, stamped water from his boots and pants, made his way aft.

"Jonas? But what's happened?" Michelle stood in the wheelhouse, staring at the trawler.

"We're on the beach, intentionally, and our friends are on the beach, accidentally. They can't get off for several hours and they can't wade ashore for a little while either, because they still have better than six feet of water around them. But you can. And better had. When next they get around to opening up that rifle there is going to be a lot of dodging to be done. Come on now. Let's have the old girl-guide bit."

The oars were laid on the deck, and he made a mattress of warps, secured at each end of each oar and then tied crosswise. On this he laid two blankets. "Will you girls get ashore now, please, and I'll pass this lot down to you."

Almost instinctively they lined up: Catherine, tall and gangling and wet, sodden black hair plastered to her head; Ilse, small and blond and anxious, her face paler than ever; and Michelle, taller even than Catherine, her dark hair dried and neatly waving once again, her face serene.

Catherine was first to look over the side. "Ugh," she said, "it's wet."

"Use the bow; there's only a couple of feet up there." The three of them dropped over the bows with a succession of plashes. Wilde handed them the stretcher. "Get up the beach."

He returned aft, gazed at the trawler. They were attempting to lower a boat, and had swung the davits out to the listing starboard side; now the dinghy hung just above the waves, with one person in it, and three others heaved at warps on deck. Those were very long odds, and he did not suppose he was looking at the full crew.

The catamaran was quiet now; although each wave still broke against the stern, she did no more than shudder to the big ones. He went into the cabin. *Regina B* was a shambles below decks, with water slurping ankle deep in each hull, having come in through the bullet holes while they had been on the water line and unable to run back out now that the sea had receded, with the fibreglass splinters caused by the bullets themselves scattered everywhere. In the midst of the confusion lay Paul Fine. Catherine had done a splendid job on his chest, even if she must have used the entire contents of the First Aid Box; he was totally enclosed in bandages from his neck down to his navel, although why they had found it necessary to undress him completely to attend to his thigh, Wilde could not figure. With what had been left in the way of bandages, Michelle had also strapped up his legs, and he was beginning to resemble a mummy. She had also, apparently, fed him all the morphine she could find, for he was unconscious. Which, Wilde decided, was just as well.

With great care Wilde scooped him from the floor, thanking his good fortune that Fine was a little man, and then made his way up the cabin steps into the cockpit.

Behind him, the dinghy from the trawler hit the waves. The wind brought him shouts of alarm as she bounced, settled in the next trough, and rode against the side of the ship, while the following wave broke over her stern. But the boat was launched, and it was only a short ride to the beach. They had to be stopped. If possible.

He laid Fine on the deck, ran back to the cabin, and picked up the Very pistol. A second oilskin clad figure was slowly lowering himself, or herself, from the deck of the trawler. Wilde took careful aim, made every possible allowance for trajectory and wind, and fired. The rocket hit the water beside the dinghy, but the hissing splash caused the new crew to lose his grip, and he tumbled in. The man already on board released the painter, and the boat drifted away from the side of the ship. The two people left on deck were shouting and gesticulating.

Wilde had already reloaded, and his next shot dropped into the dinghy itself. He was becoming quite a good shot with his unusual weapon. And this one worked wonders. The dinghy had drifted well away from the shelter of its parent without being yet under control. Now as both its crew leapt the same way to escape the ball of fire which had joined them, the little boat was struck amidships by a curling roller and a moment later was capsized. They'd be occupied for the next few minutes, anyway.

Wilde picked up Fine and made his way forward, swaying in the wind. Ilse and Catherine had carried the stretcher ashore, but Michelle remained up to her knees in the frothing water, waiting for him. He laid Fine on the deck, swung himself down beside her, and then reached back up for the injured man. Slowly they inched Fine over the hull and caught him as he fell forward into their arms.

"Okay," Wilde gasped, "go get the stretcher."

He peered round the side of the hull. The dinghy still floated upside down, even farther away from the trawler. One man still clung to it; apparently he could not swim. The two people on deck were busily throwing him a lifebelt at the end of a long line. But the second member of the dinghy's crew *was* swimming, towards the shore. Wilde turned to peer towards the shore, but still the mist clung to the horizon not farther than a quarter of a mile away, and there was nothing up there that he could see which even vaguely resembled cover.

The girls had come back with the stretcher. "Now," he said, placing Fine on the blankets, "you three beat it. Keep on going until you come to civilisation."

"But," Ilse said, "where do we go?"

"Keep the wind on your backs and you're walking southwest. Remember that. But I think you want to keep it on your left shoulder and make sure the sand is rising all the time. I'll follow your tracks whenever I can."

"You're not serious," Michelle said. "We're not exactly dressed for civilisation."

"Just keep the sweaters pulled well down and they look like miniskirts," Wilde assured her. He held her shoulders for a moment. "Don't let me down, ma'am. I can't stop this lot worrying about where you happen to be at the moment."

"But you mean to stop this lot."

"It's the job, remember?"

She nodded thoughtfully and turned and hefted one end of the stretcher. "Come on, Cathy."

"You have Ilse," Catherine objected.

"Now look here," Wilde said.

"You seem to forget that I'm the boss's wife," Catherine pointed out. "I have to be humoured. For God's sake, Jonas, I was in at the beginning. If you don't mind, I'll be in at the end, too."

"You might just need help," Michelle said. "I wish I could stay as well."

"But it's your duty to go," Wilde said.

She nodded, her lower lip sucked in between her teeth. Then she turned, waited while Ilse picked up the back of the stretcher, and staggered up the sand. In moment they were lost in the mist.

CHAPTER 9

"What happens now?" Catherine asked.

Wilde peered round the bow of the catamaran. The attempts of the people on the trawler to regain the dinghy had been unsuccessful; it had drifted out to sea and was almost lost to sight, presumably with the man still clinging to it. But that meant one less to worry about. Because this was, after all, what he was employed to do. To kill. And these people had put themselves beyond the pale of the law. His law.

But the other man was already in the shallows, splashing wearily to his feet and staggering up the beach. And now Wilde could recognise him. It was Dave.

"Sit tight," he told Catherine. "Get the Very pistol and prepare to make yourself a nuisance to the chaps on board."

He left the shelter of the cat, raced down the beach. Someone on board the trawler saw him, because he heard shouts. But no shots; they had left the rifle on the bridge.

Dave also heard him, and checked, ankle deep in water, exhausted with swimming through the surf while wearing a heavy sweater and sea boots. But there was a pistol tucked into his belt, and he reached for the weapon, dragged it clear, and brought it up. Too late. Wilde had already taken his seaman's knife-lockspike-unshackler from his pocket and opened the blade. Now he checked, steadied himself, right arm drawn back, and as Dave raised the pistol, the gleaming steel whipped through the air. Dave took the knife in the centre of the chest and tumbled backwards, hitting the water with a tremendous splash. Wilde dived beside him, scrabbling under the shallow surface to regain the pistol.

The rifle exploded from the bridge of the trawler. Wilde

never knew where the bullet went. He found the pistol, scrambled to his feet, feeling remarkably naked, and was reassured by the soft bang from behind him and the burst of the starshell over the trawler. The next shot from the rifle was equally wide of its target, as the ship was buffeted by another wave, and a moment later Wilde was slithering across the sand into the shelter of the catamaran.

Catherine's face was pale. "Is he . . ."

"We're in this thing for keeps, darling," Wilde gasped. "Here." He gave her the pistol. "You haven't forgotten how to shoot, I hope."

"Of course not. But I shouldn't think I'm as good as you."

"It's the thought that counts. Remember there are only nine shots in there. Just keep them going, one every few seconds, at the trawler's bridge. And when they run out, start up the Very pistol again."

"While you do what?"

"I want to get out to the ship. We'll never stop those two blokes from here." He pulled off his boots.

"But . . ."

"I'm going to be swimming, darling."

"Yes, but why can't we just keep them pinned down until . . ." she frowned.

"You were saying? They have more ammunition than we do, and we don't have the option of time. I want to be out of here on the next tide, and before the mist lifts. So keep shooting. Like now."

He left the shelter of the cat before she could argue any more, splashed through the shallows, caught a long breath, and then dived deep to the bottom of the shallow sea, clinging close to the sand for several long seconds and working his way to the left. Water drummed at his ears, and many other sounds, but they had all merged into a general growl. And his lungs were bursting. He kicked down, pushed against the sand, and surfaced. Now he was out in the surf, which immediately picked him up and rolled him over, but gave him the time to take another breath before diving into the following wave—all, he figured, without being spotted by the people on the trawler.

He was in deeper water now, perhaps five feet or more; the ship was not far away. And the man with the rifle, having lost him, would not be at all sure where to look or whether it was worth looking at all. Wilde skimmed the bottom, eyes searching the sand-filled gloom, and saw the huge bulk of the trawler only a few yards distant. He came up, brought his head above the water, and gasped for breath. Above his head the rifle fired, and again, but not at him. And there was no answering fire from the shore. He thought, oh God, and wanted to turn. But to give up now would not help Cathy, and this was what he had come for.

He was in against the rust-streaked iron hull, treading water, his feet touching the sand in every trough as the waves surged past the stranded vessel. The rail was only a few feet above his head, and he could reach it in a single thrust. But once that was done he really would be out in the open. And there was no sound from above him, at this moment.

He looked towards the beach while he sucked air into his lungs. The cat was almost dry now, with just a ripple of surf still playing around her stern. She looked almost embarrassed; the shattered windows of the doghouse suggested a gap-toothed grin. There was no sign of Catherine.

Astern of the yacht, face down in the wet sand, lay Dave. Each wave covered him, but soon he too would be derelict on the beach.

And then, to his horror, he did see Catherine. She stepped away from the shelter of the cat, apparently unharmed. Wilde stared at her for a second and then looked up. Yves stood above him, a pointed boathook in his hands, smiling as he watched Wilde, preparing to drive the wooden harpoon down the moment Wilde raised himself from the sea.

From the bridge, the rifle exploded. But it was lost in a perfect flurry of shots from the beach. Catherine had used her head and saved her entire magazine for just this moment. One bullet pinged off the iron hull with a gigantic noise, and another struck the water not very far from Wilde. But at least three hit Yves. He turned away from Wilde, gazed at the beach with an expression of surprise, while the boathook slipped from his hands. It came down the side of the trawler, missing Wilde by inches, and Yves, overbalancing, followed it. His body struck the water beside Wilde, raised a splash, and went down. But now was the moment. Wilde's fingers locked around the rail, and with a single vault he was on board.

The deck was empty. The firing had stopped, and the trawler might have been deserted, a ship of the dead. He turned his head to give a last glance at the beach before boarding. Catherine had disappeared again. She had regained the shelter of the cat, and to do that she had to be unharmed. His heart gave such a tremendous surge of relief he felt physically sick. And then he did feel physically sick, for out of the mist beyond the yacht there walked Michelle Smith, gazing at *Regina B,* and no doubt at Catherine, at the trawler beyond, hesitating, wondering . . . above him the trawler suddenly came to life. The rifle opened fire with more haste than accuracy, and a stream of shots scattered across the sand, licking miniature dust clouds into the air.

Michelle checked, her whole body a picture of confusion. There was a flash of flame from the side of the cat as Catherine fired her last bullet at the trawler, and then she was out from shelter, running up the beach, shouting at the bemused girl, her long hair flowing behind her in a black cascade, her red nylon oilskins making a splash of colour against the drabness of the beach.

"Christalmighty," Wilde muttered. It was almost a prayer. In front of him was the short ladder to the open wheelhouse door. And the rifle had ceased firing, for the moment. Wilde checked at the foot of the ladder, looked back at the beach.

Michelle Smith stood, legs apart, hands held in front of her as if she too was praying. She watched Catherine, who had dropped her pistol, and staggered. As Wilde watched, the stagger became a droop, and she landed on her hands and knees, while the sand around her turned dark.

Michelle stepped forward, and the rifle fired again. Wilde took the steps in two bounds, burst in the door, feet first, struck the heavy-set, dark-haired man on the shoulder with his heels, sent him flying down the sloping cabin. His elbow struck the wheel and the rifle was flung out of his hands to clatter against the bulkhead and then fly through the window.

Wilde steadied himself, taking great breaths of air into his lungs. "Up, Olly," he said. "I never figured you for much, after the first time."

Oliver Parks pushed his hands against the bulkhead behind himself, slowly forced his body upright. "You don't seem surprised to see me, Jonas."

"Relieved is the word," Wilde said. "It had to be one of you three. When Ilse Weenink was dumped on board *Nemo* with Michelle and me, to drown, it eliminated her. And I would have hated to think it was Carl. But I knew who it had to be, even before I met Ilse. Only you could have given Zita all that information about the working of the Section, of the personnel of the Section. Only you knew that much about us, Olly."

Now he breathed evenly, and the strength had returned to his muscles. And still Parks waited. Wilde remembered that here was an absolute expert in unarmed combat. He watched the policeman's fingers clawing over the chaotic chart table, looking, seeking, and finally closing on the dividers, thumb testing the needlepoint on each arm.

"So tell me," Wilde said, "where *is* Carl?"

"Oh, Carl is dead," Parks said. "He was too like you, Jonas. One of those men who never quite give up. He tried to make a break for it only a few minutes after the yacht had been taken." Slowly Parks began to move, pawing at the wheelhouse sole with his deck shoes, testing the foothold, the dividers still held in his left hand, but ready now to flick them across to his right. "Of course, then he thought he could count on me. And there was only Johann and Wilbur. They never amounted to much. As you found out, Jonas. He said, 'They don't really think much of us, Olly, leaving us with these two boys.' And went into action."

"So you got him from behind."

"Wouldn't you? In the circumstances. In our line of business, old man, it's the result which counts."

The dividers moved, with tremendous speed, flicking from left hand to right and surging forward, aimed low as Parks himself came low, falling to the floor and thrusting at Wilde's belly. Wilde sidestepped, struck the binnacle, and brought up short, and Parks turned on his elbow, his fall broken by his slapping left hand, the dividers turned upwards in case Wilde was tempted to drop on him.

Wilde kicked instead, sending his toes into the side of Parks's knee, bringing a grimace of agony to those fresh, schoolboy features, sending the lying man twisting over on his other side in pain. Wilde moved forward, and Parks reached his feet, striking behind him with the dividers as he turned, carving the air in an arc over his shoulder. But Wilde had checked, and the lethal pinpoints crunched into the wooden bulkhead. For the moment Parks still stood, half turned away from his opponent, shoulders hunched. Already he was wheeling. But his movements quick as they were were yet too slow. Wilde had anchored himself to the deck, all his weight centred in the balls of his feet and transmitted from thence up his body and into his right shoulder, hurled the length of his arm even as the arm itself swept round from left to right, in a backhanded blow which carried the edge of his hand, held rigid and hard as a length of steel piping, smashing into the base of Parks's skull. One hundred and eighty pounds of concentrated power burst over the medulla, shocking heartbeat and respiratory system into inertia much as the knot on a hangman's noose would have done.

Parks was dead before he hit the deck.

Wilde glanced at the beach again. Michelle Smith knelt beside Catherine Light, had raised her head from the sand, and seemed to be pawing at it. Behind her, Ilse Weenink had also re-emerged from the mist and gazed at the holocaust in front of her with an utterly bemused expression. For the moment, at any rate, they were in no danger. But his job was not yet finished.

He knelt beside Parks, checked for pulse or heartbeat, and was satisfied. He went out of the wheelhouse and down the ladder, opened the door to the cabin underneath. Zita Richmond lay on the bunk in the far corner, her wrists and ankles bound, her face bruised, her long dark hair tumbling over her face and shoulders as she stared at him.

"Oh, God," she whispered. "Oh, God. I didn't, Jonas. I swear it. I didn't know they meant to kill you all along. I didn't want *any* bloodshed, Jonas." Her voice rose an octave. "I swear it. They told me killing Weber was an accident."

"Carl Weber," Wilde said. "Your friend Wilbur, your friend Dave, your friend Yves, your friend Johann, another friend I don't know, and Olly Parks. And Cathy Light."

"Cathy?" she whispered. "Cathy? But how . . . I didn't even know she was around."

"Yet she's dead," Wilde said. "God help the world if you should ever *try* to do any damage, Zita."

"But I didn't *mean* it," she screamed. "It shouldn't have happened this way, Jonas. Never. Jonas, listen to me. I didn't want the money for myself. Honestly, I didn't. I was horrified by what I saw, what I heard, what I learned out there. I just had to do something about it. And people wouldn't listen. Nobody would listen. And when you think what that child earns. Earns, there's a funny word. What she *gets,* she, and everyone like her, for doing nothing. But still I didn't bear her a grudge. I didn't want to harm her, Jonas. And God knows I didn't want to harm you. I still hoped we might meet again, some day . . . it was Dave. Dave and Olly who decided to kill you all. They knew *Nemo* would get into trouble in that sea."

"Oh, I believe you, Zita. I don't think you *are* a murderess."

She sucked air into her lungs, and her shoulders heaved as she tugged against her bonds. "Then . . . then you won't . . ."

"Trouble is," he pointed out, "I don't suppose you could describe any of the people who start wars as murderers either. Just careless with other people's lives."

She gazed at him, her mouth sagging open.

"And you have made the cardinal error of even being careless with your own," Wilde said. "You may not approve of the institution to which Michelle Smith belongs, but that's not reason enough for causing all of this. And the institution is important, Zita. It makes for stability, and God knows, we could all do with a bit of that. She tells me you took some photographs of her."

"Over there," she gasped. "Over there. In that locker."

The suitcases were there as well. Wilde threw up the lid of one, gazed at the untouched notes. *What* a bloody stupid world. He opened the locker, found the photographs, riffled through them. He thought it remarkable how dignity can come through the most unfortunate situations. "Got a match?"

"There," she gasped.

He found her lighter, burned each photograph carefully, stamped the ashes into the deck. Zita watched him, her breathing slowly settling down. Her eyes lost their stare, and some of the colour returned to her cheeks.

"So what happens now?" she demanded. "You've destroyed the photos. I bet you still won't dare put me in court, Jonas. Gerald Light wouldn't dare. Because people would believe what I had to say about her. And about you. And your setup."

"I have no doubt of that at all." Wilde sat beside her. "You should have thought of that a while ago. You told me, on board *Nemo*, that everyone was in the kidnapping, hijacking game, nowadays. What you really meant was, everyone is trying to buck the system. But when you get so many people living so close to each other on such a small planet as earth, sweetheart, we just have to have a system. And it has to work."

He heard her catch her breath, watched her mouth again sag open. "No," she said. "You can't *mean* that, Jonas. You can't."

"It's my job," he said, and wrapped his fingers around her throat.

(ii)

The tide had turned, and the water lapped at the hull of the catamaran. Michelle Smith still knelt beside Catherine's body,

Ilse Weenink still stood, a few yards away, gazing at them. The mist still shrouded the morning.

Wilde waded ashore, stamped on the sand.

"She's dead," Michelle whispered. "The bullet must have gone straight through her heart. She was trying to save me, Jonas."

"I told you not to come back," Wilde said.

"I . . . we . . ." she glanced at Ilse. "I was afraid of getting lost. Don't you see, there was nothing but sand. We must have walked about a mile, and we saw nothing but sand and then there was water again. I didn't know what to do, Jonas. We followed our footprints back."

"So where is Paul?"

Her head jerked. "Over there. He's all right, Jonas. I think he's going to be all right."

Something saved. Wilde glanced at the water, at the still trawler, at the empty sea which had claimed the dinghy and no doubt the man clinging to her. At Dave, lying on the sand, the water lapping over his legs. At Catherine Light. Olly and Zita were out of sight. Like Carl Weber, and the crew of the trawler. Something saved.

"It's my fault," Michelle whispered. "I know that. Not just Catherine. Everything. Oh, God, why didn't she let them shoot me down. Wouldn't that have been better, Jonas? Wouldn't it?"

Wilde gazed at her and then at Ilse. The Dutch girl returned his gaze, her face hard. "There's fibreglass filler on board the cat," Wilde said. "Let's get those holes plugged. And while I'm doing that, bring Fine back on board. We want to be out of here the moment she floats." He turned, hesitated, then stooped and lifted Catherine into his arms.

(iii)

As it was a private cemetery, there were only a few people. Sir Gerald Light stood at the head of the grave, next to the priest. Rodrigues, the butler, stood a few feet away, next to Melanie Bird. Mocka was behind them. On the other side of the grave,

Michelle Smith and Ilse Weenink were so heavily veiled as to be invisible.

Farthest away of all, Wilde stood by himself.

But now the coffin had disappeared, and the sextons were waiting. Michelle advanced slowly. It was a perfectly magnificent summer morning, a day to be drifting slowly around the Baltic in bathing suits. Just two people on an empty cat, one in a bikini.

Michelle stopped in front of Sir Gerald, spoke for a few moments. Then she turned away, came towards Wilde. Beyond the gate the engine of the Rolls-Royce stirred into life.

"We must leave," Michelle said. "There is an aircraft waiting for us."

Wilde nodded.

Michelle sighed. "Life must go on, Mr. Wilde. But I want you to know . . ."

Wilde shook his head. "No, ma'am. As of this moment, I don't exist. I never existed. That's what you want to remember."

She hesitated, then nodded and turned away. No one else moved until the gate had closed behind her. Then Sir Gerald left the grave and came across the lawn, Mocka and Melanie Bird flanking him. Still there was no expression on Sir Gerald's face. He had just buried his wife, but there was no expression.

"It will be several weeks before Fine is fit again," he said. "An unfortunate way to begin his career. I would like a full report, of course."

Wilde took an envelope from his breast pocket and handed it to him. Sir Gerald opened the paper, glanced at it, nodded.

"You'll be pleased to learn that the Germans are treating the mystery of the shot-up trawler and its dead crew as a mystery. A mutiny, perhaps, who knows."

"Then you've nothing to worry about," Wilde said.

"Except the money."

"It's in the boot of that car," Wilde said. "Untouched."

Sir Gerald nodded. "I didn't suppose you would have forgotten that." He half turned his head, and Mocka and Melanie stepped away out of earshot. "I want you to know that I do not blame you for what happened, Wilde."

Wilde gazed at him.

"You understood my orders," Sir Gerald said, "even if I had to give them in a somewhat oblique manner, and you carried them out. That Catherine joined you was my fault. I was, ah, indulging myself at her expense without understanding how much she cared for you. But then, had she not joined you, as I understand it, Michelle Smith would have been killed."

"So she did her job, like a good operative," Wilde said. "You must be pleased about that."

"One must always count the gains, rather than the losses, Wilde. I think you need a rest. Take one. Oh, you'll want this." He reached into his side pocket, took out a wad of notes secured by a rubber band.

Wilde held the notes for a moment, then with a single twist of his wrists he tore the wad into two halves, allowed the loose pieces to scatter in the gentle breeze.

"My God," Sir Gerald said. He stared at Wilde as if he was truly seeing him for the first time in his life. "You really loved her. My God. Do you know, I believe she really loved you, too?"

Wilde turned away.

"I shall be in touch, of course," Sir Gerald said.

Wilde hesitated, then he opened the gate and stepped through. He walked down the lane. It twisted, and in a moment he was lost to sight.